THE FRANCHISE OPTION
A LEGAL GUIDE

by

MARK ABELL, LLB
Partner in Field Fisher Waterhouse, Solicitors

First edition 1989
© Mark Abell 1989

Waterlow Publishers
Paulton House
8 Shepherdess Walk
London N1 7 LB

A division of Pergamon Financial and Professional Services PLC

ISBN 0 08 040118 X

British Library Cataloguing in Publication Data
Abell, Mark
    The franchise option : legal guide.
    1. Great Britain. Franchising law
    I. Title
    344.103'84

ISBN 0-08-040118-X

Typeset by Type Out, London SW16, 01-769 9242

Printed in Great Britain by Dramrite Printers Limited, London SE1, 01-407 4077

FIELD FISHER WATERHOUSE

Field Fisher Waterhouse is a firm of solicitors based in the City of London whose origin dates back to the 1820's. It has been actively involved in franchising and licensing for over 25 years and boasts a wide spectrum of international and domestic franchising and licensing expertise in all relevant legal disciplines.

Field Fisher Waterhouse is an affiliate of the British Franchising Association.

THE AUTHOR

Mark Abell is the partner who leads the Field Fisher Waterhouse franchise and licensing team which comprises a total of ten lawyers all working in different aspects of franchising and licensing. This includes property, intellectual property, taxation, labour law, immigration, litigation, commercial law and anti-trust.

Abell has written numerous articles in journals such as the *Law Society Gazette, Franchise World, Franchise Business Magazine* and the *International Financial Law Review.* He has also lectured widely on franchising and licensing both in the UK and abroad at academic institutions such as Queen Mary College, London and McGeorge University in Austria, and commercial organisations such as the Confederation of British Industry and the Japan Franchise Association in Tokyo. He is a member of the Licensing Executives Society and is on the editorial board of, and a regular contributor to, the legal periodicals, *Patent World, Trade Mark World* and *Copyright World.*

Abell is also the co-author with his partner, John Nelson-Jones of the chapter on franchising in '*Intenational Business Transactions*', published by Kluwer, and author of the chapter on the legal aspects of entering the Japanese market in *Legal Aspects of Business Transactions and Investment in the Far East,* also by Kluwer.

ACKNOWLEDGEMENTS

I would like to thank all of those whose help and patience made this book possible, particularly my partners John Nelson-Jones for his valuable comments and guidance; Richard Bagehot for his assistance with chapter 7 on intellectual property; Nick Rose who made a major contribution to chapter 8 concerning the litigious aspects of franchising; and Graeme Nuttall who helped out with the taxation aspects of chapter 10. Thanks to Stewart Brown, assistant manager of the Franchise and Licensing Department of The Royal Bank of Scotland plc. Thanks also to Suzanne Middleton-Lindsley for her help with that part of chapter 5 relating to property; Ron Campbell and Ian Doig of The Royal Bank of Scotland plc, John Perkins of Barclays Bank plc and Ron Delnevo of Tie Rack plc for their comments and guidance; to my wife Shizuka for her encouragement and support, and to Janice Salt and Caroline Winzer for their support with the endless typing involved.

FOREWORD

Properly constituted business format franchising is one of the most successful methods of marketing goods and services in the world today.

Franchising works in practice because of the benefits, incentives and the exclusive relationships it brings to the parties concerned – the franchisor and the franchisee.

The franchise relationship is an extremely complex one based upon highly involved and technical documentation. This documentation needs to be drafted with a full understanding of the practical ramifications: ramifications of which the franchisor must also be aware.

Mark Abell, in his legal guide, appraises companies considering franchising, and their legal advisors, not only of the legal issues involved, but also of many of the fundamental commercial points that they need to consider.

If you are seriously considering franchising your business, then this legal guide should form part of your research.

James W Watson
Chairman
British Franchise Association

The law is stated as at 1 August 1989. The book does not deal with Scottish law which in some cases may be slightly different.

Mark Abell

Dedicated with affection to Mum, Dad and Shizuka

CONTENTS

Appendices

Chapter 1
WHAT IS FRANCHISING?

The general concept

Franchising is a much abused word and means many different things to different people. In simple terms it is the granting of certain rights by one party (the franchisor) to another (the franchisee) in return for a sum of money. The franchisee then exercises those rights under the guidance of the franchisor. Such a wide definition encompasses many different forms of licensing arrangements and ranges from the right to manufacture denim jeans under a particular brand name to the right to run a local radio station under the auspices of the Independent Broadcasting Authority.

This book has a much narrower focus and is concerned only with business format franchising which is defined by the British Franchise Association as:

"A contractual licence granted by one person (the franchisor) to another (the franchisee) which:

(a) permits or requires the franchisee to carry on during the period of the franchise a particular business under or using a specified name belonging to or associated with the franchisor; and

(b) entitles the franchisor to exercise continuing control during the period of the franchise over the manner in which the franchisee carries on the business which is the subject of the franchise; and

(c) obliges the franchisor to provide the franchisee with assistance in carrying on the business which is the subject of the franchise (in relation to the organisation of the franchisee's business, the training of staff, merchandising, management or otherwise); and

(d) requires the franchisee periodically during the period of the franchise to pay to the franchisor sums of money in consideration for the franchise or goods or services provided by the franchisor to the franchisee; and

(e) which is not a transaction between a holding company and its subsidiary (as defined in S736 of the Companies Act 1985) or between subsidiaries of the same holding company or between an individual and a company controlled by him."

In many ways franchising can be regarded as essentially a marketing exercise. The consumer's perception should be that, save for any express statement to the contrary, (see chapters 4 & 10 below) there is no difference between one of the franchisor's corporate outlets and a franchised one. The decor of the shop premises, the livery of vehicles, the selection of the goods or services and uniforms of the staff should be identical to the franchisor's own outlets. The franchisor is selling the franchisee the right to use its business format; hence the name 'business format franchising'.

The commercial bargain

In crude commercial terms the reason for both the franchisor and franchisee entering into a contractual relationship with each other is to make a profit. The franchisee makes a profit from supplying the goods or services to the customer. The franchisor makes it from allowing the franchisee to use its package of know-how and intellectual property rights. The bargain is struck between two independent legal entities of supposedly equal bargaining power. In reality however, the more successful and established the franchise becomes the more eager the franchisee and the wider the choice of potential franchisees the franchisor enjoys. To obtain a *Body Shop* franchise for example is nowadays a major achievement.

In order to be able to strike a bargain both parties must have something to offer. The franchisor must have a proven business format comprising continually developing know-how and a package of intellectual property rights. The franchisee must have sufficient capital to invest in the franchise and be of appropriate character and ability. Without the requisite 'assets' neither party can enter into the bargain.

Ironically however, as the franchisors' bargaining power grows with the growth of the franchise network so does the chance of the value of its package being eroded by existing franchisees or pirates. For example, the value of the *Yum Yum Pizza* franchise is the reputation it enjoys for producing a uniform quality product. If a franchisee starts to experiment on its own accord or a pirate sets up shop, the goodwill in the franchise will suffer and decrease in value accordingly. The franchisor must constantly police the franchise, ensure that its standards are carefully maintained and that pirates swiftly dealt with.

The advantage to the franchisee

The franchisee is the proprietor of its own business and owns the tangible assets of the franchise outlet. What it does not own is the goodwill. Like any other business proprietor the franchisee buys materials, pays rent and staff salaries and takes the profit of operation, less royalty and service fees. Subject to various restrictions, it can sell its business when it wishes (usually subject to the franchisor's pre-emption right and on condition that the purchaser is approved by the franchisor). What makes the franchise different from any other business is that it obtains from the franchisor the entire business concept with full training, assistance in every aspect of setting up and running the business, and access to necessary materials and supplies.

In essence, it can be said that the franchisee does not have to worry what to do or how to do it, but merely follow the developed concept. This makes failure less likely. According to the Department of Employment over 25% of ordinary businesses fail whilst the BFA (British Franchising Association) quotes failure for only 5% of franchised outlets.

Obviously the franchisees' start-up costs entail more than paying the franchisor an up-front fee; it must invest in premises, fittings, equipment, materials and working capital until the inward cash flow commences. In addition, it must make regular payments to the franchisor in the form of royalties or management services fees or, in some cases, an agreed mark-up on supplies obtained from the franchisor.

The disadvantage to the franchisee

The franchisee is not an independent *entrepreneur*. It is what might be called an *intrepreneur*. In the final analysis the franchisee must follow the franchisor's instructions. The lower risk is off-set by the lower reward for success.

The advantage to the franchisor

The main advantage of franchising to the franchisor is that it allows the latter to increase its number of outlets with minimum capital outlay and so accelerate the network's growth. Self-employed franchisees are generally more highly motivated than salaried managers, and are more likely to produce better results for less expenditure of capital on behalf of the franchisor.

The disadvantage to the franchisor

The disadvantage of franchising to the franchisor is that it has to control and co-ordinate a network of semi-independent businessmen and ensure that they build and maintain a favourable image for the whole franchised operation. This means that the franchisor's own role changes drastically. The policing and monitoring of standards by the franchisor is vital.

It will be quite apparent from the above that the franchisee is in no way an agent or representative of the franchisor. The complexities of the relationship may however lead the courts to speculate that the franchisor could in certain circumstances be a shadow director of a corporate franchisee (see chapter 2).

The origins of franchising

Franchising has experienced a dramatic growth in the last decade. The number of franchisors and the average number of franchisees per franchise has increased. Franchising as a commercial concept goes back many hundreds of years and has been practised worldwide. In China and 'Chinese Colonies', from Shanghai to San Francisco, the *Mai Toi* (or table rent) agreement for operating restaurants has existed for centuries. In Japan the *Norenkai* system, by which a former employee opens an independent branch operation in return for a royalty, has operated since before the Tokugawa era, which commenced during the early 16th Century. In England, during the Middle Ages, King John offered franchises to individuals to become tax collectors. The prospective tax collector (the franchisee) would pay a fee to the throne for the privilege of collecting taxes and passing them on to him, reimbursing himself with a small percentage of the taxes.

During the 17th Century the breweries found it increasingly difficult to find guaranteed outlets for their produce and so started to buy up public houses and developed the tied house system to guarantee outlets for their own branded beer. This has many similarities to modern day franchising, particularly the basic rationale; that of establishing a marketing and distribution system.

During the 1960's, licensing was employed in many areas to expand distribution networks in the UK particularly in the motor trade with petrol stations, car dealers and franchised spare parts dealers. These agreements were franchises of a sort and are often referred to as second generation franchises. The roots of these second generation franchises lie in the United States with the *Singer Sewing Machine Company* which was the first corporation to develop an elaborate franchise system network. Manufacturing franchises, such as *Coca-Cola* still operate successfully all over the world.

Business format franchises, the focus of this book, can be seen as third generation franchises. These franchises originally started in the USA in the early 1960's and gradually infiltrated the UK. Some are small firms started by individuals or companies with little capital, but a lot of energy. Others are run by large corporations seeking to expand their networks. Such franchises cover many different areas ranging from fast food to bridal wear and plumbing. Some of the earlier franchises in the UK include *Wimpy* and *Dyno-Rod*.

How big is franchising?

In the United States, franchising accounted for sales of an estimated US$591 billion in 1987. It is also extremely well established in other countries such as Canada and Japan. A recent survey commissioned by the British Franchise Association and the National Westminster Bank indicates that annual sales through franchising amount to up to £3.8 billion in the UK, and that turnover may reach £9.895 billion by 1994. Annual growth is 33% year on year over the last four years. In the last 25 years over 20,000 separate businesses have been created using the franchise concept, directly employing nearly 150,000 people. Today there are over 200 different types of business being franchised by about 440 franchisors with nearly 20,000 franchised outlets. According to former EEC Commissioner, Peter Sutherland, franchising accounts for some 10% of all retail sales in Europe. Even so, few franchised operations in the UK claim to be fully mature, or to have reached market saturation point.

The UK is one of the fastest expanding franchise areas in Europe, and is second only to France. After 1992 Europe, with its 320 million consumers, could surpass the United States in overall turnover through franchising. This is the result in the main of the fact that EC law is sympathetic to franchising (see chapters 3 and 4 below).

Why is franchising growing so rapidly?

Apart from the commercial advantages it offers to franchisors, there are several reasons for the dramatic increase in the growth of franchising. These range from organic factors such as the industry's relative lack of maturity to socio-economic factors such as high unemployment. Factors also include recent government policies favouring small businesses and moving away from a welfare state. The retail revolution evidenced by the building of new shopping centres has also had an effect. Lease requirements are often so heavy that they eliminate small independent

5

businessmen. The greater involvement of the major clearing banks and an increased willingness to lend to franchisees is important, and the single market which is to be created by 1992 provides another great opportunity for business to expand into Europe through the franchise approach. This is discussed in more detail below (see chapter 12).

What types of franchise format exist?

There are no strict definitions or distinctions between different types of business format franchises. The EC Commission, in its study "*The Co-operation Between Firms in the Community: Franchising*" (series Commerce and Distribution 1978 No 5), identified five different types of franchise, namely manufacturer and wholesaler; manufacturer and retailer; wholesaler and retailer; service industry and retailer; undertaking in the same distributive group (the voluntary chain group).

In the Franchise Block Exemption preamble (3) (see appendix 3 below) the Commission took a slightly different approach and categorised franchises as industrial distribution and service franchises. These definitions are wide and incorporate more than merely business format franchises (industrial franchises rarely have a business format). They also omit service/processing franchises such as *McDonalds* and *Wimpy* which do more than merely sell goods or provide a service.

It is possible to categorise franchises by other criteria; for example on the basis of the franchisees they attract.

(1) The 'ordinary' franchise, under which the franchisee is trained by the franchisor and then commences business under the franchisor's name and guidance. This would include franchises such as *Dyno-Rod* and *Fastframe* and allows previously unskilled individuals (or those with different/irrelevant skills) to run their own business. The franchisee's investment can vary from £85,000 (plus £5,000 working capital), for *Prontaprint*, to £12,500 (plus £4,000 working capital) for *Dampcure Woodcure/30*.

(2) The 'conversion' franchise is taken on by franchisees already carrying on the same business as the franchisor. Such franchises tend to, but do not always, involve specific skills, (eg hairdressing) which could not be imparted to ordinary unskilled franchisees. In such circumstances it is the way of doing business and most importantly the name and trade marks in which the franchisees are most interested. A good example of such a franchise is *Alan Paul Hairdressers*. It should be noted that any one franchise may attract

both franchisees who wish to 'convert' and those who have no previous experience of that type of work, (eg estate agencies such as *Land & Co* and *Agency No 1*).

(3) The 'investment' franchise is usually entered into by a company or syndicate, rather than an individual, as a result of the heavy capital investment (often several million pounds) required by such franchise opportunities. In these cases, the company or syndicate (the franchisee) is more interested in its return on investment, payback period and other financial indicators, than the product range which the business is actually marketing. The franchise is merely a form of investment for the franchisee. It will have no involvement in the day-to-day running. A profitable return on investment, rather than a day-to-day personal income is the prime objective. The jobs created from this type of franchise can vary from, around ten to several hundred at any one outlet. Examples of investment franchises include large retaurants and hotels such as *Holiday Inn*.

By far the most common franchise opportunities on offer in the UK are the 'ordinary' franchises, where the franchisees are in essence purchasing a source of profitable employment.

Franchising a business

Franchising is not the panacea for all business difficulties and is not a guarantee of success for franchisors who have adopted it to market their package. It is a concept which is vulnerable to abuse and demands a high degree of co-operation from both the franchisor and the franchisees. According to the BFA and National Westminster Bank's Power Report in 1988, 9 franchisors went out of business out of a total of 253 and only 4.9% of all franchisees. Nevertheless, this is still significantly below the rates applicable to individual entrepreneurs.

The subtleties of franchising take time to undertstand and not all businesses can be successfully franchised. Any entrepreneur must take a good, long, hard look at his business concept before jumping head first into franchising. The failure of a franchise can be disasterous not only for the franchisor but also for the franchisees who have invested in it.

In order for a franchise to stand a chance of succeeding, the basic concept must be a sound one, the franchisor must have sufficient resources to support the chain, and the franchisees must be properly managed.

An idea cannot be franchised. In order to franchise a concept it must first be proved to work as a business. The franchisee is paying for the right to use a system that has proved to be successful; not to put someone's bright idea into practice.

As Moshe Gerstenhaber, the Chairman of *Kall-Kwik Printing*, has explained it; "business format franchising can be considered a system leasing arrangement. The franchisee acquires from the franchisor the licence to duplicate the franchisor's existing and successful system of providing a product/service to the end user" (Directory of Franchising 1989).

The potential franchisor must therefore ask itself whether or not it has anything worth franchising. The right to sell a particular product by itself is not a business format franchise. It is an agency or distributorship which may well prove to be a profitable business in its own right, but it is not a business format franchise.

For a business to be franchiseable there must be definable know-how, a distinct way of doing things that distinguishes the business from others. Each element of the know-how taken by itself may well not be unique; there are for example, only a limited number of ways to grill a hamburger, fry chips and mix a milk shake. The combination of them however may be unique. When coupled with the franchisor's name and trade marks the system should be identifiable and distinctive. It is this that will create the value of the franchise.

This means that the know-how must be carefully identified and easily communicable. Intensive training courses and an operations manual will therefore be necessary. The potential franchisor must ask itself whether or not the concept lends itself to this. A franchise consultant may be useful in this regard (see Appendix 13 below).

Once the potential franchisor is satisfied that there is definable, communicable know-how in the business, it must then carry out a 'legal audit' of its intellectual property rights and make certain that the corner stone of the franchise – the name, trade marks and other intellectual property rights – do in fact belong to it. A franchisor cannot grant its franchisees the right to use a name and trade marks over which it does not have any proprietary rights (This subject is dealt with in more detail in chapters 7, 8 and 9).

Once a concept has been developed and its name and marks protected, it follows that it must be tried and tested in the market through a pilot operation. This will further test its profitability as a business for franchisees and allow the potential franchisor to further refine the system on the back of further practical experience. If conventional bank funding does not satisfy the capital requirements of the pilot operation, the government's Small Firms Loan Guarantee Scheme may prove to be very useful.

Once the concept has been piloted, or indeed before, the potential franchisor must decide upon how it will make money for itself from the franchise business. This is considered in chapter 5 below. The banks are usually keen to fund respectable franchisors with sound concepts, but the franchisor should also consider the possibility of utilising venture capital or even attracting finance under the Business Expansion Scheme (see chapter 10 below).

In addition to arranging the funding and determining the financial structure of the franchise, before actively recruiting franchisees it is essential that good quality legal documentation, is prepared by a solicitor knowledgeable of both the legal and commercial subtleties of franchising. This is dealt with at length in chapter 5.

Once the franchise has been set up, the finances arranged and the appropriate documentation prepared it is of course important to arrange the effective marketing of the franchise to franchisees. The best franchises require the least marketing effort. Once potential franchisees have seen outlets running and have had the opportunity to speak to happy and successful existing franchisees there will be little need to seek actively to sell the franchises. *Tie-Rack* is a notable example. It does not exhibit at the various franchise exhibitions yet for the year ending January 29th 1989 the net figure of outlets in the UK grew by 26 (a further 20 were opened in the USA, Europe and Australia during the same period).

Most franchises however, particularly to begin with, do have to market themselves carefully, and to this end the franchise press, particularly *Franchise World* and *Business Franchise Magazine* are highly reputable and extremely useful advertising media which are widely read by both potential franchisees and members of the franchising fraternity.

The various franchise exhibitions run by Blenheim Exhibitions at metropolitan centres around the country are also extremely useful as franchisee oriented marketing tools.

Once franchise applications are received they must be carefully considered and full financial forecasts presented to short listed potential franchisees. This will allow them to judge properly the value of the franchise (see chapter 6 below).

Finally, when considering franchising its business the potential franchisor must be aware that it is contemplating radically changing its own role within it. It is no longer on the 'sharp end' of the business, working with customers on a day to day basis. It should instead be continually developing and improving the system, planning its strategic growth and monitoring the franchisees to ensure that the high standards of the system are being maintained. Failure to understand this change of role will result in both franchisor and franchisees experiencing unnecessary difficulties.

Appendix 16 contains two case studies of successful franchises which will be of great use to anyone considering the franchise option. The first is an account of how *Kall-Kwik Printshops*, elected 'Franchise of the Year' in 1989 by members of the British Franchise Association became established in the United Kingdom. The second details the growth of *Alan Paul PLC* which in summer 1989 was floated on the USM. *Alan Paul PLC* own the *Alan Paul Hairdressing* and *The Body & Face Place* franchises.

Chapter 2
THE REGULATION OF FRANCHISING IN THE UK

"... Fraudsters induce investors to buy franchises, ... holding out the prospect of large returns on the investment. But once the payment has been made, the franchise proves worthless... ".

That, at any rate, is how the Fraud Trials Committee, chaired by the Right Honourable Lord Roskill PC described the dangers of entering into a franchise in its 1986 Report (HMSO ISBN 011380088 page 228).

Despite this danger, however, there is no specific franchise legislation in England and Wales to protect franchisees. Franchising, probably more than any other form of investment, is open to abuse. It is therefore necessary to protect franchisees from the sharp practice of wayward franchisors.

This important issue is complex but is often oversimplified for the purposes of popular debate. However, there can be no real disagreement on the key issue that franchisees do need protection. The difficulty is in agreeing the form that such protection should take. Should it be voluntary or compulsory? In either case, how should it be implemented? Further, there is the question of what exactly needs to be regulated; merely the sale of franchises, or the carrying on of franchised businesses as a whole.

Franchisors in the UK are on the whole opposed to specific franchise legislation for fear that it might hamper their expansion and development. In order to judge whether or not there is anything in this fear it is necessary to consider the situation abroad and the existing regulatory bodies in other areas of UK commerce/industry.

Regulation of franchising in other jurisdictions

America

The protection afforded to franchisees in the United States is often held up as a model which the UK should adopt, by those favouring a statutory regulatory system. In the United States, where franchise sales are seen as basically dealings in securities, there is a complex web of federal and state laws imposing differing requirements upon the franchisors. At federal level it is necessary to consider the Trade Commission's *"Disclosure Requirements and Prohibitions Concerning Franchising and Business Opportunity Ventures"*.

These require franchisors and area developers to provide would-be franchisees and sub-franchisees with copies of the franchise agreement, or related documentation, and a disclosure document. Matters such as the franchisor's litigation and bankruptcy histories, the description of the franchise to be purchased, details of any initial and continuing payments, details of any obligations to purchase goods, details of available finance, the precise nature of the franchisee's participation and a summary of the termination, cancellation, training, site selection and reporting provisions of the agreement are included in this disclosure document.

It is common practice to use a 'Uniform Franchise Offering Circular' (UFOC) which has been developed by the American Securities Administrators' Organisation in place of the actual disclosure document. Timing is crucial and disclosure must be made at the earlier of either the first 'personal' meeting or the time for making of disclosures (at least 10 business days prior to the execution of binding agreement or the payment of consideration by the franchisee).

All related documentation, including the agreement to be executed by the franchisee, which is materially different from the standard form of agreement must also be registered within 5 working days before execution. Further, unless the UFOC is used for disclosure purposes, an 'earnings claims document' must also be delivered to the franchisee if the franchisor makes projections of earnings or incomes of the franchisee or discloses history or information concerning the company and/or franchise operations. However, if the claims are made in the media the separate earnings claim document is compulsory even if UFOC is used.

Most states also have registration/disclosure requirements as well as provisions for covering such things as termination and renewal which are too detailed for the purposes of this book. It is enough to say that they are many and various and that the interface between state and federal laws requires a great deal of consideration and keeps the American franchise lawyers well supplied with highly remunerative work.

The problems in such a system are that franchisors find it difficult to deal with the administration necessitated by expansion into other states, and the highly technical rules tend to gain a momentum all of their own. The rules continually change as their shortcomings become evident.

Australia

By comparison, in Australia a specific franchise law was proposed in 1986 along the American lines. However the development of Australia's common law, which is basically the same as that of England, was eventually found to afford more than adequate protection to franchisees and so the proposed law was abandoned.

Japan

In Japan the Ministry for International Trade and Industry (MITI) has agreed a voluntary code with the Japanese Franchise Association which if|complied with exempts JFA members from extensive laws covering distribution in general, whilst the Fair Trade Commission has issued guidelines on desired disclosure by franchisors.

Other EC States

In other EC Member States there has so far been no specific franchise legislation. This is, however, soon to change. In France the *"Loi Doubin"*, due to be adopted in Autumn 1989, apart from shifting the legal emphasis of franchising towards the French legal concept 'credit bail', or the sale and lease-back of a business system, also requires disclosure of certain key provisions of the franchise agreement 10 days prior to its execution. In other states such as the Netherlands and Belgium existing legislation views franchising as something akin to employment and agency and affords franchisees considerable protection.

Regulation of industries in the UK

In the United Kingdom there are several different examples of industry based regulatory bodies which might be considered models for any proposed regulation of franchising in the UK.

The Press Council

The Press Council is charged with the regulation of the press, the monitoring of articles published by it and the handling of complaints raised by the public. Its authority is not backed by statute and its board comprises of a number of well respected public figures. Its powers include ordering papers to print retractions and apologies, but there is no power for it to enforce compliance with its judgments. The machinery is cumbersome and its authority doubtful, but the importance attached to preserving the so-called freedom of the press means that this is unlikely to change. The government refusal to support proposals for a harsher regime in April 1989, suggests that the Press Council will continue for some time to come.

The Law Society

The Law Society is the solicitors' professional body and was charged by the Solicitors Act 1974 with the regulation of the solicitors' profession. Membership is mandatory for practising solicitors and failure to comply with the society's rules can result in a solicitor being struck off of the membership roll on a permanent or temporary basis, preventing the solicitor from practising. This form of regulation is, despite various problems, essentially reasonable but is aimed at controlling licensed individuals rather than firms and its suitability for a non-professional industry is somewhat doubtful.

The Financial Services Act

The Financial Services Act 1986 probably affords the best example of a regulatory system in the United Kingdom. This piece of legislation was passed to control the carrying on of investment business in the United Kingdom following the liberalisation of the investment markets in London known as Big Bang and the coming to light of a number of abuses in the industry.

The legislation is incredibly complex and has required the establishment of a series of self-regulatory organisations (SRO's) namely, TSA, IMRO, FIMBRA, AFBD and LAUTRO, each controlling different sectors of the investment industry and all under the auspices of the Securities Investment Board (SIB), which is in turn responsible to the Department of Trade and Industry. All firms, subject to certain minor exceptions, wishing to carry on business in the United Kingdom must join the appropriate SRO.

Each SRO has had to produce extensive rule books, each several inches thick, and to impose experience, independence, best execution and many other requirements upon its members. The time and cost of joining and complying with the membership rules (by for example issuing extensive documentation to clients and writing manuals) is enormous. The cost of an IMRO application form alone is £250, whilst the total cost of compliance for one large insurance group has recently been estimated by its compliance officer as being in the region of £10 million!

The irony of this regulatory system, which may well result in London losing its place as Europe's financial centre, is that it imposes massive burdens upon large, reputable financial institutions such as the major clearing banks, but still allows investors to suffer at the hands of sharp practitioners such as *Barlow Clowes*, which was an IMRO member at the time of perpetrating its fraud. By trying to use a mallet to crack a nut the FSA has given the investment industry in London a very sore thumb!

Current protection of franchisees

Article 85 of the Treaty of Rome, the Restrictive Trade Practices Act 1976, and the Fair Trade Act 1973 (see chapter 3) afford protection to consumers against certain practices of both franchisors and franchisees but do not on the whole offer any protection to franchisees themselves. However, it should not be thought that English law does not afford protection to the franchisee. As became evident in Australia, the common law and a number of statutes do offer franchisees a great deal of protection.

All franchise agreements are subject to the law of contract, and a franchisee can sue a franchisor for breach of contract if he does not fulfil his obligations under the agreement. If a franchisor makes false representations to the franchisee, the franchisee can sue for misrepresentation and/or breach of an implied term, warranty or representation. The Misrepresentation Act 1967 and the Unfair Contract Terms Act 1977 may also afford redress to the franchisee in certain circumstances. The franchisee can sue for damages for loss of the bargain and also in certain circumstances, for specific performance.

If a franchisor fails to fulfil his obligations under the franchise agreement he may well be liable not only for breach of contract but also for negligence or even breach of fiduciary duty in which case the franchisee also has a right against the franchisor in both damages and, specific performance.

One particular source of protection afforded to franchisees which is often overlooked is that afforded by the Company Directors Disqualification Act 1986. Section 56(1) of this is a complicated piece of legislation but in basic terms it provides that a director of an insolvent company can be disqualified from being a director for a period of 2 to 15 years if he can be proved to be unfit to manage the affairs of a company. There is not a great deal of case law upon this point.

The relevant point to note is contained in s741 of The Companies Act 1985 which provides that a 'director' includes any person occupying the position of director by whatever means, including a shadow director. A shadow director is defined as a person in accordance with whose directions or instructions the directors of the company are accustomed to act. Case law also uses the term *'de facto* director' which is basically the same as a shadow director. This means that it is quite possible that the franchisor could, in certain circumstances, be deemed by the court to be a shadow or *de facto* director of a franchisee company and if the franchisor behaves in a commercially culpable manner (eg does not perform his obligations under the franchise agreement) it may well be that he could be disqualified as a director.

A mere distributor or licensee could obviously show that any directions were given under a *bona fide* arm's length commercial agreement. The franchisor, however, is far more intimately involved with the franchisee and has power to control most aspects of its business including management and accounting procedure, coupled with powers of inspection. Indeed, most franchise agreements provide for the franchisor to manage a franchisees' outlet in certain circumstances such as the franchisee's incapacity or even death. This would mean that not only could an individual franchisor be prevented from being a director of his own company, he could also be disqualified from being a shadow director of any other company, and therefore from being a franchisor. This bar is not restricted to individuals but extends also to corporate franchisors. Thus the UK law arguably goes further than most others in this respect in providing protection for franchisees.

If it could be shown that the franchisor, in acting as a shadow director, has lacked commercial probity, or even been merely negligent, he could become subject to a disqualification order. This grey area of law really requires some clarification; ideally by franchisors being expressly excluded by statute. However, until such amendment passes into law, the franchisor must take steps to monitor carefully its franchisees and ensure that it avoids acting without commercial probity or negligence. It should also be noted that any dishonesty by the franchisor could be an offence under the Theft Act 1968 punishable by fines and penal sentences.

The British Franchise Association

The British Franchise Association constitutes another avenue through which franchisees can seek redress against erstwhile franchisors. One weakness however is that not all franchisors are members. Some are not members because they do not satisfy the BFA's criteria. Others, however do, and are large and established, for example, *Body Shop* and *McDonalds*. The reasons why such franchisors refuse to become members differ. Some are disaffected because the BFA did not offer them support in the early years when they most needed it (which is why an Early Development Category has been introduced) whilst others feel that they are so large that they do not need the BFA's support (this is often the case with franchises owned by large public companies).

Individual franchisor's are usually small corporations and so lack political and economic muscle. As a result in most countries National Franchise Associations have been established. These associations lobby politicians to promote a positive image of franchising and establish proper ethical guidelines for it.

By 1973, pyramid selling schemes (a practice which is most definitely not business format franchising, but through loose terminology was wrongly associated with it) were widespread in the UK. They caused a large number of individuals to lose considerable sums of money. For example when the *Minnie Pearl Chicken System* collapsed in 1969, it had sold 1,800 franchises but opened only 161 outlets (see chapter 3 below). After a lot of adverse publicity, these schemes were declared illegal business practice by the Fair Trading Act 1973. This was successful in stamping out the practice of pyramid selling but by then it had already tarnished the image of franchising. The British Franchise Association was formed in 1977 by a number of leading franchise operations to resurrect franchising as an ethical way of doing business. The objectives of the BFA were to establish a clear definition of ethical franchising in order to assist the public, press, potential franchisees and government bodies in differentiating between real franchise opportunities and other suspect investment offers, and generally to 'clean up the image' of franchising.

BFA membership

The BFA is comprised of members; associates; affiliates such as solicitors, accountants, bankers and consultants; and members of the early development category.

There were 97 BFA members as at 1st May 1989 who were entitled to use the BFA logo, which apart from anything else, helps to attract potential franchisees. (A list of BFA Members, Associates and certain affiliates as at 1st May 1989 is contained in Appendices 1, 11, 12 and 13.) They are also allowed to stand for election to the BFA Council, its ruling body.

In order to become a full BFA member a franchisor must satisfy certain basic criteria. It must have run a correctly constituted pilot scheme for at least one year, and have had at least four franchised units successfully running for two years. Its franchise agreement and accounts must also be examined by the BFA. Membership subscription is £1,000 per annum plus VAT.

In order to become an associate, (there were 33 at 1st May 1989), the franchisor must show that it has run a correctly constituted pilot scheme for one year and has been successfully franchising with at least one franchisee for at least one year. The registration fee is £750 per annum plus VAT.

The early development category was introduced by the BFA in 1988 and is designed to help franchisors through the early, difficult period when they have little experience and great problems. The 'Early Development' scheme offers several benefits to the prospective franchisor such as eligibility to attend all BFA functions which include in-house seminars and conventions etc. A reduced rate is available for Early Development franchisors who exhibit at the various exhibitions. Category members have their progress monitored on a quarterly basis and interviews with the BFA director, a legal advisor and other officers are encouraged. In addition to the practical help it offers, a listing as a member of the Early Development Category shows the franchisor's commitment to ethical franchising.

The British Franchise Association's present functions

The BFA's stated aim is to promote franchising as an ethical way of doing business. The appointment of Lord Ezra as the BFA's president sought to add more credibility to this claim. The BFA presently performs this function in a number of ways, the first of which is the vetting and accreditation of members and affiliates as described above.

The BFA also helps to establish approved education programmes such as seminars for developing franchisors, has published a Code of Ethics with which franchisors should comply, instigates acceptable arbitration procedures and acts as a common voice in lobbying and liaising with government bodies. Its most recent initiative, backed by the Royal Bank of Scotland, is to establish a training programme for its members.

The BFA's Code of Ethics (Appendix 14 below) seeks to provide for disclosure by franchisors in what it sees as the main areas of concern. These include the franchisor's financial status, details of those involved in the franchise, a full description of the franchise package (including existing franchisees), financial projections, details of the agreement and a recommendation to take independent advice.

The British Franchise Association also offers an avenue through which franchisees can seek redress against erstwhile franchisors. The BFA's moral power over its members grows annually but it is still far from being total. It is not known, for example, how rigidly its members comply with the Code of Ethics. Its arbitration procedure does, however, afford franchisees a quick, cheap and private way of enforcing their rights against a franchisor.

In order to become a proper regulatory body with unquestionable authority, however, the BFA has far to go, and must gain the trust of both government and franchisees. It must also have teeth with which to bite offending franchisors. It must prove itself sufficiently independent, responsible and tough with offending franchisors, to be able to police franchising.

The stronger the BFA becomes (be it the result of moral or legal pressures) the more effective will be its policing role. Backed by the ultimate sanction of refusing membership to a franchisor, the BFA's great knowledge of franchising potentially allows it to act in a sensitive and positive manner for the good of not only individual franchisees and franchisors but also of the franchising industry as a whole. The problem is therefore how to make membership so important that franchisors will be afraid of not being granted it or losing it. The choice is simple; moral coercion or legal obligation. The decision is mostly in the BFA's own hands.

Conclusion

Abuse of franchising cannot and should not be tolerated. Franchisees, often investing their life savings and borrowing heavily to enter a franchise, must be protected. Exactly how this should be effected is however a difficult question which can only be answered after a great deal of careful thought and research.

The present system is not perfect. Specific franchise legislation should be genuinely considered and not dismissed out of hand. However, upon examining other regulatory systems both abroad and in the UK, (and taking particular note of Australia's experience) lessons can be learned. It would seem that careful evolution of statutory and common law coupled with a strong, more independent, professional British Franchise Association probably offers a more sensitive and considered response to the abuses of franchising than rushing headlong into hastily prepared specific franchise legislation.

If the BFA does not rise and meet the challenge, however, legislation is inevitable. Unfortunately, such legislation is usually passed in haste but repented at leisure and could therefore prove potentially dangerous to an industry that if properly nurtured will offer a good living and a worthwhile return on investment to a great number of people.

In order to prevent this therefore, legislation, if it comes, must result from the substantial input of franchisors, the BFA and those professionals involved in franchising, rather than public outcry and hysteria. It should be used to bolster the role of a leaner BFA rather than involve civil servants who know little of the commercial reality that is franchising.

Chapter 3

THE LEGAL IMPLICATIONS OF FRANCHISING IN THE UK

General background

The basic concept of franchising discussed in chapter 1 is not a novel one, and has existed around the world in one form or another for centuries. Nevertheless, franchising still succeeds in causing problems for both lawyers and legislators throughout the world. In The United States (discussed in chapter 2 above), a complex network of both Federal and State laws closely regulates every aspect of a franchise and imposes arduous registration and public disclosure requirements on the franchisor. In Australia attempts to draft a specific franchise law have, after years of frantic negotiation between government and interested parties recently been abandoned (see chapter 2 above).

In the European Community, Article 85 of The Treaty of Rome has until recently created difficulty for some franchisors by, amongst other things, creating obstacles to, the grant of exclusive territories to franchisees. The recently adopted EC Block Exemption (see chapter 4 below), part of the hundreds of reforms creating a single market by 1992, considerably reduces these difficulties.

In the UK however (as distinct from the EC) complex legislation still means that precisely drafted legal documents are necessary to prevent the franchisor falling foul of the Office of Fair Trading and the courts. However, the government White Paper suggests that the system will soon be simplified (see below).

The main reason for the difficulties faced by franchising is that its basic rationale runs against the grain of the popular economic theory embodied in the law. In many countries the law has become obsessed by the right of small traders to go about their business unrestricted. It is seen as inequitable that larger enterprises should be able to impose their will upon smaller ones merely by virtue of their differing economic strength. The various anti-trust or anti-monopoly laws therefore try to reduce this inequality in bargaining power by the imposition of various restrictions. This perception of commercial relations as being based upon a conflict of interests does not really take account of franchising. The interests of both the franchisor and franchisee are similar to a far greater extent than in other commercial relationships. The result is that franchises often have to operate within legal jurisdictions that do not really accommodate or understand their way of doing business. It is essential that the franchisor has a basic understanding of the legal restrictions within which it must operate its franchise. Such an understanding will allow it to plan properly and structure the franchise in a way that will avoid the many traps the law has set for the unwary franchisor battling to achieve the success it may well deserve.

English and European Community law

Since the UK joined the Common Market, the franchisor has had to deal with two very different sets of legal restrictions. Those of the English legal system, which are contained in a patchwork of statutes and legal precedents, and those of the EC which are contained in the Treaty of Rome and the recently adopted Block Exemption (see chapter 4 below).

These two parallel legal systems are very different. English law is concerned with how a transaction is structured and is preoccupied with the form of agreements. Simply put, it is not concerned with what anti-competitive effects are achieved provided that the documentation complies with, and does not contravene, its highly technical provisions. EC law, on the other hand, cares little about the form of a transaction and concentrates upon its ultimate affects.

This divergence of approach makes the lawyers' job an exceedingly difficult one presenting numerous conflicts and contradictions with which to deal. Hopefully, this will no longer be a problem once proposals in the government's White Paper (Cm 727) passes into law in the next eighteen months. Until such time, however, lawyers and their clients must deal with a complicated tangle of laws.

While it should not be forgotten that franchises are of course subject to the laws which govern all businesses, this chapter, will concentrate only upon those which are of particular relevance to franchising. Some of the wider legal implications are dealt with in chapter 10 below. To present this complex web of law in a simple form, this chapter will consider first of all basic EC law and then English law. Chapter 4 will consider in detail the EC Franchise Block Exemption which came into force earlier this year and could have a profound effect upon franchising in the EC over the next few years.

European Community law

Article 85 of the Treaty of Rome

Article 85.1 is concerned with any practice the purpose or effect of which is to 'prevent restrict or distort' trade between Member States. It concentrates upon the anti-competitive effects of a franchise agreement rather than upon its particular provisions.

Article 85.2 specifies that such practices are void and makes the franchisor liable for fines. Article 85.3 allows for individual exemptions to be granted (see page 27 below).

The European Court of Justice has built up a good deal of complex case law analysing the impact of Article 85 (1) on trade between member states.

In the *Technique Minière* case (Case 56/65 *Societe Technique Minière v Maschinebau Ulm* [1966] ECR 235) it was considered necessary to first consider the 'object' of the agreement (exclusivity does not mean *per se*, that the object is to restrict competition). The next step was to consider the 'effect' of the agreement upon competition, taking into account the competition that would exist in the absence of the disputed agreement, the parties market shares, whether or not it was part of a network of agreement (eg a franchise agreement) and its effect upon parallel imports. The court considered that to come within Article 85 (1) the agreement must have an appreciable effect on competition.

In the cases of *Consten and Grundig* however, (Cases 56 and 58/64 *Consten and Grundig v Commission* [1966] ECR 299) the European Court of Justice established the basic principle that agreements which prohibit exports within the Common Market of their nature restrict competition within the meaning of Article 85 (1), irrespective of their actual facts.

These cases therefore distinguish between two kinds of agreement. Those that do not necessarily restrict competition and those that 'of their nature' do.

The *Brasserie de Haecht* case (case 23/67 *Brasserie de Haecht v Wilkin* (No 1) [1967] ECR 407) confirmed that the whole economic context must be taken into account when considering whether or not an agreement has the effect of restricting competition within the meaning of Article 85 (1). This means not only that the existence of a franchise network, for example, must be carefully considered, but also that an agreement in only one member state may still affect trade between member states.

In the *Völk* case (case 5/69 *Völk v Vervaecke* [1969] ECR 295) the 'rule of reason' approach adopted in *Technique Minieret* was endorsed and provides that if market analysis shows the effect on the market to be insignificant Article 85 (1) does not apply despite the existence of absolute territorial protection.

The *'de minimis'* rule is of great importance and is embodied in the Commission's Notice on Agreements of Minor Importance (see below).

The *Metro* cases, (Case 26/27 *Metro v Commission (No 1)* [1977] ECR 1875 and Case 75/84 *Metro v Commission (No 2)* [1986] ECR 3021) however suggested an alternative approach to assessing what amounts to a restriction on competition. The court came to the conclusion that certain restrictions do not come within Article 85 (1) if they can be 'objectively justified' by overriding policy considerations; eg ensuring the distribution of sufficient high quality or high technology products.

The *Nüngesser* or *'Maize Seed'* case (Case 258/78 *Nüngesser v Commission* [1983] ECR 3151) endorsed the *'per se'* approach outlined in *Consten and Grundig,* whilst the *Remia* case (Case 42/84 *Remia v Commission* adopted a *'rule of reason'* approach instead. This *rule of reason* approach means that an agreement is not considered to fall foul of Article 85 (1) if its restrictions are reasonable in both time and scope.

Thus when considering whether or not a franchise agreement falls within Article 85 (1) and has as its 'object or effect the prevention, restrictions or distortion of competition' it must be appreciated that there is a variety of possible approaches that may be adopted by the European Court of Justice and the Commission.

Fortunately however, exactly how Article 85 (1) impacts upon distribution franchise agreements was laid down by the celebrated *Pronuptia* case, which exhibits a mixture of the *Consten and Grundig* 'of their nature' approach and the *Technique Minière 'per se'* approach, together with the more liberal approaches contained in *Metro,* the *Maize Seed, Brasserie de Haecht, Völk* and *Remia.*

The Pronuptia Case

In this case (case no 161/84) *Pronuptia de Paris GmbH Frankfurt am Main v Pronuptia de Paris Irmgard Schillgallis Hamburg* (OJC 191, 19/07/84), the French company, *Pronuptia de Paris SA's* German subsidiary *(Pronuptia de Paris GmbH),* granted three exclusive franchises in Germany to *Firma Pronuptia de Paris Irmgard Schillgallis* (see Appendix 3 for full judgment). Following a bitter disagreement between *Pronuptia de Paris GmbH* and the franchisee, Mrs Schillgalis, the German subsidiary sued her for unpaid royalties. The case passed quickly through the German courts and eventually came before the European Court of Justice raising a number of issues regarding the validity of the franchise agreement and its compatability with Article 85. It should be noted that whilst this case concerned only distribution franchises, the judgment has commonly been taken by lawyers involved in franchising to be indicative of the EC's approach to other forms of franchise.

In *Pronuptia* the provisions in a franchise agreement which are indispensable for the purpose of protecting know how from competitors and those which create controls indispensable for the preservation of the identity and reputation of the network, were considered to be acceptable by the European Court of Justice. These include obligations to apply business methods and know how, to sell goods in premises decorated as directed, to locate outlets as directed, to purchase from the franchisor, franchisees or nominated suppliers, and for the franchisees' advertisement to be vetted by the franchisor. The court ruled that a franchisor can protect the image of his franchise by inserting the appropriate restrictions in the franchise agreement. For a comparison between the *Pronuptia* judgment and the provisions of the block exemption see chapter 4 below.

However, perhaps, more important to note is that, in *Pronuptia* market sharing and concerted practices to put into effect indicative prices were judged *prima facie*, to be anti-competitive practices and therefore not acceptable under Article 85.1. The grant of exclusive territories also falls foul of Article 85 unless it obtains individual exemptions under Articles 85.3 (see page 27 below).

The European Court of Justice ruling in the *Pronuptia* case is very important but ultimately it will be up to the national courts to decide in each case (subject to the block exemption) on the voidness of clauses which may offend Article 85.1. Such a ruling of voidness could have far reaching effects on a franchise. Even if the blue pencil approach of deleting only offending clauses, is adopted by the courts in considering such agreements, the danger is that the entire agreement may be unenforceable, on the grounds that the deletion of the clause changes the whole nature of this agreement. At very best the royalty payment may be greatly reduced, at worst the franchisor will not be able to stop the franchisee setting up in competition using his know-how.

The 'De Minimis Exemption'

There is a *'de minimis'* exemption of which advantage can be taken by franchisors. It is contained in the Notice Concerning Minor Agreements as amended by the Commission Notice [1986] OJC 231/02. Franchises which come within it are automatically exempted from Article 85.1. The franchise must not represent more than 5% of the total market for such goods or services in the areas of the common market affected by the agreement, and the aggregate annual turnover of the participating undertakings must not exceed 200,000,000 ECU (approximately £132,000,000). This is very relevant to most franchises. It means that a franchisor who operates on a small scale can grant exclusive territories under Community law [irrespective of whether he is protected by the block exemption].

Care must be taken to monitor the growth of the franchise, and to identify the relevant market, which is extremely difficult. For example, in the case of a Cardiff based franchise selling factory workers' clothing and uniforms, the market could be the clothing market, the uniform market, the factory clothing market, or the factory clothing market in only particular industries. It could also be the market in the EC, the UK, or Wales. The EC Commission have in the past held a market to be as narrow as the spare parts for a particular brand of cash register. This does not mean that the *de minimis* provision is of no use to franchisors, it merely means that they must carefully consider the market position before relying on it. The Restrictive Trade Practices Act 1976 described below also makes the *de minimis* exemption less attractive than it may seem at first, although the adoption of the White Paper (see below) will render it of somewhat greater significance in future.

Notification

Regulation 17, Article 4 of the Treaty of Rome, provides that in order to take advantage of the exemption to Article 85.1 (available under Article 85.3), or to obtain negative clearance, the agreements must be notified to the EC Commission. Most notifications request both individual exemption and negative clearance in the alternative. Such notification is made by filing form A/B at the Commission together with 11 copies of the agreement. This form can be obtained from the Commission's offices in Brussels or London. Basically, the form gives details of the identity of parties, the purpose of notification, a brief description of the arrangement or behaviour, the market, further details of the parties, details of the arrangements and reasons for the notification.

Notification does not exempt an agreement from Article 85.1. It merely provides interim protection from the time of its notification until the time that the Commission reaches a decision on it.

Failure to notify an agreement which contravenes Article 85.1 results in the parties becoming liable to substantial fines and makes the offending clauses void (see page 25 above). It is possible to approach the Commission for a comfort letter which states (unofficially) that the agreement is not notifiable. Certain agreements which are potentially void under Article 85.1 are exempt from notification under Regulation 17, Article 4.2.

However, this is not of any great relevance to franchise agreements and it will not be dealt with here.

Negative clearance

The Commission has the power, under Regulation 17, Article 2, to certify that upon the facts available to it there are no grounds under Article 85.1 (or Article 86) for action by it in respect of the agreements. Such negative clearance should be sufficient for a franchisor, but really only confirms that Article 85 does not apply. It does not grant any exemption.

Individual exemptions

Since the *Pronuptia* case applications for individual exemptions by *Pronuptia, Yves Rocher, Computerland, Servicemaster* and *Giles Jourdan* have been successful. The *Yves Rocher* agreement, for example, allowed exclusivity of retail outlets to be granted to the franchisee, whilst reserving for the franchisor the right to sell into the territory by way of trade fairs and mail order.

It was considered that in these individual circumstances there were special grounds for allowing terms that might otherwise have been considered to 'prevent restrict or distort' trade between Member States. Such applications should only be made after carefully weighing up the special circumstances that may justify an individual exemption. The popularity of such applications may well decrease now that the EC's Franchising Block Exemption has passed into law.

The block exemption

The most important development in EC law as regards franchising is undoubtedly Regulation 4087/88, the Franchising Block Exemption. In order that it can be fully explained, it is dealt with separately in chapter 4 below.

Article 86

This article (Appendix 2) aims at preventing the exploitation of a dominant position. The use of trade marks and other intellectual property rights to impose 'tie-ins' (ie forced purchasing of goods by franchisees) could possibly amount to such an abuse. The evidential burden of providing not only dominance but also abuse, however, is heavy and it is unlikely that Article 86 will be breached by franchisors as the result of their size.

English law

The relevant English legal provisions of particular interest to franchisors come mainly from four different statutes and case law, rather than one particular Article. Nevertheless, they still succeed in restricting the scope and development of a franchise. In view of the government's White Paper, dated July 1988 and entitled *Opening Markets: New Policy on Restrictive Trade Practices (CM 727)*, English law is likely to assume a form more resembling Article 85 by the early 1990s. These proposals are considered briefly below in appendix 17.

The Restrictive Trade Practices Act 1976 (RTPA)

This highly complex and technical piece of legislation is the most important source of UK law affecting franchising. It necessitates detailed legal drafting of franchise agreements and related documentation. The detailed provisions of the Act must be carefully studied.

The RTPA provides, in brief, that any contract between two or more parties for the supply of goods or services in the UK which contains 'relevant restrictions' accepted by both parties must be registered at the Office of Fair Trading (OFT).

Section 6(1) provides:

"This Act applies to agreements (whenever made) between two or more persons carrying on business within the United Kingdom in the production or supply of goods, or in the application to goods of any process of manufacture, whether with or without other parties, being agreements under which restrictions are accepted by two or more parties in respect of any of the following matters:

(a) the prices to be charged, quoted or paid for goods supplied, offered or acquired, or for the application of any process of manufacture to goods;

(b) the prices to be recommended or suggested as the prices to be charged or quoted in respect of the resale of goods supplied;

(c) the terms or conditions on or subject to which goods are to be supplied or acquired or any such process is to be applied to goods;

(d) the quantities or descriptions of goods to be produced, supplied or acquired;

(e) the processes of manufacture to be applied to any goods, or the quantitites or descriptions of goods to which any such process is to be applied; or

(f) the persons or classes of persons to, for or from whom, or the areas or places in or from which, goods are to be supplied or acquired, or any such process applied."

Section 11 provides that:-

"(1) the Secretary of State may by statutory instrument make an order [*no order has been made yet*] in respect of a class of services described in the order . . . and direct by the order that this Act shall apply to agreements (whenever made) which:
(a) are agreements between two or more persons carrying on business within the United Kingdom in the supply of services brought under control by the order, or between two or more such persons together with one or more other parties; and
(b) are agreements under which restrictions, in respect of matters specified in the order for the purposes of this paragraph, are accepted by two or more parties.

(2) The matters which may be specified in such an order for the purchases of sub-section (1)(b) above are any of the following:
(a) the charges to be made, quoted or paid for designated services supplied, offered or obtained;
(b) the terms or conditions on or subject to which designated services are to be supplied or obtained;
(c) the extent (if any) to which, or the scale (if any) on which, designated services are to be made available, supplied or obtained;
(d) the form or manner in which designated services are to be made available, supplied or obtained;
(e) the persons or classes of persons for whom or from whom, or the areas or places in or from which, designated services are to be made available or supplied or are to be obtained."

It is important to note that it is not necessary for the parties to accept the same relevant restriction. It should also be noted that at least two parties must be carrying on business in the UK. Thus if the agreement is with, say, a Danish company, with no presence in the UK, to establish an area developer in Denmark, the RTPA will not apply.

Sections 6 and 11 are totally separate, If, for example, the franchisor accepts a restriction under s11, not to offer a cleaning service to the public and the franchisee agrees not to sell cleaning fluids (s6), this does not amount to an exchange of relevant restrictions within the RTPA.

Registration at the OFT means that the agreement is placed upon a public file (which could create problems if the operations manual (see chapter 5) is incorporated in it). There is, however, a special confidential section. The Secretary of State can permit any confidential information to be filed in this section if disclosure could substantially damage the franchisor's business. The agreement may be referred to the Restrictive Practices Court (RPC), which can rule the agreement or parts of it to be void. This procedure is very time consuming and expensive. It is, however, possible to negotiate with the OFT under s22 of the RTPA on the grounds that any restrictions are insignificant and so avoid an RPC referral. Failure to register the agreement will result in all such restrictions in the agreement becoming void. Any party giving effect to it will be transgressing the law and a court can order its cessation.

It is important that the franchise agreement, if at all possible, avoids the necessity of registration at the OFT by drafting the agreement in such a way that it does not contain an exchange of restrictions. There is a body of opinion, however, that believes that in any event the agreement should be registered to prevent possible challenges by franchisees in the future.

If it is necessary to register an agreement, it should be done before any of the restrictions are accepted and in any event within three months of the day on which the agreement is made.

Form C2/76 should be used to register an agreement accompanied by three copies of it. In order to avoid the need to file every agreement entered into by the franchisor with a franchisee, a memorandum of other parallel agreements can be appended. This saves everyone concerned time and money, although there is no registration fee. A copy of any form A/B notifying the agreement to the EC Commission should also be filed with the OFT (see page 26 above).

The best way of illustrating the potential impact of the RTPA upon a franchise agreement is by way of a hypothetical example. Imagine a 'soft-soap' franchise with a network of ten stores retailing skin-care products in the UK through high street outlets which also operates a home delivery service. Nine of the stores are in the South East, the tenth in Nottingham. Owing to a stressed infra-structure and lack of capital the company has decided to offer 'soft-soap' franchise packages to suitable would-be franchisees in the Midlands area.

The franchise agreement provides that each franchisee will be given the sole right to operate an outlet in a specific area, but that it must not use its home delivery service to sell into the areas serviced by any other branch or franchise outlets. This is seen as being of particular relevance to the Derby franchisee who might have the opportunity of selling into the area serviced by the Nottingham branch. It also helps to safeguard the

Leicester franchisee's investment against the more aggressive neighbouring franchisee in Derby.

The reasoning behind the imposition of these restrictions may seem to be a matter of mere commercial common sense, but it is in fact out of step with the law, and the franchise agreement must be registered under the RTPA.

The grant of an exclusive territory is perhaps the most common way in which such a franchise agreement runs into difficulties with the RTPA even though exclusivity is desired by both the franchisor, to protect existing branch outlets, and to allow a more structured approach to marketing, and by the franchisee, to protect his investment from more aggressive franchisees and company branch outlets. It is seen as being against the ultimate interests of the consumer, and therefore is not permitted. By agreeing to an exclusive territory both the franchisor and the franchisee accept a geographical restriction, which is a relevant restriction under the RTPA.

Other clauses which may cause similar difficulties are those imposing tie-ins (ie forcing the franchisee to purchase goods or services from the franchisor), non-competition clauses concerning exclusive supply and purchase, and minimum price clauses (when permitted by the Retail Prices Act 1976). It should be remembered that although the Act only bites if relevant restrictions are accepted by both parties, as pointed out above; the parties do not have to accept the same restriction.

Thus, if the franchisor described above decided to remove the provision for exclusive territories and replace it with an undertaking not to itself sell into the franchisee's area, this does not bring the RTPA into play. The franchisee has not accepted a geographical restriction. It can sell wherever it wishes, and it is not protected from neighbouring franchises. The franchisor has accepted a relevant restriction but the franchisee has not. If however the franchisee agrees to purchase from the franchisor only equipment for use in the franchise operation, such as for example a warehouse shelving unit, the acceptance of such a tie-in is a relevant restriction. As both parties are accepting a relevant restriction, even though they are different restrictions, the RTPA bites.

There are exemptions available for provisions which relate 'exclusively to the goods' under s9 of the RTPA and to, amongst others, trade marks, patents and registered designs, know-how and exclusive dealing under Schedule 3 of the same Act. These exemptions should always be considered when drafting a franchise agreement but are of a very technical nature and have only limited application. For example, it may be possible under s9 to allow the introduction of a clause preventing the franchisor from supplying similar goods to other persons within a given area, although it is not certain that the restriction upon a franchisee purchasing from an alternative source could be disregarded. Schedule 3 exemptions are looked to only once any exemptions under s9 have been taken advantage of and are of an exclusive nature. This means that if, for example, the franchisor avails himself of the trade mark exemption, by entering into what is known as a s28 registered user agreement and ensuring that any restriction applies only to goods bearing the mark or the processes used to manufacture the same, it cannot also take advantage of the know-how or exclusive dealing exemption.

In trying to decide whether or not the franchise agreement is registrable under the RTPA, there are three basic questions to be asked:

(a) Do both parties accept any relevant restrictions? (See s6 for goods and s11 for services. See page 28 above)
(b) If relevant restrictions are accepted by both parties, can they be disregarded under s9 (see page 31 above).
(c) If there is still an exchange of relevant restrictions does any part of Schedule 3 afford any exemption? (See page 31 above.)

If there is still an exchange of restriction it must be registered at the OFT.

Franchisors must bear this in mind and remember that even though the original agreement itself contains no exchange of relevant restrictions, subsequent correspondence, such as a letter to a franchisee confirming the franchisor's 'off the record' intention not to appoint another franchisee in the same area, may create such an exchange and cause the RTPA to bite.

As mentioned above, the government has concluded in the White Paper that the present regime does not effectively prevent anti-competitive agreements being entered into. The RTPA is seen as over complex, technical and rigid.

The proposed new system will require an assessment of the economic impact of the franchise on the market place rather than the over-technical approach currently adopted by the RTPA. It will concentrate not on the form of the agreement but the effect it, and any concerted practices, may have.

It is proposed that certain practices will be prohibited. In terms of franchising the most important will be market sharing, price fixing, non-competition clauses and advertising. Most importantly block exemptions, similar to those granted by the EC Commission will be granted by a regulatory authority, probably the OFT. Properly drafted franchise agreements will be able to take advantage of such a block exemption. These proposals are described in more detail in Appendix 17 below.

Common law

The common law is of markedly less importance than Article 85 and the RTPA. Nevertheless the case of *Esso Petroleum Co Ltd v Harpers Garage (Stockport) Ltd* ([1986] AC 269 HL) developed some points which are relevant to franchising. It shows how a franchise agreement might be treated by the courts when a franchisor tries to enforce it against a franchisee.

In this case *Harpers Garage* entered into a solus agreement to buy petrol exclusively from *Esso* for a certain period of years and amongst other things agreed to keep the garage open at all reasonable hours, and in the event of selling the garage to a third party, to obtain the same agreement from the purchaser. In return the garage obtained a number of benefits including a discount of the price of petrol.

Examining the franchise agreement, the courts looked at the trading pattern of the whole chain, not just one agreement in isolation. The benefits of any particular restraint were weighed up against the disadvantages.

When presented with the task of ruling upon the legality of the franchise agreement or a specific clause under common law its basic approach was to adopt the 'rule of reason.' This meant asking whether or not the social and economic circumstances had changed so much since the signing of the agreement that the term was no longer reasonable. This shows the importance of updating the franchise agreement periodically upon renewal. Interesting though this common law may be to legal academics, it is true to say that it only has any real impact upon a franchisor if it becomes involved in litigation. At such time it is not uncommon to find potentially void clauses operating with varying degrees of success in the franchise agreement. In such cases the court is most likely merely to rule the offending clause to be void.

If a clause is so basic that its deletion changes the underlying nature of the agreement, the franchisee may ask the court to rule the whole agreement void on the basis that the new agreement is not what he originally bargained for. The consequences of such a request, if granted are grave for the franchisor and may include the non-payment of any franchise or management fees and the unenforceability of any non-competition clauses.

Competition Act 1980

This Act aims to foster competition, and gives the Director General of Fair Trading power to control any practice which he can identify as being anti-competitive.

The size of most franchise operations means that this Act is unlikely to apply. It does have potential relevance to public policy clauses, including price discrimination, predatory pricing and vertical price squeezing; and distribution policy clauses including tie-ins, full-line forcing, rental only contracts, exclusive supply, selective distribution and exclusive price arrangements among others. If an agreement is registrable under the RTPA it is automatically exempt from the Competition Act. Following the White Paper on Restrictive Trade Practices this Act is being reviewed by the government.

Retail Prices Act 1976

The imposition of minimum retail prices is prohibited by s9 of this Act. As it does not affect services or further processed goods, its application to franchising is somewhat limited. For example whilst it is against the law to impose a minimum price on the sale of a can of fruit juice, it is permissible for the franchisor to impose a minimum price on a hamburger, which the franchisee has made in accordance with the franchise system's recipe, or upon the costs of a courier service. The proposed new Restrictive Trade Practices Act is likely to repeal this Act.

The Fair Trading Act 1973

This piece of legislation was passed in response to the abuses of pyramid selling in the late 1960's and early 1970's. The most notable abuse, as discussed in chapter 2 above, was the *Minnie Pearl Chicken System* which, when it failed in 1969 had sold 1,800 franchises but had opened only 161 outlets.

Pyramid selling is a multi-level distributorship in which each distributor sells the goods to several sub-distributors who in turn sell on to a number of sub-sub-distributors and so on. At the end of the day, participants end up with over-priced merchandise they are unable to sell. The statute's approach is to control the advertising of such schemes and impose, amongst other things, a cooling off period.

The Secretary of State has also exercised the powers, granted to him under the Act, to issue a statutory instrument regulating the issue, circulation and distribution of advertisements, prospectuses, circulars and notices.

The common form of franchise where a franchisor grants a licence to a franchisee who sells to the end-user will not usually fall foul of this legislation. It may, however, create difficulties for an overseas franchisor, seeking to franchise through its own UK subsidiary to a master licensee, who in turn franchises to unit franchisees. The Fair Trading Act is currently being reviewed by the government.

Conclusion

It can be seen from the above that the structure and growth of franchises in the United Kingdom have, until February 1989, been restricted by the law of the EC and that of England. Despite the more enlightened parts of the *Pronuptia* judgment, key terms such as exclusivity have been difficult to impose. How the EC block exemption (and the proposed UK block exemption) affects this situation is dealt with in the following chapter.

Chapter 4
EC REGULATION 4087/88 –
THE BLOCK EXEMPTION

According to Jean Eric de Cockborne LLD Principal Administrator at the EC Commission (*Journal of International Franchising and Distribution Law*, March 1989), the block exemption:

"... does not intend to give a general definition of all possible kinds of franchise agreements, but attempts to determine a category which is sufficiently homogeneous to make it possible to assume that agreements corresponding to that definition, and fulfilling the other conditions set out in the Regulation will normally meet the conditions for application of Article 85(3)".

The adoption of Regulation 4087/88 (see Appendix 3 for full text) by the EC Commission was a major step forward for the franchising industry in Europe. It clearly signifies its coming-of-age as a method of doing business in the EC. It can be seen as giving a degree of credibility and recognition to franchising on a Pan-European level which previously it lacked. No more do the legal and administrative authorities of the European Community regard it as little more than a slight variation upon ordinary distributorship. The block exemption states quite clearly that franchising is here to stay.

Franchisors have welcomed the Commission's declaration in the introductory part of the Regulation that:

"franchise agreements normally improve the distribution of goods and/or the provision of services as they give franchisors the possibility of establishing a uniform network with limited investment which may assist the entry of new competitors into the market, particularly in the case of small and medium sized undertakings thus increasing inter-brand competition and allowing independent traders to set up outlets more rapidly and with a higher chance of success than if they had to do so without the franchisor's experience and assistance".

The Commission realises that it gives franchisors a greater chance of competing more efficiently with large distribution undertakings. Equally, the realisation by the Commission that franchises also allow consumers and other end-users a fair share of the resulting benefit is to be applauded. The block exemption was passed on 30th November 1988 and came into force on 1st February 1989 until 31st December 1999. Block exemptions are a common part of the EEC's legal armoury and are used to reduce the workload placed upon the Commission in considering applications for individual exemptions from Article 85 of the Treaty of Rome. Block exemptions have also been passed for, amongst other matters, exclusive distribution agreements, exclusive supply agreements, patent licences and know-how licences. By complying with the terms of the block exemption, franchisors will gain automatic exemption from Article 85.

The structure of the franchising block exemption is in the usual form. It commences with a preface justifying the block exemption. This is followed by:

(1) Article 1: Defining terms used.

(2) Article 2: Specifying **exempted** provisions.

(3) Article 3: Describing provisions which **can** be imposed.

(4) Article 4: Detailing compulsory provisions which **must** be included.

(5) Article 5: Listing prohibited provisions which **cannot** be included.

(6) Articles 6, 7, 8 and 9: Procedural matters including the Commission's power to oppose and/or disapply the exemption if appropriate.

Definitions

This regulation covers franchise agreements between two undertakings, the franchisor and the franchisee, for the retailing of goods or the provision of services to end-users, or a combination of these activities, such as the processing or adaptation of goods to fit specific needs of their customers. It also covers cases where the relationship between franchisor and franchisees is made through a third undertaking, the master franchisee. It does not cover wholesale franchise agreements because of the lack of experience of the Commission in that field.

Article 1 contains a number of definitions which deserve some careful consideration because only a franchise agreement as defined by this

Article can take advantage of it. This is of great importance bearing in mind Jean-Eric de Cockborne's comments above (page 35).

(a) *Franchise* means a package of industrial or intellectual property rights relating to trade marks, trade names, shop signs, utility models, designs, copyrights, know-how or patents, to be exploited for the resale of goods or the provision of services to end-users;

(b) *Franchise agreement* means an agreement whereby one undertaking, the franchisor, grants the other, the franchisee, in exchange for direct or indirect financial consideration, the right to exploit a franchise for the purpose of marketing specified types of goods and/or services; it includes at least obligations relating to:

    (i) the use of a common name or shop sign and a uniform presentation of contract premises and/or means of transport

    (ii) the communication by the franchisor to the franchisee of know-how

    (iii) the continuing provision by the franchisor to the franchisee of commercial or technical assistance during the life of the agreement

(c) *Master franchise agreement* means an agreement whereby one undertaking, the franchisor, grants the other, the master franchisee, in exchange for direct or indirect financial consideration, the right to exploit a franchise for the purposes of concluding franchise agreements with third parties, the franchisees;

(d) *Franchisor's goods* means goods produced by the franchisor or according to its instructions, and/or bearing the franchisor's name or trade mark;

(e) *Contract premises* means the premises used for the exploitation of the franchise or, when the franchise is exploited outside those premises, the base from which the franchisee operates the means of transport used for the exploitation of the franchise (contract means of transport);

(f) *Know-how* means a package of non-patented practical information, resulting from experience and testing by the franchisor, which is secret, substantial and identified;

(g) *Secret* means that the know-how, as a body or in the precise configuration and assembly of its components, is not generally known or easily accessible, it is not limited in the narrow sense that each individual component of the know-how should be totally unknown or unobtainable outside the franchisor's business;

(h) *Substantial* means that the know-how includes information which is of importance for the sale of goods or the provision of services to end-users, and in particular for the presentation of goods for sale, the processing of goods in connection with the provision of services, methods of dealing with customers, administration and financial management. The know-how must be useful for the franchisee by being capable, at the date of conclusion of the agreement, of improving the competitive position of the franchisee, in particular by improving the franchisee's performance or helping it to enter a new market;

(i) *Identified* means that the know-how must be described in a sufficiently comprehensive manner to make it possible to verify that it fulfils the criteria of secrecy and substantiality; the description of the know-how can be set out either in the franchise agreement or in a separate document, or recorded in any other appropriate form.

The table in Appendix 3 details the respective provisions and gives examples of clauses which will be affected. The real difficulties with the block exemption will be experienced by agreements which contain restrictions not referred to in it. It will then be necessary for the professional advisers to decide whether or not they fall within its general provisions.

Unfortunately full advantage cannot be taken of the block exemption in the UK until UK anti-trust law (ie RTPA) is amended to accord with that of the EC (see chapter 3 above). Following the government White Paper in July 1988, this is likely to take place by 1991.

Problems presented by the Regulation

The block exemption, like most law, is the result of negotiation and compromise. Whilst the franchising lobby, especially the representatives of the International Franchise Association (IFA) wanted complete freedom for franchisors in Europe, the Commission was concerned to ensure that its usual approach was taken and its concerns over restrictions on trade properly addressed.

As a result, though the franchise block exemption is in most aspects far less restrictive than other block exemptions (such as the Know-How Regulation). There are still a number of lacunae, deliberate or not, that franchisors may find problematic or at least illogical and inconvenient. One of the biggest 'gaps' is the omission of wholesale franchises from the Regulation (Article 1.3(a)) by the definition of a franchise being construed as one that sells goods or provides services to *end users*.

The Commission's usual approach to anti-trust issues has lead it to require that under the Regulation, parallel imports are allowed (Article 4(a)). This could seriously prejudice new product lines which may need to be adapted to the needs of a particular territory before its distribution there. This will have a direct effect on many franchisors which have outlets throughout Europe. Goods sold in Italy may not be suitable for, say, Denmark, until they are modified to accommodate Danish consumer preferences.

The prohibition on the franchisor stipulating resale prices in Article 5(e) presents even greater problems. Not only is it not allowed to set maximum prices, it is not even allowed to set minimum ones. This lack of control over pricing structure could create major difficulties for many franchisors and may well mean that several are unable to take advantage of the Block Exemption with any ease. It must be said, however, that price fixing is such anathema to the Commission that it is unlikely that individual exemption will be granted unless there are exceptional economic reasons for the pricing structure. The implications of this inability to control pricing are that the franchisors' common identity and reputation are likely to suffer as a result.

As in all other block exemptions, the EC Commission has elected to maintain the rather artificial distinction between passive and active selling. The issue touches the very heart of the Commission's dilemma in trying to reconcile the need to facilitate free trade between Member States with the commercial importance of exclusivity. The solution opted for is to allow franchisees to make unsolicited sales out of their territory and into a third party's exclusive territory, ie passive selling. Solicited sales, ie active selling, outside of the territory are not, however, permitted. Commercial reality means that this distinction is somewhat difficult to enforce. A franchisee might sell goods to consumers living in a neighbouring franchisee's territory as a result of his price cutting habits. When the goods need guarantee/warranty work to be carried out, it is a condition of taking advantage of the block exemption that all franchisees provide such a service (Article 4(b)). This could therefore result in an uneven burden being placed upon one franchisee.

Article 2(e) excludes spare parts from the permitted prohibition on competing goods. This could lead to considerable quality control problems, especially as regards guarantee work. Thus, if spare parts are essential to the franchise, it would seem that it will be necessary to apply for individual exemption rather than seeking to take advantage of the block exemption.

The requirement that a franchisee must be able to hold a financial interest in a competitor so long as it does not allow it to influence the economic activity of such an undertaking (Article 3.1(d)), could cause the franchisor considerable problems. The leaking of know-how and general threat to confidentiality is a reality which cannot be ignored, and the policing difficulties present still further difficulty for the franchisor.

Finally, the definition of a Master Franchise Agreement (Article 1) is somewhat restrictive and means that there is probably little scope for structuring such agreements through, for example, a joint venture between the franchisor and area developer.

Taking advantage of the block exemption

When drafting a franchise agreement (see chapter 5) it is necessary to pay careful attention to the terms of the block exemption. This means excluding the prohibited clauses contained in Article 5 and including the mandatory clauses described in Article 4. Further, Article 3 must be carefully scrutinised to ensure that 'grey' clauses are properly drafted. Such an approach will mean that the exempted clauses contained in Article 2 can be incorporated.

The important point to bear in mind is that if any 'black' clause is included – for example, price fixing – advantage cannot be taken of the regulation. In such a case, however, the franchisor may be able to obtain an individual exemption if there are strong enough economic reasons for its inclusion.

Another example of an agreement which may not be able to take advantage of the block exemption is a conversion such as a hairdressing franchise by which existing salons adopt the franchisor's know-how, names and marks, etc. (*Alan Paul* is an example). The agreement will probably be between two competitors and therefore prohibited from taking advantage of the block exemption by Article 5. The need to define the market is crucial in such a case.

Definitions are also important and need to be considered. For example, Article 1.3(b) suggests that the agreement can only be between two parties; the franchisor and the franchisee. It is suggested that it is, however, possible to include further parties, such as guarantors, and still be able to take advantage of the block exemption if it amounts to a bundle of bilateral rights and obligations rather than ones which are trilateral.

Types of restrictions permitted

The draftsman should particularly note the following points when drafting the franchise agreement:

Territorial exclusivity

Exclusivity is desirable from the stand point of both franchisor and franchisee. The Regulation recognises this and allows three types of exclusivity. The franchisor can agree:

(a) not to appoint another franchisee in the contract territory;

(b) not to exploit the franchise itself or to market the goods and services which are subject to the franchise in the contract territory;

(c) not to sell its goods to third parties in the contract territory.

As in the patent block exemption and the know-how block exemption the Commission draws an uneasy distinction between passive and active selling (see page 39 above) which is hard to justify on a strictly commercial basis.

Non-competition classes

The Regulation allows three types of non-competition clauses:

(a) The franchisee may be required not to compete directly or indirectly in a similar business in the territory in competition with a member of the franchise network for a reasonable period of up to one year (it should be noted that one year will not always be seen by the Commission as being reasonable).

(b) The franchisee may be required not to acquire financial interests in the capital of a competing undertaking sufficient to give him the power to influence its economic conduct.

(c) The franchisor may impose a customer restriction by requiring the franchisee to sell only to end-users and other franchisees where these goods are not sold through other channels by the manufacturer or with his consent.

41

Location clauses

The block exemption allows two types of location clauses:

(a) The franchisee may be compelled to obtain the franchisor's consent to any change in the location of the premises. However, if the franchisor unreasonably refuses consent, ie for reasons other than for protecting its industrial/intellectual property rights and maintaining the common identity and reputation of the network, the benefit of the block exemption can be withdrawn.

(b) The franchisee may be required to exploit the franchise from the named premises only.

Quality controls

'White' clauses permitting the imposition of quality controls include:

(a) The application of the franchisor's commercial methods and use of the licensed intellectual property rights.

(b) Compliance with the franchisor's standards as regards equipment, premises and transport.

(c) Co-operating with any inspection by the franchisor.

(d) Refraining from assigning any rights or obligations.

Withdrawal of benefit

Merely drafting an agreement to comply with the block exemption is not sufficient, however. The franchisor must ensure that its conduct also complies. Franchisors must note that Article 8 allows the Commission to *withdraw* the benefit of the block exemption if the effects of the agreement, even though it complies ostensibly with the block exemption, are contrary to Article 85. This poses a particular threat to exclusivity which, according to Article 8, could be deemed to be contrary to Article 85 in certain circumstances. This is acceptable in principle, but not all of these specified circumstances seem to be as anti-competitive as the Commission suggests. Of particular concern are:

(a) A parallel network of similar agreements by competitors restricting access to a market or competition. This provision fails to see the economic reality that if other networks are able to offer exclusivity the franchisor may find it difficult to attract new franchisees or retain existing ones.

(b) The isolation of markets by use of different specifications. This is unrealistic in many circumstances because even after 1992 many technical barriers to a single market will remain, often making differing specification for each EC Member State essential.

(c) Concerted practices by franchisees concerning resale prices. This means that great care must be taken by franchisees at franchisee meetings and precautions must be taken to help prevent any allegations of a concerted practice. This is however very difficult for the franchisor to effect as he is more often than not excluded from franchisee meetings.

(d) The abuse of the franchisor's rights to check premises and transport, and to give prior consent for relocation of premises and assignment of the franchise. A franchisor should not, of course, commit such abuses, but this provision could lead franchisees to make allegations of such to the Commission and so threaten to remove the benefit of the block exemption from the franchisor if there is some legitimate disagreement between them.

Which franchises will it affect?

The future for franchising in the EC, in general terms, seems to be rosy, but exactly what effect the block exemption will have at grass roots level, upon franchisors currently established in the United Kingdom, is open to some discussion. Does it really amount to a change in the EC Commission's approach and attitude to franchising? How does it fit in with the law of each EC Member State? In order to answer these questions fully, the block exemption must be seen in its proper legal perspective. It is not, as some lawyers might suggest, the 'be all and end all' of franchising law. Nor should it be a 'fatted calf' upon which lawyers gorge themselves.

As has been pointed out (chapter 3), franchising in the United Kingdom is currently governed by two sets of laws. Firstly, there is EC law in the form of Article 85 of the Treaty of Rome, and secondly, English law, particularly the Restrictive Trade Practices Act 1976. These two sources of law are quite different and do not always sit well together.

Article 85 of The Treaty of Rome prohibits anything that tends to prevent, restrict or distort trade between Member States, which in terms of franchising (according to the *Pronuptia* case) means exclusive territories, price controls and restrictions upon sales between franchisees.

By drafting an agreement which accords with the block exemption the franchisor is now able, amongst other things, to grant exclusive territories, impose location clauses, limit tie-in requirements and prevent franchisees from selling competing goods without offending against Article 85 (1). It might therefore be supposed that, freed from the shackles of the *Pronuptia* decision, franchisors would take advantage of the block exemption to issue new franchise agreements containing, amongst other things, grants of exclusive territories to franchisees. This (in the author's opinion) is unlikely to be, as in reality the effect of *Pronuptia* is somewhat remote from many franchisors in the United Kingdom who, instead of living in reluctant compliance with the *Pronuptia* decision, take advantage of the *de minimis* exemption described in the previous chapter, despite the associated difficulties discussed.

A second reason why there is unlikely to be a flood of new franchise agreements is that those larger franchises which are not able to take advantage of the '*de minimis*' exemption, or those which fear that they will soon exceed the turnover/market share requirements are nevertheless able to apply for individual exemption from the agreements under Article 85 (3) (see chapter 3 above).

Many notified agreements, not only franchise agreements, spend years in the filing cabinets of the Commission without being looked at. Others, however, such as those of *Yves Rocher, Computerland, Servicemaster* and *Giles Jorudan* have been scrutinised by the Commission and, after some negotiation, amended to comply with the demands of the Commission following which they have been accepted and validated.

A comparison of these decisions with the block exemption is interesting. Not surprisingly, the decision of the Commission in such cases tends to be somewhat similar to the approach of the block exemption.

The ability to grant absolute exclusive territories and impose location requirements under the block exemption will no doubt be of some value to larger franchises but it should be borne in mind that as mentioned in the previous chapter, the Commission has previously granted limited exclusivity under Article 85 (3), to *Yves Rocher* for example. In this case a competing mail order trade in the contract territory was considered sufficient to grant the franchisees exclusive retail rights. Although the block exemption does introduce certain substantive changes, together with complete procedural changes in EC law, it would be wrong to suppose that it amounts to a complete change and liberalisation in the Commission's approach to franchise agreements. Indeed, those obligations referred to in Article 3.1 are permitted only 'as far as necessary' to protect the franchisors' intellectual industrial property rights or maintain the common identity and reputation of the network.

Further there are in certain provisions of the Regulation 'double-necessity' tests such as the duration of a post-contractual non-competition clause in Article 3.1 (b). Even objective quality requirements for products sold by the franchisee (Article 3.1 (a)) are conditional upon necessity, whereas the court in *Pronuptia* accepted it without any such condition. This leaves a good deal of discretionary power to the national courts and may lead to uncertainty and differences between individual Member States.

As regards English law, the Restrictive Trade Practices Act 1976 (as discussed in chapter 3 above) concentrates upon the detailed form of the agreement rather than its effect. The provision giving rise most commonly to such an exchange of restrictions is the granting of an exclusive territory by the franchisor to the franchisee.

As current legal opinion is against registration with the OFT in most cases, a third reason why the block exemption will not have a significant, immediate effect on franchisors in the UK is apparent; the general approach in drafting franchise agreements for use in the United Kingdom is to ensure that all of the restrictions are imposed upon the franchisee and not the franchisor. This means that exclusive territories as such are not usually granted because such a grant necessarily means that the franchisor accepts the restriction not to appoint any more franchisees in the territory. Until English competition law is substantially amended, as is likely to be the case in the next few years, the freedom to grant exclusive territories under the block exemption is unlikely to benefit most franchisors in the United Kingdom unless they have first been registered at the OFT and any relevant restrictions have been deemed to be insignificant.

Conclusion

The block exemption is certainly a step in the right direction, but the existence of other exemptions (individual and *de minimis*) and the difficulties caused by English law has to date reduced its impact. Following the adoption of the proposals contained in the current government White Paper however (see pages 28 and 32 above), it is likely to exercise a far greater influence over the drafting and structure of franchise agreements in the UK than it does at present.

Chapter 5
THE FRANCHISE AGREEMENT

Structure

Once it has been decided to franchise a business, it is necessary to consider exactly what form the franchise should take: what should be its management structure. There is no such thing as a correct or incorrect structure. The aim must be to adopt whatever structure best facilitates simple and effective control of the franchisees, and avoids over burdening the franchisor's managerial and financial resources; commercial rather than legal considerations should determine the franchise structure.

A further consideration for the structure of a franchise is of course the tax implications. The advice of an accountant or tax lawyer familiar with franchising is vital.

Negotiation

Before entering into discussions with prospective franchisees clearly it is essential that the basic legal documentation has been drafted in a balanced manner. It must be remembered that all franchisees will be signing the same documents, and it is therefore bad practice to grant different terms to individual franchisees, however desperate the franchisor may be to sign up the first few franchisees. Discussions may lead to slight modification of the basic documentation, usually by way of a side letter. However, to grant preferential terms to a number of franchisees or indeed to accept a lower calibre applicant will most likely lead to future problems. All too often such 'special deals' have given rise to dissatisfaction on the part of franchisees who were not given such favourable terms. These have, in turn, caused a general lack of trust and co-operation between the franchisor and its franchisees.

Application form

Recruitment of good franchisees, although more of an art than a science, is vital to the success of the franchise. The application form can make recruitment much easier and should give the franchisor as much information about the potential franchisee as possible. It should require full and frank disclosure of the applicant's financial status and details of individuals' background and personal circumstances. The franchisor must try to ensure that, during the first couple of years of the franchise, when the franchisee's income will be at its lowest, his domestic and other financial commitments will not be too heavy. A sudden rise in mortgage interest rates for example can sometimes create unexpected cashflow problems for the franchisee. This in turn can push the franchisee into trying to maximise his income by 'cheating' the franchisor by underdeclaring his turnover, and so underpaying the royalty/management service fee.

The aim is to enable the franchisor to sort out the chaff from the wheat at the earliest possible stage. Even the simple question; 'Why do you wish to become a franchisee of Bloggs & Co?', is often very revealing.

Once a candidate has been short listed he/she (or its shareholders and directors in the case of a corporate franchisee), should then be interviewed, preferably twice. The second occasion should take place if possible, in the candidate's own home, as this is of great help in assessing his/her suitability. If the home is untidy and dirty, you can expect the franchise outlet to be in the same condition!

Confidentiality agreement

The franchisor and potential franchisee should enter into a contract before signing the actual franchise agreement in order to protect their respective interests. The confidentiality agreement should state that in consideration of a deposit, either refundable in whole or part, the franchisor will release sufficient confidential information to the potential franchisee to enable him to construct a business plan. Such a plan will then be used to obtain finance from a bank. The most important clause from the franchisor's point of view is the requirement for the potential franchisee not to compete with the franchisor or otherwise abuse the confidential information given. Such an agreement will normally last for two to three months after which time either the franchise agreement itself will be executed or the potential franchisee will have withdrawn. It should also oblige the franchisee to take independent legal advice.

The manual

The franchise operations manual is arguably the most important document which the franchisor must produce. It contains all of the franchisor's know-how, and details the operational aspects of the business. It should of course be well presented, written in an easily understandable style on durable card or paper and be well indexed and cross referenced.

It will usually be included, by reference, in the franchise agreement to impose upon the franchisee a contractual obligation to comply with it. One of the franchisors' most important functions is continually to update and improve the manual. This is best done by ensuring that the manual is loose-leaved so that updated sections can be added easily. Each page should be properly numbered and dated.

To avoid any doubt or confusion, the franchise agreement should state that the manual kept by the franchisor at its offices will be deemed to be the current version.

The sort of detail the manual should contain is well-illustrated by the one used by a well-known fast food chain. It states, for example, that four ice cubes should be put in each soft drink (not five or three, but four). It also contains procedures for dealing with blind customers which includes, for example, giving them a menu, even though they cannot read it, to put them at ease, and telling them when you are walking away from the table so that they are not left talking to themselves. The manual is the result of the franchisor's own bitter experiences. It is exactly this for which the franchisee, to a large extent, is paying.

Drafting the manual is a long and difficult task and whilst many franchisors (in the author's opinion, quite properly) do it themselves, others hire a consultant to assist them. In either event, it will form part of the franchise agreement and so it is vital that it is vetted by the franchisor's solicitor before it is distributed to the franchisees.

The franchise agreement

There is no proper way to draft a franchise agreement, but whatever form it takes it must provide the franchisor with the power to control the franchise not only for his own sake but also for the sake of all the franchisees who have invested their own money, time and labour. It must also comply with the relevant laws (see chapter 3 above). The usual clauses include:

Recitals
Rights granted to the franchisee
Term and renewal
The franchisor's initial obligations
The franchisor's continuing obligations
Franchisee's obligations

Targets
Initial training
Continuing training
Payments to the franchisor
Premises
Invoicing
Promotion and advertising
Trade marks
Audit
The sale of the business
Termination
Consequences of termination
Waiver
Severability
Limitation of liability
Assignment by franchisor
Arbitration
Force Majeure
Notices
Whole agreement
Execution clauses

In the following pages, the basic issues to be addressed when drafting a franchise agreement are analysed in a manner which hopefully will give the reader a flavour of the issues involved and how they might be approached. Sample clauses are also included. Clearly every franchise agreement is different and the sample clauses may not be suitable or relevant to all franchises. They will also often require some expansion.

Term and renewal

"This Agreement shall, subject to the provision for termination in Clause 14 below, subsist for an initial period of 7 years commencing on the 20th day of December 1989, and be renewable, on the terms then currently being offered to franchisees by the franchisor, for a further 7 year period subject to there being no existing breach and the franchisee agreeing to refurbish the premises as directed by the franchisor."

In general the period of a franchise in the UK is shorter than its counterpart in the USA, and a 7 year basic term is not unusual. In essence it is a commercial decision which may well depend upon the nature of the franchised business. The term is not usually controversial and a good many franchise agreements provide for a shorter term (say 5 years) which is then renewable.

If the franchisee is investing a good deal of personal capital, time and labour in the franchise he will want to see a return upon his investment, above and beyond the income derived from the initial term. The goodwill of the business must of course rest in the franchise itself and not in the individual franchisee. Nevertheless it is far from equitable to expect a franchisee to give up his investment (ie the outlet), unless there is a good reason for him to do so.

On the other hand if the franchisor is to be able to maintain the high standards of his franchise he must be able to terminate franchisees who do not conform with those standards, or adopt the latest products, "get up" or methodology of the franchise.

It is good practice to provide that the franchise agreement should be renewable for a further term, subject to the franchisee adopting the then current franchise agreement and making whatever alterations to the outlet are necessary to conform to the latest image of the chain (eg shop fronts, staff uniforms, transport, etc). The franchisor must also have the right to terminate for non-performance by the franchisee. This is discussed in more detail below.

A renewal fee is sometimes charged depending upon the structure of the franchisor's income. In general terms, however, such a fee is, in the author's opinion, undesirable. Any reasonable profit should be realised through the royalty/service charge rather than by a renewal fee. This ensures the franchisor's continuing interest in the franchise.

Rights granted to the franchisee

"Subject to and in accordance with the terms hereof the franchisee shall have:

(a) the right to operate the services under the marks;

(b) the right to use in the business the marks and other symbols, insignia, distinctive designs and plans or specifications owned, or authorised to be used, by the franchisor together with benefit of the accumulated experience and knowledge relating to provisions of the Services;

(c) the royalty free right to use in the business the copyright in any printed matter, distinctive features, marks, fabric designs and drawings and any other relevant matter or materials developed by the franchisor for use in the business; and

(d) all other rights and benefits accruing to the franchisee by virtue of this Agreement."

In most cases, what makes the franchise valuable, is not what is done, but the way in which it is done and the trade marks/service marks under which it is done. The grant of the right to use the marks is therefore very important. It is consequently essential that any marks are registered by the franchisor before commencing the franchise and that their use by the franchisees is very carefully monitored. Protection of the marks is very important, and the block exemption (see chapter 4) allows a number of provisions on the basis that their inclusion is necessary to protect the marks, name and reputation of the franchisor. The right for franchisees to use the marks and other intellectual property rights should exist only so long as the agreement is valid, and appropriate non-competition clauses should be included.

The know-how granted to the franchisee is usually contained in the franchisor's manual and incorporated by reference into the actual agreement (see page 47 above).

The franchisor's obligations

"To assist the franchisee in conducting the business, the franchisor will provide or make available to the franchisee the following:

(a) initial training in the method, lasting for 2 weeks, at one of the franchisor's training centres in the United Kingdom;

(b) advice in regard to choosing a suitable site for the business ('the premises');

(c) the continual update of, and training in, any alterations and/or improvements in or to the System, together with an up to date Manual. In the event of any dispute, the authentic text of the Manual shall be the copy kept as such by the franchisor at its head office. The Manual shall at all times remain the property of the franchisor. The franchisee hereby acknowledges that the copyright in the Manual is invested in the franchisor;

(d) copies of all other advertising materials as soon as practicable;

(e) at the franchisee's reasonable request, advice, know-how and guidance in such areas as management, finance and promotion of the business and any equipment to be employed in connection therewith;

(f) up to date information regarding all conventions, seminars or franchise meetings organised by the franchisor and permit or arrange for the franchisee at its own expense to attend such events. No charge will be made by the franchisor for attendance at conventions, seminars or meetings;

(g) a sufficient number of any newsletters published by the franchisor to enable the franchisor to distribute to all appropriate members of staff and customers;

(h) an 'on the spot' trouble shooting service to enable the franchisee to deal with any operational problems which may arise."

The initial obligations of the franchisor must include giving the franchisee sufficient training, guidance and support to enable him to start up the franchise outlet as easily as possible, after all it is exactly this for which the franchisee is paying. It helps the franchisee avoid the need to take unnecessary risks and increases his chances of success. The franchise agreement should therefore provide for such assistance. The franchisor should of course make sure that it has the resources to undertake the training.

Once the operation is underway the franchisor must continue to provide support and guidance as necessary and again this should be clearly stated in the agreement. The cost of such guidance and support is usually included in a periodic service charge often based on a percentage of the gross turnover. By providing the continual support the franchisor will increase the chances of both its own and the franchisee's success.

The cost of further training will also often be included in the service charge although the expenses such as travel and accommodation incurred by the franchisor, the franchisees or the franchisee's employees will be the responsibility of the franchisee. This continual training is vital to maintain high standards and ensure a uniform image for the franchise.

In addition to this continual training, support and guidance it is also essential that the franchisor continually applies itself to improving and updating the franchise package. Failure to do so will eventually lead to the franchise's decline and likely failure.

A hypothetical case in point is the *Taste-so-Good* restaurant chain in the United States. This chain started off as a successful chain of steak restaurants, decked out in a 'wild west' type setting. The franchise was, during the first 10 years, very successful. However, the original franchisor neglected to monitor the changing eating habits and increased sophistication of the American public. As a result, in the early 1980's sales had already peaked and were falling rapidly. The health craze had turned people away from red meat towards a healthier diet. *Taste-so-Good* restaurants were suffering as a result.

In 1984 the franchisor sold out his interest, and owing to its effective and highly imaginative management the new franchisor eventually turned the chain around and rebuilt it into a highly successful franchise. This was done by re-vamping the outlets' decor, and adapting the menu to the latest tastes by introducing white meat, poultry, seafood and salad and greatly cutting back on red meats. If the original franchisor had properly monitored the market on a continual basis and adapted accordingly, the crisis of the early 1980's might have been avoided.

The franchise agreement should stipulate that continual improvement of the franchise is one of the franchisor's obligations. This obligation must be honoured as this is the basis of the franchise's long term success.

Franchisees' obligations

In order to protect the value of the franchise the franchisor must be able to control the activities of the franchisees and ensure that the know-how of the franchise concept is being practised and not adulterated. The franchise block exemption (see chapter 4) stipulates certain obligations which are forbidden if the franchisor seeks to take advantage of it. Other clauses are allowed on certain conditions, whilst a third category is allowed unconditionally. These should be carefully studied if it is intended to come within the Block Exemption. Obligations usually included in agreements are, among others:

(a) *Finance*
the franchisee should ensure that it has sufficient capital to discharge his obligations.

(b) *Commencement*
The franchisee should actually start trading within a stated period, often three months, of signing the agreement.

(c) *Standards*
The franchisee must maintain the franchisor's high standards. This takes on a particular importance in terms of limiting the franchisor's liability for any product defect above and beyond the need to protect the franchise's high reputation.

(d) *Goodwill*
The franchisee must protect the franchisor's goodwill and ensure that all customers are properly dealt with.

(e) *Confidentiality*
The franchisee must ensure that it, its officers, shareholders and employees do not breach the franchisor's confidence by publicising the know-how (unless it is within the public domain).

(f) *Competition*
The franchisee must be prevented from competing with the franchisor and abusing the know-how both during and after the term agreement. Such restrictions must of course be reasonable in order to be enforceable. Careful note must also be taken of the franchise block ememption Article's 2, 3.1 and 3.2.

(g) *Approval*
The franchisee must be required to obtain the written approval of the franchisor before undertaking any new business or purchasing goods or materials from different sources.

(h) *Other financial interests*
The franchisor should be prevented from taking any financial interest in competing enterprises which allows the latter to influence the commercial conduct of that enterprise, and in any event should declare all interests upon entering the agreement.

All of these restrictions placed on the franchisee should be based on the need to protect the standards of the franchise or, to use the block exemptions terminology, its 'industrial/intellectual property rights, reputation and common identity'.

Payments to the franchisor

"The franchisee shall pay the franchisor:

(a) £10,000 net of all taxes by way of initial fee payable by:

(i) £5,000 on the execution of this agreement;
(ii) £2,500 three months after the date of the execution of this Agreement; and
(iii) £2,500 six months after the date of the execution of this Agreement.

(b) On the first working day of each calendar month a service charge equal to 5% of the previous month's net turnover.

(c) On the first working day of each month a contribution to the franchisor's Advertising and Promotion Fund equal to 1% of the previous month's net turnover."

This is perhaps the most important clause from the franchisor's point of view. The form of the payments by the franchisees to the franchisor can vary, and will, to a large extent, depend upon the structure and nature of the franchise. The tax implications of the fee structure are of paramount importance (see chapter 9).

It is common, but by no means universal, to find that there is an up-front payment required. This is usually expressed to be the result of the grant, by the franchisor, of the right to use his intellectual property rights and know-how. The up-front sum paid for a franchise can vary greatly. For example: £10,000 for a *Wimpy* franchise (total investment £650,000); £12,000 for *Kall Kwik* (total investment £64,000); £7,500 for *Fastframe* (total investment £34,000); and £4,000 for *Das Haar* (total investment £28,000). These figures are taken from *Directory of Franchising 1989*, published by *Franchise World*.

The amount charged by way of an up-front sum will of course to a large extent determine the type of franchisee likely to be attracted. Inevitably the more established and successful a franchise the more justifiable a high up-front fee becomes. In the US, high up-front fees are quite common. However, it is suggested that it is both unwise and unethical for a franchisor to try and make a killing on up-front fees. A lower up-front fee and steady periodic payments are far better as they show the franchisor's long term commitment to the franchise.

For taxation reasons (see chapter 9) it is better to treat a periodic payment as a service charge for the services supplied by the franchisor rather than a mere royalty for the use of the intellectual property rights. Regardless of how it is expressed, it is usual for a periodic payment to be calculated as a percentage of the gross turnover. A percentage fee has the advantage of being easy to calculate, although it is sometimes thought to be difficult for the franchisee to accept psychologically. Each month it sees a slice of its profits taken away for what, after a few years, may seem to be no good reason.

Another possible form of income for the franchisor is a mark-up on the products and equipment it supplies to the franchisee. Such a source of income must be openly declared to the franchisee in order to prevent any ill-will, which often arises, when the franchisor is making a mark-up but has not declared it. Such secrecy undermines the mutual trust essential to the franchisee/ franchisor relationship. It must also be borne in mind that such tie-ins are not automatically acceptable under the EC block exemption. They can be imposed only when it is impracticable to stipulate objective standards by which goods can be manufactured.

The franchisor will need to be reimbursed for any out of the ordinary expenses such as trouble shooting and this should therefore be included in the agreement.

Whatever the remuneration package of the franchisor it is important that the franchise agreement contains a clause which clearly shows the franchisee what his total expenses will be during the term of the agreement, including any advertising charges. It should be borne in mind that if the franchisor takes the initial fee in instalments he will need a consumer credit licence under the Consumer Credit Act 1974. Likewise a licence will be required if it recommends the potential franchisee to approach a particular bank for funding (see chapter 10).

Advertising and promotion

"(a) The franchisor shall be responsible for all national and regional advertising and promotion of the business, which shall be paid for out of the Advertising and Promotion Fund.

(b) The franchisees may undertake only such local advertising and promotion as the franchisor, in its reasonable discretion deems necessary and has previously consented to in writing in order to market the Services properly in the franchisees' locality. Such local advertising and promotion shall be at the franchisees' own expense."

In order to promote the services or products of the franchise it is usual to provide for an advertising budget as described above, to which all franchisees contribute a percentage of their gross turnover.

The franchisor will use one part of this fund for regional and national advertising whilst the franchisee will usually be in charge of local advertising. Local advertising should be subject to the franchisor's prior approval to ensure uniformity of presentation with the franchise image. This is permitted by the EC block exemption.

In any event it is important that the franchisor exercises strict control over advertising and ensures that any advertising campaign does not make exaggerated safety claims which may cause problems in terms of product liability under the Consumer Protection Act 1974 (which conforms with the EC Directive on product liability, see chapter 9).

The sale of the business

"(1) The franchisee may not under any circumstances either assign or delegate his rights or obligations under this agreement. The franchisee may, however at any time after the second anniversary of the signing of this agreement sell his business with the prior written consent of the franchisor and subject to the conditions listed in (2) below. The franchisor shall grant to a purchaser of the franchisee's business who is acceptable to the franchisor, a new agreement for the period of not less than seven years. This period will commence on the date of the sale of the business. The new agreement will be in the form of the standard agreement then currently being offered by the franchisor to its franchisees.

(2) The conditions to be satisfied in order to obtain the written consent of the franchisor to the sale of the franchisee's business shall be:

(a) the franchisee must not be in material breach of any obligations to the franchisor under the terms of this Agreement;

(b) the proposed purchaser shall meet the franchisor's standards as regards business experience, financial status, moral rectitude and ability;

(c) if the franchisor has introduced the purchaser, it shall receive from the franchisee the sum of 10% of the sale price and if otherwise, it shall receive 5% (except that where the franchisor exercises these options under sub-clause (3) below to purchase the business, no such payment shall be due to the franchisor);

(3) (a) a copy of the proposed purchaser's written offer to purchase the said business from the franchisee (the Purchase Offer) shall be submitted to the franchisor by the franchisee together with a financial statement of affairs and a business history of the proposed purchaser and any further information which the franchisor may reasonably require;

(b) upon receipt of the Purchase Offer accompanied by such items specified above, in addition to its other rights the franchisor shall have a pre-emptive right to purchase the franchisee's business for the same amount and on the same terms as those set out in the Purchase Offer. This option must be exercised by written notice to the franchisee within twenty-one days after the receipt by the franchisor of the Purchase Offer during which period the terms of the Purchase Offer cannot be altered;

(c) if the franchisor does not exercise such pre-emptive right and consents to the proposed purchase it will be conditional upon the proposed purchaser depositing 20% of the purchase price with the franchisor. Upon completion of the sale the purchaser shall pay the balance of the purchase price to the franchisor (as agent for the franchisee) and the franchisor shall deduct from the said purchase price an amount equivalent to any sums due and owing to the franchisor by the franchisee together with the amount due in accordance with sub-clause (2)(a) above. Any outstanding balance of the purchase price will be remitted to the franchisee within twenty-eight days after the date of the receipt of the final amount of the purchase price by the franchisor;

(d) The sale of the business under (c) above, may only proceed on the terms of the Purchase Offer notice. If the sale price or any other significant term of the Purchase Offer notice is changed the amended terms shall constitute a new Purchase Offer notice which shall be submitted to the franchisor to be processed under this sub-clause in place of the original Purchase Offer notice;

(4) Immediately upon the completion of the sale, the franchisee shall assign to the Purchaser or franchisor as the case may be all of its rights under the franchise agreements."

The grant of a franchise to the franchisee should only be made after the franchisor has carefully considered the character, qualities and suitability of that particular individual franchisee. If a potential franchisee does not come up to scratch it should not be granted a franchise. This must be done in order to maintain the standards of the franchise. It follows therefore that the franchisor must also be able to choose, or at least have the right to reject the franchisee's choice of transferee when the franchisee desires to sell its interest in the franchise.

Complicated provisions are necessary to control such situations, especially the financial aspects. The franchisor will usually take a percentage of any payment received by the franchisee in consideration of the transfer of the business. If, however, there are undue restrictions placed upon the right to transfer its interest, the franchisee must doubt the true value of the franchise. The franchisee will, in the final analysis, want to realise its full capital investment and therefore will look for a provision in the agreement whereby it can assign a whole new term rather than the tail end of the existing term. This, however, may not be attractive to the franchisor from the stand point of his losing control over franchisee recruitment.

If the franchisor has a pre-emptive right to buy back the franchise at the market value in preference to a third party, he can still retain this control. What it does lose however is financial advantage, as the market price it will have to pay will be higher for a new term than it would for the remainder of the existing term. In the end commercial considerations must be given priority.

The same problem arises in a more acute manner when an individual franchisee dies. Provision is usually made for his personal representative to sell his interest in the franchise, or perhaps to pass it on to the deceased's beneficiary. In either event the franchisor must still retain an element of control over the transferee. If the beneficiary is the wife who has always worked in the franchise, the franchisor is unlikely to object to her taking over the franchisee's interest. However, if it is the deceased's eighteen year old niece who lives some three hundred miles away the franchisor is likely to prefer to either re-purchase the franchise himself or allow a suitable third party to purchase it, providing temporary cover in the meantime.

It may be thought appropriate for the franchisor to take a percentage of any transfer fee paid, but it is unlikely that a franchisor would require a fee merely for allowing the franchisee's beneficiary to take over.

Premises

The franchisee agrees:

(a) to decorate and fit out the Premises in the manner and style, and to a standard, approved by an architect approved by the franchisor, before commencing provision of the Services;

(b) to display on or about the Premises only such signs, posters and other advertising material as may be supplied or approved by the franchisor. Such signs, posters and other advertising material to be kept in a clean and satisfactory condition and state of repair;

(c) to ensure that the Premises, including the window and facia, are at all times kept clean and tidy and free from litter, and that the customer reception area is regularly inspected to ensure maximum cleanliness and tidiness;

59

(d) to ensure that the Premises are at all times fitted and decorated in a manner and style, and to a standard, approved by the franchisor; and

(e) to use the Premises for providing the service and for no other purpose, save and with the exception of such other purposes as the franchisor gives express prior written consent thereto."

The shop front and interior decor of the premises should of course be in accord with the franchise's required image, details of which are usually contained in the manual.

Procuring prime sites is always a difficult task for any business, and it is therefore not surprising to find that many franchise agreements contain lengthy clauses which try to ensure that the franchisee has no security of tenure once the franchise agreement has been terminated. This is often achieved by the franchisor taking a lease of the premises and then granting the franchisee a licence or sub-lease.

There are four possible situations which may be provided for in the franchise agreement.

(a) where the franchisor owns the freehold of the site.

(b) where the franchisor owns a leasehold interest in the site.

(c) where the franchisor owns neither and it is for the franchisee to find appropriate premises to be approved by the franchisor who will then take such reasonable steps to acquire the property, which if leasehold will be on such terms which are satisfactory to the franchisor.

(d) where the franchisor has no direct interest in the property, but will probably require an option on the property on termination of the franchise agreement.

Whatever the situation the franchisee's activities, as far as the property is concerned, will be regulated not only by the franchise agreement, but also, where appropriate, by the lease.

In becoming a tenant as well as a franchisee the franchisee's obligations and liabilities inevitably increase. It will not only have to comply with requirements as regards fitting out the premises, sourcing the goods and meeting financial targets contained in the franchise agreement, it will also have to comply with the added obligations contained in the leases such as repair, which although of no particular interest to the franchisor are of prime importance to the landlord.

In most situations the franchisor attempts to retain as much control over the franchisee as possible. The most efficient way of doing this is through the franchisee being the franchisor's tenant. This gives the franchisor two complementary but legally independent ways of controlling the franchisee. By the franchisee 'contracting out' under the Landlord and Tenant Act 1954 s28 the franchisor can retain valuable premises after the franchisee leaves the franchise network.

In the situation where the franchisee is obliged to find suitable premises the franchisee can consider premises that may normally be unavailable to him if he has no experience in business, for example a unit in a shopping centre which probably commands a high rent. The superior landlord would want to be assured that the rent would be paid and he would be more likely to grant the lease to the franchisor who has the financial backing, is well known and is established.

The franchisor will normally set down guidelines to help the franchisee select a site in his chosen area so that time and money are not wasted in the franchisee submitting details of premises for approval which are manifestly unsuitable. Here the franchisor benefits in that the franchisee uses his knowledge of the area in selecting the site.

Other advantages to the franchisee of the franchisor first acquiring the property and then granting a lease to the franchisee are that the franchisor has to deal with such considerations as use and planning permission and consent for alterations. The franchisee does not have to consider the burden of a commercial mortgage nor go through the costly process of acquisition. Renting is generally cheaper than buying property with mortgage finance and this can lead more rapidly to healthier and more encouraging balance sheets.

The disadvantage to the franchisee of the franchisor acquiring the property is that it gains no possible profit from investing in the premises at which he is going to carry on his franchised business. The franchisee must also consider the impact of rent reviews and the possibility of sharp increases in rent if the value of the commercial premises has increased. Property is also a valuable asset against which finance can be raised for business expansion.

Another consideration is VAT. From 1st August 1989 landlords have been able to elect to charge VAT upon rents. This they will no doubt do if they themselves are charged VAT upon rent in the case of their holding a leasehold interest, or upon purchasing new commercial premises. The new legislation giving effect to this election is complex and convoluted and will not be considered here in any further detail.

From the above it can be seen that commercial property implications of franchising are considerable. If there is to be a lease to the franchisee by the franchisor the lease goes hand in hand with the main franchise agreement and must complement rather than conflict with it.

If there is a lease taken by the franchisee from an independent landlord the lease must be drafted carefully to ensure that the provisions of each do not conflict in any way.

Termination

"(1) The franchisor may terminate this Agreement forthwith by notice in writing to the franchisee:

(a) if the franchisee shall have committed any material breach of his obligations hereunder or shall have failed to remedy any remediable breach within a period of twenty-eight days of the receipt of a notice in writing of the franchisor requiring him to do so;

(b) if the franchisee shall commit an act of bankruptcy or have a receiving order made against him or make any arrangement or assignment with or for the benefit of his creditors or suffer distress or execution to be levied or threatened on any of its properties;

(c) if any sum or document required under the terms of this Agreement is not paid or submitted at the latest within twenty-one days following its due date;

(d) if the franchisee ceases or takes any steps to cease his business:

The termination or expiry of this Agreement shall be without prejudice to any rights and obligations conferred or imposed by this Agreement in respect of any period after such termination and shall also be without prejudice to the rights of either party against the other in respect of any antecedent breach of any of the terms and conditions hereof."

The franchisor must retain the right ultimately to terminate a franchise agreement for non-performance, and bankruptcy of the franchisee, etc to protect the franchise from bad franchisees. Likewise the franchisee should be able to terminate, although it will inevitably prefer to assign it instead, to realise his capital investment.

Audit

"The franchisee will maintain proper books of account relating to the business and shall employ a Chartered Accountant to prepare annual accounts for the business and the franchisee shall supply the franchisor:

(a) within sixty days after the end of each financial year, with an audited certificate as to the franchisee's gross turnover during such period calculated in accordance with this Agreement;

(b) within one hundred and eighty days (180 days) after the end of each financial year with a certified copy of the audited profit and loss accounts and balance sheet of the franchisee's business and such other accounting and financial information relating to it as may reasonably be required by the franchisor; and

(c) the franchisee shall provide to the franchisor any certificates, etc set out in (a) and (b) above which shall be prepared after the termination of this Agreement but which shall relate to any financial period of the franchisees which falls in whole or in part within the period of this Agreement."

To enable the franchisor to examine the franchisee's accounts and other books of record there should be one system for all franchisees to follow. The franchisor should be allowed access personally or through its agents at any time to carry out random checks and a regular audit. This helps to prevent cheating by the franchisees and makes the franchisor's own accounting far simpler. There should also be a timetable for any monthly payments etc with provision for interest to be charged on arrears.

Arbitration

"If any dispute shall arise between the parties hereto concerning the construction, interpretation or application of any of the provisions of this Agreement whether during the continuance of this Agreement or after the termination thereof by what ever cause, such dispute shall be referred to the arbitration of a single arbitrator to be appointed by the Chairman for the time being of the British Franchise Association, provided always that this Clause shall have no application to terms of this Agreement concerning restrictions against competition and non-disclosure, and the parties hereto agree to be bound by the terms of such arbitration and to bear the costs of such arbitration in equal shares."

Arbitration can save both parties a considerable sum of money. More importantly, for the franchisor, arbitration is private and so avoids or limits embarrassing press coverage which could discourage potential franchisees.

Conclusion

The above is not a comprehensive list of the clauses which will be found in a franchise agreement. For example target clauses, setting out minimum turnover requirements are favoured by some franchisors. Franchisees who fail to achieve the target are liable to have their agreements terminated. Quite rightly, however, in many cases the BFA do not favour such clauses which can be used to bring undue pressure to bear on a franchisee who may well be unable to achieve the target due to insufficient support from the franchisor.

Each franchise is unique in respect of its operation and this will need to be reflected in the agreement itself. There is for example, a great difference between a mobile franchise such as *Dyno Rod* and a retail premises based one such as *Snappy Snaps.*

There should of course also be included the standard clauses concerning notices, waivers, whole agreement, force majeure, etc. It is also important that franchisors are obliged to take full independent advice on the agreement before entering into it (see chapter 6 below).

The franchise agreement and all other documentation should not only protect the interests of the franchisor and the franchisee, it should be drafted in as simple and easily understandable manner as possible. Franchisees are not, as a whole, particularly sophisticated in commercial or legal matters. It is therefore in the franchisee's own best interests to ensure that they fully understand exactly in what they are becoming involved. More easily understandable documentation is one definite step the franchisor can take to achieve this end.

Chapter 6
THE FRANCHISEES

Franchisee prudence

It is an unfortunate fact of life that franchise outlets sometimes fail. When they do there is often a lot of bitterness on the side of both the franchisee and the franchisor. Both blame each other for the failure. The press has a field day. The franchisee is portrayed as an innocent victim suffering as a result of the franchisor's sharp practice or inadequate commercial ability. It is clearly in the franchisor's interests therefore to take great care in its recruitment of franchisees. Good recruitment practice will help to save a great deal of trouble in the future (see chapter 5 about application forms).

When a franchise fails the ultimate responsibility must lie in most cases with the franchisor, but the personal involvement of each individual franchisee in such a franchise is the responsibility of the individual franchisee himself. This must be made very plain to the franchisee *before* he signs up. It is, usually, inequitable to blame the franchisor entirely for the franchisee's losses if the franchisee failed to take the appropriate steps to investigate the franchise fully and test its true worth and viability before entering into the franchise agreement. Unfortunately this does not stop the media from doing their worst.

The franchisee must be encouraged to invest both time and money vetting the franchise. Indeed it should be required by the confidentiality agreement and the agreement should contain a declaration that the franchisee has done so before entering into it.

If a person purchases a house, it is unlikely that he/she will hand over the purchase price merely because he/she likes the look of the house front. Indeed, most purchasers will spend many hours looking at the house and deciding whether or not it is suitable for their needs. Once this has been decided, a surveyor will report upon the structural soundness of the house and a solicitor will investigate the potential vendor's title to the land and ensure that he/she is purchasing exactly what he/she intends to purchase. The purchaser would be less than pleased if the back garden did not, in fact, belong to the house, but to the neighbouring property instead.

When entering into a franchise, the potential franchisee must undertake exactly the same process, both for his sake and that of the franchisor. If, after a few months, the franchisee becomes disillusioned an immense burden will be felt by the franchisor and the other franchisees.

After examining the franchise concept and deciding whether or not it is one in which it could comfortably function and make a success, the franchisee should be given full information by the franchisor about its financial status, as well as the opportunity to test the reputation and reliability of the franchisor by speaking to others involved in franchising such as the British Franchise Association and especially to other franchisees of that particular franchisor.

Another useful source of information can be his own bank, as most of the high street banks have central franchise units which are intimately involved with franchising in the United Kingdom and have a great deal of expertise and knowledge to offer (see Appendix II for details of banks affiliated to the BFA).

By ensuring that franchisees undertake such prudent measures the franchisor will in the long run save itself time, money and worry. There are many sad stories of franchisees who thought that they would rather save on the costs involved in taking proper advice and found out only too late that what they had assumed they were obtaining in exchange for the franchise and service fees was somewhat different to what they finally obtained.

Franchisee recruitment

In the words of the director of the British Franchise Association, Mr Tony Dutfield: "Franchisee selection is one of the greatest problems facing franchising in the UK today".

As noted in chapter 1 success will attract more potential franchisees which means the chances of selecting good franchisees is much higher. Failure will drive them away. However capable franchisees are, without support, and lacking direction from the franchisor, the operation cannot and will not maintain its position in the market.

In today's competitive economy, probably the single most important advantage that one franchised operation can have over another is the calibre of its franchisees. To maintain this advantage, the franchisor must ensure that its recruitment policy and practice are sound and to this end carefully drafted application forms and an understanding of what frachisees are looking for are essential (see chapter 5 above).

Franchisee scrutiny

The franchisor should bear in mind exactly what the prudent prospective franchisee, who has taken proper advice from a solicitor, banker and accountant, will be looking for in a franchise. This will enable the franchisor to further streamline its recruitment process, saving both time and money.

Before considering the franchise itself in too much detail the franchisee will require general information about the market in which the franchise operates including competitors and details of any failures. Any information upon this and the performance of the franchise in the market will usually be independently checked by the potential franchisee.

Once satisfied about this the potential franchisees' concern will then turn to the track record, financial strength and structure of the franchisor. A company search is often used to this end, although the auditor's end of year accounts usually only tell half of the story, and the franchisors' bankers' reference is also useful.

The business experience of the franchisor (and if a limited company, its directors) and the progress of the pilot operations are also of paramount importance in this regard and the well advised potential franchisee will require full details.

The next stage in the would-be franchisees' enquiries will concern the actual mechanics of the franchise and include the following questions:

(a) What is the selection and training policy of the franchisor?

(b) How are sites and territories selected and allocated amongst franchisees?

(c) What degree of support is actually given to franchisees?

(d) How, and from where, does the franchisor source any goods tied into the franchise?

(e) Does the franchisor actually own the trade marks and other intellectual property rights which are being franchised?

(f) What control/monitoring system is used to maintain the standards of the franchise?

(g) What is the full 'up and running' cost of the franchise, including any assets that the franchisee will need to purchase?

(h) How does the franchisor make its income? What is the gearing of the 'upfront fee' and the 'on going' fees? Is there a mark-up on tied-in products?

(i) Is the franchisor a BFA member – if not, why not?

(j) Has the legal agreement been either notified to the EC Commission or registered at the Office of Fair Trading (see chapter 4 above)? If so, full details will be requested.

The franchisor should expect these sort of enquiries and indeed welcome them as a sign of the potential franchisee's prudence and common sense. A pro-forma 'disclosure document' addressing these points will save both franchisor and potential franchisee a good deal of time. The franchisor should also encourage the potential franchisee to visit existing franchise operations. Talking directly and candidly with successful franchisees will help remove many of the reservations the potential franchisee may have about the operation. It will enable him to decide more easily whether or not he is suited to it. This could save both parties a great deal of difficulty in the future.

Franchisee finance

The importance of screening franchisees to ensure that they are not financially over-committing themselves has been discussed in chapter 3 above. Most franchisees will however need to borrow some money. This brings to light one of the many real advantages of franchising from the franchisee's point of view.

All of the major clearing banks have specialised central franchise units which offer advice to clients and more importantly in this regard, to their branch managers on franchising. The franchise unit's internal function is twofold. Firstly, it is to 'educate' bank staff in the subtleties of franchising as a business concept, so that they are better able to understand the proposition being put to them by a franchisor or a franchisee. Secondly, it is to compile a record of each individual franchise. This report will assess the attractiveness of the franchise from the bank's point of view and will be made available, on request, to all branch managers considering a request for funds from a franchisee. Competition between the banks is fierce and a full list of those affiliated to the BFA is contained in Appendix II.

The banks are usually willing to lend to franchisees of an 'approved' franchisor on a 2:1 ratio rather than the 1:1 ratio it generally extends to non-franchise small businesses. The advantage is marked. If £30,000 is required to invest in a business the franchisee will usually be able to raise £20,000, whereas the non-franchisee will have access to only £15,000.

It must be said however that each loan is approached on a case by case basis. It is for the discretion of the branch manager involved, who will obviously take account of the personal status and circumstances of the franchisee. A bank will not lend to a 'bad risk' individual merely because he is taking on a franchise.

The franchisor should therefore make it a priority to establish cordial relations with the franchise managers of the major clearing banks and provide them with whatever information they require to enable them to form a full picture of the franchise. This again will streamline the recruitment process and impress the potential franchisee.

The franchisee's working capital requirement will as in any business be divided into basic capital (to purchase and set up the franchise) and working capital (to fund the day-to-day running of the business). The franchisor will have to help the franchisee draft up a business plan to present to the bank when applying for a loan. The importance of a confidentiality agreement in these circumstances cannot be too strongly emphasised (see chapter 5 above).

The banks usually provide the initial lump sum of capital on a reducing loan with repayment over a period of years at a fixed or variable interest rate; obviously always less than the initial term of the franchise. It may however be possible to negotiate slightly different terms in particular cases. Working capital is usually provided by way of an overdraft facility.

Franchisee Associations

Once franchisees have been involved in the franchise for a year or so they often begin to question the franchisors' wisdom. As a result, they may start to agitate. Franchisee associations sometimes result.

Franchisee associations can be a very positive thing, but more often than not turn out to be a can of worms for the franchisor. If the franchisee association is not properly organised or fails to direct itself to appropriate issues, it can become a centre for discontent. A franchisee which is ill disposed for whatever reason, to the franchisor, can ferment trouble which if not properly handled, could possibly lead to the break-up of the whole franchise chain. The success or otherwise of a franchisee association therefore depends to a large extent upon the individual franchisees involved, and the franchisor's political adroitness.

The franchisor is faced with some difficulty if it is not particularly welcomed as a participant in the franchisee association and it may therefore wish to take the incentive. If a franchisee association seems appropriate the franchisor should take a leading role and structure it formally, with rules of procedure and voting rights. It should allow discussion and the putting forward of positive ideas. It can also act as a 'pressure valve'. It should not, however, be allowed to become a forum dominated by malcontents.

As discussed earlier in chapter 3, Article 85 of The Treaty of Rome prohibits any practice which prevents, restricts or distorts competition. These restrictions, preventions or distortions may be contained either in agreements between undertakings, decisions by associations of undertakings, or concerted practices.

A franchisee association may well amount to a concerted practice even if only the franchisees themselves participate and take certain decisions. If the franchisor also participates, there may be an ever stronger case to be argued that a concerted practice exists.

Concerted practice may arise from any practice which substitutes practical co-operation for the risks of competition. In other words any consensual action, even a gentleman's agreement could amount to a concerted practice.

The Commission's general approach is that in a horizontal relationship. eg amongst franchisees, common behaviour can be sufficient to amount to a concerted practice. In a vertical relationship, however, eg franchisor/franchisee something far more definite is required before a concerted practice is likely. Thus, if the franchisee association discusses pricing policies, it may be running foul of Article 85, and therefore make the franchise chain, but not necessarily the franchisor, subject to fines for not notifying the commission of the practice.

Similarly, under the Restrictive Trade Practices Act if the franchisees exchange relevant restrictions, the franchise agreements may become registrable, and failure to register will again cause the franchisees, and therefore the franchisor, substantial difficulties.

It will be clear that although a franchisee association may be desired by the franchisees, it is very much a two edged sword. If a franchisor is to permit such an association, it must try to ensure that it is property structured and run, and that it will not unintentionally wreck the franchise ship on the rocks of legislation.

Chapter 7
PROTECTING THE FRANCHISE
– STATUTORY PROTECTION OF
INTELLECTUAL PROPERTY

A franchise is basically a package of intellectual property rights and know how and the protection of these rights is of paramount importance. This chapter deals with the available statutory protection. The following two chapters consider how to prevent abuse, and the remedies available against it.

Trade marks

Introduction

Trade and service marks are the most important form of protection of which the franchisor can avail itself. Under the Trade Marks Act 1938 the owner of a trading name, or device which is used in connection with goods, can register that name or device as a trade mark in the appropriate choice of forty two classes of trade marks. Registration of a mark confers a statutory monopoly in the use of that mark in relation to the trade for which it is registered.

To be registrable a trade mark has to relate to *goods*, and must:

(a) be distinctive;
(b) not be deceptive in any manner; and
(c) not conflict with any existing registered trade mark.

It is not possible to register trade marks which contain geographical names, are descriptive, or which are otherwise considered by the registrar not to be sufficiently distinctive.

Registration of a trade mark is *not* compulsory. The main legal difference between an unregistered trade mark and a registered trade mark is that an unregistered trade mark must rely upon the concept of passing off for protection (see chapter 8), whereas a registered trade mark gives statutory protection. Certain words, eg royal, are prohibited from use.

A European Trade Mark system is being considered and the recent

Trade Mark Directive (89/104/EEC) requires further harmonisation between EC Member States (see chapter 12).

Service marks

Until the Trade Marks (Amendment) Act 1984 there was no mechanism to enable trade marks for *services* to be registered. The first applications for the registration of service marks under the 1984 Act commenced on 1st October 1986. Parliamentary approval for the receipt of applications was, however, obtained by the Registry from 4th August 1986.

The 1984 Act extends and modifies the 1938 Act to refer to services as well as goods, and to adapt the requirements of the 1938 Act accordingly. Trade marks for goods and service marks for services will all be treated as trade marks for registration and protection requirements. The definition of a service mark under the 1984 Act is:

"a mark used, or proposed to be used, in relation to services for the purposes of indicating or so as to indicate that a particular person is connected in the course of business with a provision of those services whether with or without any indication of the identity of that person."

For registration the same criteria of distinctiveness, non-deceptiveness and non-conflict with existing marks will apply, as will the criteria relating to geographical names, surnames and descriptive words. Service marks which are not registrable will be protected by the common law only.

It is possible to gain dual protection by registering a particular trade mark registered in the relevant class where it can be connected with goods, and the relevant class where it can be connected with services.

Classes of marks

The forty-two trade mark classes of goods (fully described in Appendix 9) are reasonably successful in separating out specific goods so that the overlap between classes is minimised. There are examples where applications in more than one class are necessary to protect one particular product. For example, playing cards would be registered as paper in one class and as games and amusements in another. It is more difficult to separate out potential areas of services.

If a franchisor has a wide ranging area of activities using either one mark to identify the whole of its business, or several marks for divisions of activity within its business, the possible scope of each of the classes for services will have to be examined to establish which will be applicable.

The World Intellectual Property Organisation (WIPO) has published two books entitled *"International Classification of Goods and Services"*, which give a detailed description of the areas of services which would be applicable to each of the above service marks classes.

When making any trade marks search there must also be a search against service marks. The difficulty is how to cross reference the searches as between goods and services.

Defensive and certification marks

All references to defensive trade marks or certification trade marks have been omitted in relation to the extension of the 1938 Act to services. These are used where a trade mark consisting of an invented word or words has become well known in respect of any goods for which it is registered. The result can be that when it is used in respect of other goods it indicates a connection, which does not in fact exist. The proprietor of such a mark may apply to register the mark as a 'defensive' trade mark in respect of those other goods, even though he has no intention of using it for those goods.

A defensive trade mark is deemed to be associated with the original trade mark and has all the rights of a trade mark except that it is not liable to be removed or limited on the ground of non-use.

A certification trade mark is a mark adapted to distinguish, in the course of trade, goods certified by any person in respect of origin, material, mode of manufacture, quality, accuracy or other characteristic from goods not so certified.

Certification trade marks are not common, and need the consent of the Secretary of State for registration. Such marks are normally owned by trade associations. A primary feature of a certification trade mark is that its use is open to all traders who attain the relevant standards laid down and who otherwise qualify under the regulations as being able to make use of the certification trade mark when attached to the goods.

Registered user agreements

Under the 1938 Act, it is prohibited by s28 to 'traffic in trade marks'. Trade marks can only be registered in connection with specific areas of goods belonging to the proprietor, normally the manufacturer.

When the franchisor licences the area developer to market and sell its goods or provide its services, one of the key parts of the deal is licensing the use of the trade mark, possibly by means of a registered user agreement.

The franchisor is entitled to grant a whole series of registered user agreements to different parties for the use of that service mark. It is not necessary to register all of the user agreement. It is sufficient to register only one or two agreements if all of the others are identical save for the identity of the registered user. Franchisors who have never used their mark but have licensed it out to the area developer must be careful. There will be no intention on the part of the franchisor to use it itself. In this case the application will be invalid under s26, which insists that it be made with *bona fide* intention to use. Fortunately this problem may be overcome where there has been *bona fide* use by a licensee, providing it is registered use.

It has been suggested that even though the mark's owners only intended to use the mark through a licensing arrangement, if a mark is filed without indicating that any registered user is appointed, and the owner starts to use it within 5 years of the date of registration then the mark will withstand attack. It is safer, however, for the applicant to use the mark in a pilot scheme initially.

The idea of effecting a registered user agreement may not appeal to some franchisors because of the administration involved. If so, it may be possible to avoid signing such an agreement but the franchisor must bear in mind that by not doing so there is a danger to the mark if he does not himself trade in the goods or services. Further, only a registered user agreement is exempted from the provisions of the Restrictive Trade Practices Act 1976 (see chapter 3).

Another problem often encountered in franchising is found when a company has been set up specifically to run a franchise, but the intellectual property rights, including service marks, remain with the shareholders of the franchisor company. It is not possible for the service mark to be licensed to the company which in turn sub-licenses to the franchisee. This particular problem can be overcome by the franchise agreement containing a clause which states that the franchisor will procure a licence for the franchisee and then a separate agreement is concluded with the owner. Alternatively an agency relationship can be arranged in which the franchisor, by virtue of the agency power, acts on behalf of the owner in issuing a licence to the franchisee. The franchisor should also be appointed agent for the purpose of quality control.

In short, whether or not a registered user agreement is necessary depends upon the nature of the franchise and the terms of the franchise agreement. It may be that the franchise agreement itself allows the franchisor to exert sufficient control. However, where the franchisees actually manufacture the goods a registered user agreement is desirable. In other cases, it is certainly safer, although not always necessary.

Problems

The registrar may have difficulty in distinguishing between applications. Many marks are descriptive of the service or product. Particular words are universal or commonly used as part of marks; for example the word *pizza* in the mark *Eat-a-lot-a-Pizza*.

If a commonly used word is included in a registered mark for goods, the registration normally proceeds on the basis that there is no exclusivity in relation to that particular common word.

Geographically localised services which operate under an abbreviation of their corporate name, or under a descriptive explanation of the services, seldom seek to protect the goodwill and recognition generated beyond the locality within which they carry on business and have established their reputation. A registered service mark will instantly give national protection.

Priority

If there are a number of applicants for a mark, the important question is which of them will have their application granted? There is no right of prior use to a trading name which becomes the subject of a service/trade mark application to give the applicant priority over another applicant for the same or similar service mark. On the other hand, it would be inequitable for an established reputation, goodwill and business to be at risk if an entrepreneur tries to register the name as a trade service mark. The Registrar can permit registration by more than one proprietor if there is *honest* concurrent use.

The procedure for applying for trade and service marks and a list of the various classes is contained in Appendix 9 below.

Copyright and designs

Prior to the Trade Mark (Amendment) Act 1984 the non-registerability of service marks meant that it was necessary for the franchisor to rely upon the protection afforded by the law of copyright as contained in the Copyright Act 1956.

Under this Act an original, distinctive representation of the franchise chain's name, and logo are protected 'irrespective of their artistic quality.' Copyright rests automatically in the author and there is no registration procedure. However under the Universal Copyright Convention (as reviewed by the 1971 Paris Protocol) use of the symbol © on all published copies of the work together with the name of the proprietor and the year of its first publication gives notice of a claim to copyright. These details must be sufficiently prominent to give notice of the claim to protection.

Under the Registered Designs Act 1949 it is also possible to register a new design and so obtain protection for a period of 15 years.

The new Copyright Designs and Patents Act 1988, which came into effect earlier this year, changes this situation somewhat by introducing a concept unique to English law; the unregistered design right, and amending the law of copyright and registered designs as regards industrial designs.

Unregistered design rights, as their name suggests, do not need to be registered and are similar to copyright. They represent a property right subsisting in creation of an original design which is any aspect of shape or configuration (external or internal) of whole or part of an article. They do not subsist in a method or principle of construction or any features necessary to enable it to perform (the so-called 'must fit' and 'must match' exceptions). An example of such a design is the face of an electrical plug the metal pins of the plug would not be protected as a result of the 'must match' and 'must fit' exceptions.

The law of copyright and designs is extremely complex. Design rights, registered and unregistered, and especially copyright can be useful to the franchisor as a way in which to protect the franchise package depending upon the nature of the franchise but the advent of service mark registration (see above) has made them less important than they were previously.

Patents

It is unlikely that patent protection (previously under the Patents Act 1977 and now the Copyright and Designs and Patent Act 1988) will be relevant as a means of protecting the franchise package. Business format franchises are usually low-tech and do not entail technology which would qualify for a patent registration. Furthermore, patent applications are expensive and time consuming to make and relatively expensive to maintain. They also publicise the technology and provide a monopoly right for a limited period only.

Know-how

Know-how is defined in the EC franchise block exemption (see chapter 4) as:

"A package of non-patented practical information, resulting from experience and testing by the franchisor, which is secret, substantial and identified".

The only way to protect the know-how as a package is contractually to restrain franchisees and their employees from using it without authorisation. Such restraints of trade cannot, however, be unreasonable and a skilled legal practitioner is required to draft clauses that are as all-embracing and protective as possible whilst avoiding the danger of becoming too restrictive and therefore unenforceable.

The new EC know-how block exemption came into force in spring 1989 but will have no effect upon franchise agreements, which are covered by the franchise block exemption (see chapter 4 above).

Chapter 8
PROTECTING THE FRANCHISE – PREVENTION

Why protection is needed

When a franchisee or area developer (for the distinction between the two see the International Bar Association's publication, *International Franchising: Commonly Used Terms* by Alexander Konigsburg. The basic distinction is that the master franchisee sub-franchises and an area developer does not), buys a franchise it is basically paying for the right to use the franchisor's name and other intellectual property, such as trade and service marks. The franchisee/area developer will also be obtaining some know-how, but the most valuable asset of the franchise is undoubtedly the goodwill vested in its name and reputation.

Smith's Hamburgers may be just as tasty as *Wimpy's* but given the choice the majority of consumers will purchase a *Wimpy* in preference to a *Smith's* burger. To the public, *Wimpy* means consistent quality and a uniform flavour. That is why a franchise can be a good investment for the franchisee. The name has consumer pulling-power. The same product sold at the same price under a different name will fare less well than one sold under a well-known, respected name.

The name of the franchise may be its most valuable asset, but it is also its most fragile one. The franchisor must, therefore, take definite steps to protect his name, and the franchisee must make sure before entering into the franchise agreement that the name, which it is buying the right to use, is not being abused by third parties, and is in the gift of the franchisor.

There are a number of steps which the franchisor in the UK must take to protect the franchise package or, in other words, its name and associated intellectual property rights. The franchisor who omits to take such steps is a liability to both itself and its franchisees.

Suggested procedure for a franchisor

Before choosing a name for use in the UK the franchisor must take positive steps to ensure that the name it has chosen is available to it. In order to do this, it should take the following basic steps:

(a) make a search of the companies registry

(b) make a search of the trade marks registry, and

(c) check trade and area directories.

When it is satisfied that the name is available, it should then take the following extra steps:

(a) If, as would usually be the case, the franchisor is carrying on business through a limited company, it should ensure that whenever possible, the trading name is registered as its proper company name at the Company Registry in Cardiff. If it is an overseas company which does not intend to establish a subsidiary it should consider establishing a place of business under s691 of the Companies Act 1985. This will prevent any other company registering the same name. This does not prevent a third party trading under that name, but it at least asserts an initial claim to the name under the Companies Act 1985.

(b) Immediately ensure that both trade and/or service marks are registered at the trade mark registry in the appropriate classes. As discussed in the previous chapter, a registered mark gives the proprietor a statutory monopoly over the use of the name in the class of use in which it is registered.

(c) It is important not merely to register the mark, but to ensure that it is registered in the appropriate class or classes (see Appendix 9). The proprietor of, for example, the *Pizza Hut* mark in class 42 (miscellaneous) will not, under trade mark law, be able to stop a third party using it in connection with say, the building industry, or even registering it in class 37 (construction and repair) and so acquiring a statutory monopoly over its use in such a class. However, there are other ways of preventing such an abuse, which are described in the previous chapter.

(d) On a more practical level, the franchisor must take positive and effective steps to police its name and marks by regularly checking, for example trade magazines and the telephone directories. Very often, a small regional operator can be found working under the same or a similar name in a local services directory.

(e) Finally, trade mark agents can be instructed to carry out periodic, swift, up-to-date searches of the Trade/service mark Register and recent applications.

Suggested procedure for an area developer

The potential franchisee area developer, when considering taking on a particular franchise, will usually investigate the name and marks, carefully, and take steps to satisfy itself that they are not being used by unauthorised third parties. This would usually include:

(a) A search of Companies House, the trade mark registry, national and regional trade magazines, the *Yellow Pages* and regional directories etc.

(b) Check with the BFA (and IFA in the case of an American franchise), the franchising department of the franchisor's bank and a solicitor, about any franchise industry based background information on the franchisor's name and any current disputes over the name. The BFA and the professionals who are involved heavily in franchising have a great deal of wisdom to offer on such matters.

(c) Asking the franchisor directly about its proprietorship of the name, and insisting upon the appropriate statements and guarantees, warranties and indemnities being formally incorporated into the franchise agreement. The franchisor should ideally have taken the appropriate steps described above before commencing negotiations with the area developer.

The warranties should state clearly that the franchisor is the sole proprietor of the name and the other intellectual property rights and that it has a full unfettered right to grant the franchisee/area developer a licence to use them.

The indemnities will usually provide that if a third party uses the name, or other intellectual property rights, without the franchisor's authority, then the franchisor will take whatever steps necessary to enforce his monopoly over them and reimburse the franchisee/area developer for any reasonable costs which it is forced to bear as a result.

The franchisee/area developer will in return have to agree to assist the franchisor in policing the name and other intellectual property rights by immediately reporting to him any abuse of which it becomes aware and also assist him in enforcing his rights if appropriate, subject, of course, to the indemnity.

Chapter 9
PROTECTING THE FRANCHISE – REMEDIES AGAINST ABUSE

Whatever preventative steps are taken by the franchisor, the area developer and the unit franchisee, it is quite possible that at some time a third party will come to light who is, without consent, using the franchisor's name and/or marks; possibly without even knowing of the franchisor's existence. In such circumstances, the franchisor must act quickly in order to protect its investment and that of its franchisees. Every franchisor must therefore be aware of the possible remedies if they detect any infringement of its mark or abuse of its reputation.

Difficulties arise for the franchisor when a third party uses a similar name, perhaps in a different field of activity, and although the franchisor's trade mark may not have been infringed, the public may still confuse the franchisor with the third party (see chapters 7 and 8).

If the franchisor discovers a third party using its name, or a similar name, and/or a similar logo in a similar business dealing with similar goods or services, then the franchisor may be in a position to bring a trade mark or passing off action against the third party.

Trade mark infringement

The registration of the franchisor's trade mark, in a particular class or classes of goods or services, is important and should prevent abuse of the franchisor's name and reputation in most cases. Infringement of the franchisor's trade mark can be readily proved and prevented. The franchisor may also apply to the trade marks registry to ward off a third party's application to register a trade mark if the franchisor has prior rights over the mark.

Passing off

Whether or not the franchisor has registered any trade marks will not have any relevance to any action for passing off. The franchisor will have a separate right of action against a third party who has infringed its trade marks and may apply for an interim injunction to prevent any further infringement and also claim damages.

Passing off, as it is called, is a very complex area of the law and in basic terms the franchisor will have to establish:

(a) That its trade mark, including its name, logo or any similar device, applies to a class of goods or services which it is selling in England.

(b) The class of goods must be clearly defined. The public must distinguish the trade name attaching to the franchisor's goods from other similar goods. For example, the 'golden arches' will distinguish *McDonalds* hamburgers from any others.

(c) That its goods have a reputation and therefore, goodwill is attached to the trade mark of its goods. This is regardless of whether or not the franchisor is the only person who sells these goods, or merely one of a class of such persons. There are many shops selling hamburgers, but there is only one *McDonalds*.

(d) That it has suffered and is likely to suffer substantial damage to the goodwill of its business because the third party is selling goods which are falsely described by the trade name to which the franchisor's goodwill is attached.

It is only by understanding the definition of passing off that a franchisor will be able to identify those third parties who pose a genuine threat to its business. The essence of any passing off action is that, as a result of the third party's actions, the public will confuse the third party's goods or services with those of the franchisor. Confusion is the key point, and clearly the public will only be confused if the two businesses and names used by them are similar, and that the name is sufficiently unusual for the franchisor to have a monopoly in the name.

Clearly, anybody trading under a commonly used name is unlikely to be able to bring a passing off action because it will not be able to claim any monopoly in the name, as in, for example, a newsagent called *Smith's Newsagents*.

If the franchisor detects a possible abuse by a third party, the areas of confusion on the part of the public with the franchisor's business may be as follows:

(a) Customers may be confused into placing repeat business with the third party instead of the franchise outlets.

(b) Customers may be confused into thinking that the local franchisee outlet has been taken over by the third party and that in future the franchise outlet may be providing a narrower or poorer service.

(c) Potential new customers may think that a recommendation by existing customers to the franchisee is, in fact, a recommendation of the third party's similar but unsuitable competing service.

(d) Both new and existing customers may think that the franchisee's promotional material refers to the third party.

(e) Existing customers may believe that the franchisee has decided to expand, or change the nature of its business, if the third party has a similar name but is in a different field of activity.

If the franchisor or its area developer/master franchisee or franchisees discover a third party using its name or a similar one, then the first step would be for the franchisor's solicitor to write a letter to the offending third party requesting that the third party should immediately change its name or cease all business under its current name.

If this letter does not produce a satisfactory response then the franchisor may apply to the court for an interim injunction preventing the offending third party from continuing business under its present name. This procedure is quick and effective, and an injunction can be obtained within a matter of days.

To obtain an interim injunction, the franchisor only needs to show that it has a good arguable case and that some confusion by the public is the likely consequence of the offending third party's business.

The court, at the initial hearing, is not in a position to consider in detail the merits of the franchisor's case. However, if it is satisfied that the franchisor has at least an arguable case, then the court may grant an injunction in favour of the franchisor. It must be satisfied that, on the balance of convenience, the franchisor's interests must be protected, pending trial of the action at a later date. If an interim injunction is awarded but at the trial the court decides that the franchisor has not proved sufficient evidence of passing off, then the franchisor may have to compensate the defendant financially for any losses it has suffered as a result of the interim injunction being awarded.

Obviously before rushing to obtain an injunction, the franchisor would be well advised to obtain some evidence of the public, probably from its own customers, being confused between the offending third party's goods and the franchisor's goods. It is the evidence of confusion by the public which will have most influence with the court.

A comprehensive survey, or poll taken by professional pollsters, is another option open to the franchisor, although there is unlikely to be sufficient time to prepare such a poll before an application for an interim injunction and so it is more likely to be used at the trial.

At the interim hearing, the application will be dealt with by way of affidavit evidence, and so affidavits from the franchisor's customers claiming confusion with the third party will be of great assistance to the franchisor.

Any claim for damages to compensate the franchisor for any losses it may have suffered as a result of the passing off will only be considered by the court at the trial and cannot be dealt with at an interim stage in the proceedings.

Infringement by the franchisor

It must be remembered that passing off is a two-edged sword and that it can be used against the franchisor as well on his account. A franchisor anxious to avoid any allegation of passing off by a third party should avoid using a similar name or logo of not only large companies and household names, but also of small unknown companies. The little known company may still bring an action for passing off against a franchisor with a larger and more widely-based operation, if the smaller company can show that some goodwill attaches to its name and business. For example, there may be a small, relatively unknown business in Cornwall which has been trading under the name *Quaint* for 10 years. A franchisor, in the same or similar business, having carried out all the usual searches and enquiries, may not be aware of its existence and so may adopt the use of the trade name *Quaint* and operate on a national scale.

If the original *Quaint* business subsequently brought a passing off action against the franchisor, such an action may succeed on the basis that the public may be confused into thinking, for example, that the original *Quaint* business is only a pirate company, trying to imitate the franchisor and this would damage the original *Quaint* business.

Copyright

It is also possible to bring an action against a party for breach of copyright. Such litigation is usually long and protracted and is far less useful to the franchisor than actions based in trade mark law or passing off. This relative lack of importance means that this issue will not be considered further in this book.

Patents/registered designs/unregistered design rights

These rights also give rise to a right to issue a claim against any infringer, but like copyright are of little importance to franchisors.

Conclusion

The franchisor must investigate its own name and trade marks carefully and then take such steps as are possible to obtain a statutory monopoly over them. It must then continually police them and act swiftly to prevent abuse.

Chapter 10
OTHER LEGAL IMPLICATIONS

Franchising a business has very wide implications and this chapter reviews a number of points that deserve consideration even though they are not all, with the exception of taxation, central to franchising as such.

Shadow directors

One possible disadvantage of franchising is that it is possible that in certain circumstances the franchisor might be found by the courts to be a shadow director of an insolvent franchisee under s56(1) of the Company Directors Disqualification Act 1986 (see chapter 2 above). This has not, to date, occurred but as such a finding could lead to disqualification as a director, including a Shadow Director and hence a franchisor, for up to 15 years it must not be ignored.

Product liability

The Consumer Protection Act 1987 (the CPA) has had a great impact on the question of liability for damages. Its effect upon franchising is not always appreciated.

In essence, the CPA imposes strict liability upon manufacturers and other defendants, so removing the necessity to prove negligence. The legislation is too complicated to examine in full detail here but it is likely to impact most heavily upon those franchisors who manufacture goods, those who place their name and trade marks upon goods manufactured by others and those who import them into the EC. The legislation does not concern damage to, or defects in, the goods themselves but the damage it causes to other property or persons.

There are a number of ways in which a franchisor can seek to protect itself. The most obvious one is to take out good, comprehensive product liability insurance. However, insurance alone will not be sufficient. The franchisor must reduce the risks by exercising strict quality control upon the franchisee, avoiding exaggerated safety claims in its advertising and ensuring that clear warnings and instructions are given with goods.

The risks can also be transferred from the franchisor in certain circumstances and so it should keep careful records of all supplies, negotiate appropriate terms in contracts and ensure that neither it nor the franchisee make unnecessary admissions.

Taxation

The tax implications of franchising are of prime importance and must be clearly understood before franchising a business. The full implications will not be considered here.

It is important to analyse the franchise fee. Part of the monies paid by the franchisee to the franchisor will probably be royalties for the rest of the franchisor's intellectual property rights and part as payment for the provision of continuing services such as management, support, advertising, etc. It is then possible to establish, for instance, whether any part of the fee should be paid under deduction of income or corporation tax.

Taxation of intellectual property royalties (income/corporation tax) is a particularly complicated subject and varies depending on whether it is a trade mark, patent, know-how or copyright.

As regards trade marks, which are the most common form of intellectual property in franchising, if the trade mark owner exercises effective control over the mark and provides additional services, then the payments can probably be made gross. If this is not the case, the monies could be treated as pure income profit and, as annual payments, will then be subject to tax at source by the franchisee. Such deductions are calculated at the then current rates and clearly cause severe cash flow difficulties.

In simple terms, if the monies paid to the franchisor by the franchisee are in consideration of support services then they are likely to be considered by the Inland Revenue as income derived from a trade carried on by the franchisor and so the franchisee will not, in most cases, be obliged to deduct tax at source on the payments. Failing this they could be treated as investment income.

Another aspect to consider is the deductions of payments. Any payments to the franchisor by the franchisee in respect of know-how will most likely not be treated as a normal trading expense on the part of the franchisee. Instead a 25% writing down allowance should be available. There are various other tax issues. For example, the franchisor must charge VAT on its taxable supplies such as the services provided covering administration and training. The tax residence of the franchisor can also have a great impact upon the tax implications of the franchise. There may also be reliefs under any relevant double tax treaty to consider.

Business Expansion Scheme

The Business Expansion Scheme (BES) exists to encourage private individuals to invest in UK companies run by other parties and provides a relatively cheap form of finance. In essence it allows an investment up to £40,000 per tax year as a deduction against the investor's income if it has been invested in subscribing for shares in an unquoted company carrying on a qualifying trade wholly or mainly in the UK. Franchisors experience some difficulty in obtaining the benefit of the BES as they cannot have a qualifying trade if it consists to a substantial extent of the receipt of royalties or licence fees.

Consumer Credit Act 1974

The basic philosophy of this Act is to promote 'truth in lending' and to give uniform protection to individuals, including sole traders and partnerships, but not limited companies, who incur debts not exceeding £15,000, though there are numerous exceptions. It is clear therefore that it is only concerned with the franchise agreements granted to individuals, sole traders and partnerships but *not* limited companies.

The Act is concerned with credit agreements between an individual and any other person by which the creditor provides the debtor with credit not exceeding £15,000. If an agreement falls within this definition it is known as a regulated agreement and the creditor is deemed to be carrying on a consumer credit business. In the same way, a consumer hire agreement is defined as an agreement made by a person with an individual (the hirer) for the hiring of goods to the hirer, being an agreement which:

(a) is not a hire purchase agreement, and

(b) is capable of subsisting for more than three months, and

(c) does not require the hirer to make payments exceeding £15,000.

If a trader falls within the above definition he will be deemed to be conducting a consumer hire business.

It is clear therefore that if the franchisor falls within the definition of either a consumer credit business or a consumer hire business then a licence from the Office of Fair Trading will be required.

If the franchisor proposes to lend money to potential franchisees to enable them to enter into the franchises, then provided the amount of credit falls within the above definitions a licence will be required.

As regards arranging factoring facilities for franchisees and possibly introducing franchisees to equipment leasing companies, it is necessary to determine whether the franchisor would be regarded as conducting a credit brokerage as defined by the Act.

In essence, this consists of the effecting of introductions of individuals desiring credit or goods on hire, to firms offering such facilities or to other credit brokers. In simple terms, if the franchisor introduces its franchisees to either consumer credit businesses or consumer hire businesses as previously defined, then the franchisor would be deemed under the Act to be carrying on an ancilliary credit business in the form of a credit brokerage and therefore a licence from the Office of Fair Trading would be required.

There is a school of thought that suggests that even if the agreements entered into by the franchisees, whether they be credit agreements or hire agreements, are not in the normal course of events regulated by the Act, it is nevertheless possible that merely by arranging such credit or the hiring of goods, the franchisor would still require a licence under the Act.

Whether the franchisor would be deemed under the Act to be acting on credit brokerage depends to a large extent on to whom introductions are made. In short, if the credit organisation or hiring organisation would fall within the definition of consumer credit business or consumer hire business respectively, then in all likelihood a licence is required.

Where an individual franchisee is raising a sum of £15,000 or less to purchase the franchise, attention needs to be paid to the possibility of the franchise agreement being a linked transaction in relation to the loan.

For example, a franchise agreement would be deemed to be a linked transaction and thereby require a licence under the Act if the franchise agreement is entered into by the franchisee in compliance with a term of the actual or prospective regulated agreement.

A franchise agreement is likely to come within the definition of a linked transaction if the franchisee is forced to opt out of the franchise if the regulated agreement is cancelled; moreover, if on a termination of the regulated agreement the franchise agreement is terminated.

There is no doubt that if a franchisor lends money directly to franchisees and the consumer credit agreements fall within the Act, a licence will be required. (see Appendix 15 for example of application form)

Further, a franchisor may be deemed to be a credit brokerage under the Act with regard to either arranging factoring facilities for franchisees or introducing franchisees to equipment leasing companies or to banks for finance. It should always be borne in mind that depending on the circumstances, a franchise agreement might be deemed to be a linked transaction under the Act, thereby requiring a licence.

Franchisor's liability

The novelty of franchising and the lack of legal decisions upon commercial disputes arising out of it means that there are a number of areas which are uncertain from the legal point of view. The extent of the franchisor's liability is perhaps the most important of these.

Clearly the franchisor owes a duty of care not only to the franchisee but also to the public. The difficult question is whether or not it would be liable to the public for the acts and defaults of the franchisee.

If the franchisor's negligence causes loss or injury to a third party, would that third party sue the franchisor, even though it had not acted incorrectly itself?

Common law addresses this question of agency in three basic ways being; master and servants; principal and agents, and independent contractors. None of these provides a totally satisfactory answer.

In English law, an employer is vicariously liable for the acts and omissions of its employees in the course of their work. If a lorry driver knocks down an old lady, she can sue both the driver and his employers. The reason for this right of action is the employer's ability to control the employee. This would seem to be inappropriate for the franchisor/franchisee relationship.

As the franchisee, in many instances, holds himself out as the franchisor's agent, and the franchisor allows this, it may be that a third party has a right of action against the franchisor. Such an action would be based in the concept of agency by estoppel or holding out.

This means that where the one party, the franchisor, represents that another, the franchisee, is his agent, it will not later be allowed to deny it. The key point here is what amounts to a representation. The uniform appearance, products, services and trade marks may well prove a sufficient representation.

Another possibility is that the franchisor and franchisee might be considered to be in partnership with each other under s5 of the Partnership Act 1890. As partners are jointly and severally liable this could form another course of action against the franchisor.

It would seem that there is plenty of scope for the franchisor to be held liable for the acts or omissions of its franchisees. It is absolutely vital that the franchisor limits this liability as much as possible by stating prominently on all advertising, stationery, etc the exact nature of the franchisee's relationship to the franchisor.

Chapter 11
INTERNATIONALISING
THROUGH A FRANCHISE

Commercial considerations

When considering whether or not to embark upon the internationalisation of a business through franchising it goes without saying that certain key questions must be asked about the commercial desirability of the venture.

(a) Is there a ready market for the product/service?
(b) Is the market big enough?
(c) Will the product/service work in that market?
(d) Is it too far away for the franchisor to provide effective supervision?
(e) Is there a language barrier?
(f) Should the franchise package be modified for local conditions, and if so how by whom?
(g) Is the local distribution network familiar to the franchisor?
(h) Is the locality politically stable?
(i) Are there any exchange control or inward investment controls to be considered?

Who participates in international franchising?

Franchising is only one way of internationalising a business, but there are others each of which involves problems of its own. They include

(a) Establishing branches abroad
(b) Establishing overseas subsidiaries
(c) Entering into joint ventures with local partners
(d) Appointing overseas agents and distributors
(e) Trade mark and know-how licensing
(f) Acquisition of a local corporation

Of the companies that do opt for the franchise route there are basically two types. One is the established domestic franchisor who wishes to expand abroad. It has demonstrated its ability to operate a successful franchise network and has a tried and tested franchise package. However, such previous experience can sometimes result in the franchisor being too inflexible in his approach to international franchising, and failing to appreciate the need to modify the existing package in the face of a different economic and cultural environment.

The second type of international franchisor is one which wishes to franchise a tried and tested product or service which it has not franchised in its own country. Such franchisors are often more open minded in assessing the needs of the target country franchisees. They lack any preconceived ideas but obviously suffer in other ways from their lack of franchising experience. For example, they may find it hard to understand fully the role of the franchisor and tend to still concentrate upon dealing directly with customers rather than the franchisee/area developer.

Both types of prospective international franchisor require the advice of a lawyer and accountant who are able to point out the advantages and problems involved in international franchising and place it firmly in its proper perspective. They should also consider taking advice from a local franchise consultant on the general suitability of their products or service for that particular market.

The advantages of international franchising

The advantages of using franchising as a method of international expansion include:

(a) The franchisor does not have to invest large amounts of money into the business in order to expand and establish it overseas.

(b) A less developed infra-structure is required by the franchisor because a compact central office can manage and develop the organisation without becoming heavily involved in personnel management and other day to day issues.

(c) More rapid expansion of the network is possible, as the franchisor's resources are not as thinly spread as they would be when employing any other method of marketing.

(d) As the area developer and franchisees will usually be local to the territory being developed, the franchisor is able to take advantage of their local knowledge, and so usually conduct business more efficiently.

(e) Franchisees are usually more highly motivated than ordinary managers or agents, and may well prove cheaper than expatriate managerial staff.

(f) The area developer, if one is appointed, will cope with the area's specific problems.

(g) Political problems such as overseas investment restrictions may be more easily overcome by passing the control of day to day affairs over to an area developer.

(h) The appointment of an area developer may alleviate various tax and tariff problems which would otherwise be experienced by the franchisor.

The disadvantages of international franchising

Problems which are particular to franchising include:

(a) Once the area developer/franchisee has been trained in operating the franchise, it may decide to carry on the business without the franchisor, and so become an effective competitor.

(b) Training the area developer/franchisee to a sufficiently high standard, and then maintaining and monitoring standards can be difficult.

(c) It is very difficult to select the best area developer/franchisee, but as the success of the franchise will turn upon the chosen candidate, this must be a carefully made decision.

(d) The franchisor/area developer or franchisor/franchisee relationship is founded on a large measure of mutual trust.

(e) The keeping of appropriate records by the area developer/ franchisee and the monitoring of these can prove difficult for an inexperienced franchisor.

Structure of the franchise

Once it has been decided that franchising is the most suitable way in which to internationalise a particular business, a franchise structure that best suits the company's needs and resources must be chosen. This is an immensely important task, as an unsuitable structure will make the franchise difficult to manage. It may bring about the failure of a potentially successful international franchise. The company must obtain reliable counsel as regards the commercial, cultural, legal and tax environment of the intended target territory from advisors who are knowledgable about the company's activities, resources and aspirations.

It has been stressed before that there is no correct structure. Every possibility will throw up different problems. The aim must be to create a structure which enables the franchise package to operate in an efficient manner without putting undue demands upon the franchisor's financial or managerial resources. It is vital that the international franchise structure chosen should ensure the maximum tax benefits, whilst at the same time limiting the exposure to domestic taxes. This is considered in more detail below.

The main reasons for choosing a particular structure will usually be *commercial* rather than legal. The four basic ways of structuring the franchise are listed below:

Direct franchising

This involves the franchisor granting a franchise directly to a franchisee in another jurisdiction, in exactly the same way as it would appoint a domestic franchisee. This may be very appealing to an established domestic franchisor, but is really only practical when franchising into a jurisdiction that is geographically, culturally, linguistically and legally close to the franchisor's home territory. Thus, there is a good deal of direct franchising from the USA into Canada, and from Australia to New Zealand. In both cases there is a wealth of homogeneity between the home and target territory. The EC single market which is supposed to be with us from the end of 1992 would also seem to invite direct franchising. This is discussed in more detail in the following chapter.

Franchising through an overseas subsidiary

In this way the franchisor retains direct control over, and contact with, the foreign franchisees. Whilst this may be attractive to the established franchisor, it detracts from one of the main advantages of becoming a franchisor, the need for only limited managerial resources. Further, whilst it is more versatile than direct franchising, it is still best suited to target countries with similar cultural, commercial and linguistic backgrounds. This way the franchisor can continue to operate his domestic franchise system with little or no amendment.

Franchising through a joint venture

Establishing a joint venture company with a local corporation provides the franchisor with a reservoir of local knowledge which will facilitate the more successful exploitation of the target territory. The selection of the joint partner is clearly of paramount importance, and in an ideal world, should be made only after the careful screening of a large number of possible candidates.

The joint venture will of course share the risk of the project between the partners, but joint ventures are often short lived affairs, and can create potential future competitors. In addition, equal voting rights at board and shareholders' meetings can make management of the joint venture vehicle slow and laborious, taking up a good deal of the franchisor's own management time. The franchisor is placed in the position where not only must it carry out the duties of a franchisor, but must also monitor and safeguard its own interests within the joint venture company. On top of this, the franchisor may well find that his role in, and the versatility of, the joint venture is severely hampered by foreign investment legislation.

Appointing an area developer/master franchisee

The franchisor appoints an area developer/master franchisee to exploit a territory, usually a particular country. This greatly reduces the franchisor's involvement and the demands on its managerial and financial resources.

This is often the best structure to adopt for countries with different commercial, cultural, linguistic and legal backgrounds from those of the franchisor's own jurisdiction. Choosing the right area developer/master franchisee is if anything more difficult and important than choosing a suitable joint venture partner. The consequences of a bad area developer/ master franchisee can be traumatic, and ruin later attempts by the franchisor to re-enter the territory.

It is not sufficient merely to decide to operate through an area developer, it must also be decided how that area developer will function. The options are broadly as follows:

(a) The area developer/master franchisee is given the right to open and operate franchise outlets within the teritory for its own account, or

(b) The master franchisee is given the right to appoint unit franchisees within the territory on the basis that it will, in relation to them, perform the role of a franchisor. The unit franchisees may also include the area developer's own subsidiaries.

The decision on which of the approaches to adopt is entirely a commercial one; it depends upon the size and resources of the area developer and the tax implications of both choices.

The block exemption discussed above now makes this approach to franchising a more appropriate one inside the EC as the granting of exclusive territories makes it a more financially attractive proposition for the area developer (see chapter 12).

Specific franchise laws

Clearly once the franchisor commences business abroad it must deal with the law of foreign jurisdictions. Whilst many jurisdictions are struggling to come to terms with the concept of franchising, others have, to one degree or another, introduced specific franchising laws. Whilst this establishes a previously unknown certainty in franchising matters, such laws can also be unduly restrictive and stunt the growth of franchising.

Not all franchise laws are as positive and constructive as the EC block exemption. The franchise law proposed in Australia in 1986 would have had exactly this stunting effect.

Specific franchising laws often lay down precise reporting or disclosure requirements with which the foreign franchisor must comply if it is to avoid severe legal penalties.

In the United States, generally acknowledged to have the most fully developed franchising legislation, there are both Federal and State requirements, with which both domestic and foreign franchisors must comply. At the Federal level it is necessary to consider the Trade Commission's *"Disclosure Requirements and Prohibitions Concerning Franchising and Business Opportunity Ventures"*. (see chapter 2 above).

These require franchisors and area developers/master franchisees to provide would be franchisees and sub-franchisees with copies of the franchise agreement, all related documentation, and a disclosure document. Matters such as the franchisor's litigation and bankruptcy histories, a description of the franchise to be purchased, details of any initial and continuing payments, details of any obligations to purchase goods, details of available finance, the precise nature of the franchisee's participation and a summary of the termination, cancellation, training, site selection and reporting provisions of the agreement are included in this disclosure document.

Timing is crucial and disclosure must be made at the earlier of either the first personal meeting, or the time for making of disclosures, which is at least 10 business days prior to the execution of the binding agreement or the payment of consideration by the franchisee.

All other related documentation, including the agreement to be executed by the franchisee, if materially different to the standard form agreement must also be registered 5 working days before execution.

An earnings claim document must also be delivered to the franchisee if the franchisor makes projections of earnings or income of the franchisee, or discloses historical information concerning company owned, or franchised operations.

Many states have registration and disclosure requirements, as well as provisions governing, *inter alia*, termination and renewal, which are far too detailed to comment upon here.

Taxation

The main aims of the international franchise tax planner must of course be to minimise or defer taxes overall, by a combination of:

(a) Minimising exposure to income and withholding taxes in the country where the franchise is granted.

(b) Minimising or deferring taxes in the franchisor's resident jurisdiction.

(c) Maximising foreign tax credits. Minimising local taxes involves ensuring that the franchisor has little or no presence in the jurisdiction to which the BFF has been granted, taking advantage of any available Double Taxation Treaties, and ensuring that the money paid to the franchisor is described in the most tax efficient manner.

Withholding taxes can be avoided if a suitable Double Taxation Treaty exists between the area developer's/master franchisee's country and the franchisor's country. If there is no such treaty, it may be appropriate to establish an intermediary to which the franchisor licences the relevant commercial and intellectual property rights, and which then licences them in turn to the area developer/master franchisees. Such a subsidiary would usually be based in a country such as the Netherlands, which has favourable tax laws as regards not only withholding tax, but royalty taxes in general.

It may also be possible to structure the franchise to minimise or defer liability for taxes in the franchisor's home jurisdiction, by for example, assigning the rights to an offshore company which in turn licenses the area developer/master franchisee, or by establishing a number of subsidiaries spread throughout the world, in order to collect profits there and eventually remit them to the franchisor.

There are numerous alternative structures available to minimise taxation liability, but the suitability of a structure naturally depends upon the location of the relevant parties, and the lawyer must therefore be aware of all of the possibilities.

The harmonisation of the taxation system in the EC prior to 1992 will possibly lead many established EC franchisors to re-examine their structures.

Exchange control

The purpose of the franchisor deciding to enter into franchising is to increase its profit. This means that not only must the franchisor be able to invest in the chosen jurisdiction in an acceptable manner, but it must also be possible to receive payments from the area developer/master franchisees, be it through intermediaries or otherwise. The foreign exchange control laws of the area developer/master franchisee's country are therefore of prime importance. If they prevent or severely restrict payments abroad, the whole transaction will become commercially unattractive.

Import/export controls

These are germane to distribution franchises in particular, and are a direct result of a country's economic policy. A 'protectionist' approach can severely hamper a franchise. Not all controls on imports are obvious, and a plethora of quality control and consumer protection laws may hamper and delay imports that are *prima facie* acceptable. Another indirect way of controlling imports is the imposition of high import taxes to over inflate the base price and so make the goods unattractive to the local consumer. Japan for example has long had a reputation for this practice.

Work Permits

Whatever franchise structure is adopted it is likely that the franchisor will have to post a number of its employees in the target territory for a period of time. If this is necessary it is important to ensure that they obtain the appropriate visa/work permit. Failure to do so could cause problems with the relevant government department and so severely compromise the franchisor's efforts.

Conclusion

Internationalising a business through the franchise option can be an attractive commercial proposition. It involves a great deal of research and planning however and the franchisor must ensure that it obtains the best possible advice in order to have the best possible chance of success.

Chapter 12
1992 AND FRANCHISING

Objectives and benefits of a single market

The creation of a truly common market was one of the objectives when the Treaty of Rome was signed in 1957. It was, however, not until 1985 that the EC governments made a commitment to remove all technical, physical and fiscal barriers to the free movement of people, goods, services and capital among the twelve Member States (White Paper on *Completing the Internal Market*). This commitment has been included in the package of Treaty reforms known as the Single European Act (SEA) which came into operation on 1st July 1987. The SEA also incorporates a series of important Treaty reforms to speed up decision making by extending majority voting to virtually all the major areas of the single market programme.

By 31st December 1992 not only all tariff barriers but also all non-tariff barriers should have been abolished. The benefits (as described in the Cecchini Report – *1992. The European Challenge* – Wildwood House) of creating an internal market are the following:

(a) increase in economic growth;
(b) increase in employment;
(c) achievement of a better balance in the world economy;
(d) regeneration of European industry;
(e) healthier competition (not only internally but also vis-a-vis non-EC companies, particularly Japanese and American companies);
(f) achievement of economies of scale and improved productivity and profitability;
(g) stable prices and improved consumer choice;
(h) increase in professional and business mobility;
(i) substantial cost savings by governments and companies by cutting out substantial red tape;
(j) improving plans for regional and rural developments;
(k) increased possibilities for scientific, technical and commercial co-operation; and
(l) greater unity.

Legislative implementation

In its White Paper on *Completing the Internal Market* (Brussels, 1985), the Commission produced a plan of action and timetable for the achievement of the single market by the end of 1992. This legislative programme is now well under way and is expected to be completed more or less on time. Some 300 legislative acts were necessary to remove the remaining non-tariff barriers, over 150 of which have been approved so far. The franchising block exemption (see chapter 4) further supports this aim. In summary, these Acts the impact of which upon franchising in the single market will be enormous, relate to three main areas.

The removal of physical barriers

(a) Control of goods, EC border stoppages, customs control and associated paperwork.
This will allow franchisors more freely to distribute their goods to franchisees in other Member States, and reduce management overheads.

(b) Control of individuals.

The removal of technical barriers

(a) Free movement of goods, harmonising divergent national product standards, technical regulations and conflicting business laws.
This will increase the potential market for distribution franchises.

(b) Barriers for foreign companies to enter nationally protected public procurement markets.
This will also increase a franchisor's potential market in other Member States.

(c) Common market for services:
 (i) banking
 (ii) securities
 (iii) insurance
 (iv) transport
 (v) telecommunications
 (vi) information technology
This will enable franchisors to provide more easily the necessary support to franchisees.

(d) The removal of control capital movements.
This is obviously essential. If a franchisor cannot repatriate funds easily there is little incentive to do business in other Member States.

(e) Creation of suitable conditions for industrial and commercial co-operation:
(i) harmonising company law
(ii) harmonising patent law
(iii) creating a Community trade mark system.
This is very ambiguous but will ultimately provide a legal framework much better suited to inter-state franchisors.

The removal of fiscal barriers

(a) harmonising VAT rates

(b) harmonising excise duties
This again will enable the franchisor to devote less time to paperwork and more to addressing important issues such as franchisee support and marketing.

How will franchising fare in the single market?

Franchising is the ideal medium through which the small and medium sized business can exploit the single market. The reasons are outlined in the previous chapter on internationalisation through franchising. It would be naive, however, to think that this means that franchisors will not encounter problems in the post-1992 EC. The most common problems are those which will affect all business. Despite all of the Commission's efforts to create a single market, there are still many problems which it is doubtful will be overcome by 1992.

These problems are based on the political, cultural and commercial differences that exist between each Member State. The Single Market is comprised of 12 different consumer cultures and distribution networks for which it will not be possible to adopt a single marketing plan. The 'Euro-ad', for example, is still far from a reality as shown by *Coca Cola's* spectacular failure in advertising on *Sky Television*. The advertisement was such a failure that it was withdrawn after only a short time.

A good illustration of the problem is the experience of the novelty manufacturer *Hunky Dory Designs*. This UK company makes small gifts and greeting cards and decided to market them in other EC Member States.

In Italy, Portugal and Spain the goods were successful. However, in West Germany for some unknown reason, only those gifts made from metal were popular. The other products did not sell. In France, there were no novelty gift shops to sell these sort of goods; they could not be properly presented to the consumer and so failed.

Another example is the experience of the American toy company, *Tonka*. It has found that in order to sell its toys they often have to be given a different name in each EC Member State. There are also many other variables for example, the Dutch market is very price sensitive with games. Toys associated with violence are not popular in West Germany and Italian children prefer traditional toys such as cars and dolls. These sort of differences will always cause problems in the Single Market, as they cannot simply be removed by legislation, they are cultural biases.

Other problems which will dog the Single Market are those created by international terrorism and drug trafficking. The abolition of border controls will be severely resisted by members such as the UK, France and Spain if they cannot devise a way around such problems. This will hamper the distribution of goods and so impair the growth of distribution franchises in the EC.

Areas of reform particularly relevant to franchising

There are certain areas impacted by the move towards a single market which are particularly relevant to franchising.

Research and development

The SEA provided a great fillip to the EC's Research and Development policy by way of Title VI 'Research and Technological Development' which contains 11 articles. These articles contain the aims of research and technological development in the EC and detail how they will be implemented. The budget for 1987-91 is almost £4 billion. The programmes are very diverse and responsibility for them is divided amongst various departments (known as Directorate-Generals) of the EC Commission. Smaller enterprises are eligible for these grants and it may well be that certain franchisors could use the funds to develop their concepts, as they do in effect carry out the research and development for their franchisees.

Public procurement policy

Public purchasing by Member State government agencies account for 10% of the Communities GDP. Despite the fact that under Article 30 of the

Treaty of Rome, there should be no barriers to intra-community trade including purchasing by public bodies, such restrictions still exist.

However, in accordance with the Cockfield White Paper on the creation of a single market, three draft directives have already been published covering public supplies, public works and remedies in the case of non-compliance. Certain sectors such as public energy, water, transport and telecommunications are excluded, as are services. The liberalisation of these markets may well afford inviting new opportunities to franchises in appropriate areas, and encourage their development in other EC Member States.

Intellectual property

The harmonisation of intellectual property law will do much to remove the difficulties of franchising in other Member States.

As regards patents, there has been a European Patent Convention since 1978 making it possible to site a single application for a European patent. This is processed by the European Patent Office. However, there are still considerable differences between Member States' approach to patent law and Eire, Denmark and Portugal are not yet signatories to the convention. The differences will, however, disappear when the Community Patent Convention is eventually implemented, although when this will be is still uncertain. This is unlikely to affect franchises much because of the minor role of patents in franchising.

The first step towards the harmonisation of the laws of Member States on the law of trade marks was adopted earlier this year (Council Directive 89/104/EEC). It requires the necessary amendments to national law to be effected by 28 December 1991. The Directive applies to every trade mark for goods or services which is registrable in a Member State, to collective marks, guarantee marks and certification marks, marks registrable in the Benelux Trade Mark Office and marks registered internationally and having effect in a Member State (Article 1). Trade marks may consist of any sign capable of being represented graphically, words (including personal names), designs, letters, numerals, or the shape of goods or of their packaging, provided that the signs are capable of distinguishing the goods or services of one undertaking from those of another (Article 2).

The Directive sets out the marks or signs which must be refused registration (which also serve as grounds for declaring existing registered marks invalid). Special provision is made in respect of Community trade marks, when they become available, by Article 4(3).

The rights conferred by a trade mark are set out in Article 5, but the proprietor cannot prevent a third party from using, in the course of the course of trade, his own name or address, certain indications concerning the characteristics of the goods or services, or the mark itself where it is necessary to indicate the purpose of a product or services, eg spare parts (Article 6). The proprietor cannot prohibit the use of the mark in relation to goods put on the market within the Community by himself or with his consent (Article 7). Most important for franchising, the Directive envisages the licensing of marks (Article 8) and provides for the lapse of certain rights in relation to a mark which have not been enforced over a period of five years (Article 9) or where the mark itself has not been used for such period, unless there are 'proper reasons' for its non-use (Articles 10 and 11). A mark which has not been put to 'genuine use' for five years may be revoked (Article 12).

Trade marks constitute one of the most important issues in establishing free trade between EC Member States. Before a common EC wide law is adopted, the national trade mark laws must be harmonised in line with the Trade Mark Directive described above. A Community trade mark would make it possible to make one application to register a mark in all twelve Member States. This may well create problems for existing trade marks and lead to conflicts in the short term, and language differences may mean that it is not possible to use a certain mark in particular Member States as the words have an undesirable meaning there. However, it will stimulate the development and promotion of European brands and so greatly assist the development of EC franchising.

EC company law

The harmonisation of company law in the EC will allow the franchisor to take a more flexible approach to EC-wide franchising without having to deal with different systems of company law.

This is of particular importance as it will make direct franchising through local subsidiaries far simpler to administer. Examples of moves to effect this harmonisation include the Draft Directive Extending the Fourth Directive on Annual Accounts (and the Seventh Directive on Consolidated Accounts), the Draft Fifth Directive on the Structure and Management of PLC's and the Eighth Directive on Regulation of Auditors.

The Draft Twelfth Directive aims at harmonising the law relating to the incorporation of single member state companies in the EC. The natural desire of companies to have a true European legal vehicle to operate as a single unit throughout the Common Market has resulted in the EC Commission proposal being brought forward. The main questions are which national structure should be chosen, and how should employees be represented on it? So far, only a discussion memorandum exists for this vehicle called 'Societas Europea'. The EC Commission has proposed three possible structures:

(a) Supervisory board on which employees are represented and a separate board of management

(b) a board of directors and a separate works council, and

(c) freedom for the company and employees to negotiate the form of participation by employees as they wish.

It should be noted that none of these methods except possibly (c), provides for individual plant or office participation. This is important because there are likely to be many companies with plants or offices in different EC states.

The *Societas Europea* will be an optional alternative to forming a national company and present an exciting new option for pan-EC franchisors or area developers. For tax purposes it will be resident in the country where its headquarters are located, its offices and plants in other countries being treated as branches.

Taxation

Further harmonisation of VAT throughout the EC will impact on all businesses and not just upon retail sales. It is proposed to introduce two different rates of VAT.

Zero rating is also permitted by Article 17 of the Second Directive on VAT provided that it is for clearly defined social reasons and for the benefit of the final consumer. The far-reaching effect that such reforms may have is well illustrated by provisions of the Finance Act 1989 effecting a substantial change in the imposition of VAT on commercial property. Although there will be some winners and some losers in the harmonisation, it will make administration far simpler for the EC-wide franchisor.

Corporation tax will also be affected by harmonisation, although these proposals have not as yet been developed. In basic terms, however, the amendment will remove tax liabilities which can be incurred because transactions cross national boundaries. This will greatly encourage franchisors to set up in other Member States.

Free movement of capital

The free movement of capital between Member States is a priority of the '1992 lobby'. Without it, the single market will be illusory, but to date, it has yet to be tackled head on, for example, there are still restrictions on repatriating funds from Greece to other Member States.

European Economic Interest Group (EEIG)

Regulation No 2137/85, passed on 25th July 1985, facilitates the establishment of EEIG's as from 1st July 1989. The EEIG is a new form of business medium which will more easily facilitate cross-frontier co-operation between firms engaging in certain types of joint venture activities such as franchising. It is the first truly community based legal entity and will be of particular use to small and medium sized enterprises that wish to use it as a way of minimising the individual cost of common activities.

It may well be that a franchisor establishes an EEIG with its franchisees to carry out its advertising or product sourcing activities. It could also be the medium for EC wide franchisee associations (although Article 85 may cause difficulties here).

The EEIG is perfectly suited to this as it neither replaces nor completely absorbs its members' activities and does not have to be formed or run to make profits in its own right, although profits can be made if so desired.

In order to form an EEIG, there must be at least two members with their principal activity or central administration in different Member States. It is therefore only of use to those franchisors which have outlets in at least one other Member State.

The constitution and legal existence of the EEIG is based in community law, although any 'unregulated' issues which arise out of it will be dealt with by the relevant national legislation.

The EEIG without doubt gives pan-EC franchisors the opportunity to develop a structure which is uniquely suited to their particular activity. It has infinite possibilities and will no doubt be taken full advantage of to the benefit of both franchisors and franchisees alike.

The block exemption

The EC block exemption (see chapter 4 above) is a definite step forward for franchising, and suggests that the single market will be very conducive to successful pan-EC franchising. However, as discussed above, at present the block exemption will have little effect upon the substantive legal restrictions placed upont he UK franchisors. This is likely to change somewhat once English and Scottish competition law has been amended in accordance with this government's 1989 White Paper (see Appendix 17) to resemble more closely EC law in the early 1990s.

The block exemption succeeds in recognising the definite benefits of franchising as a way of doing business. It achieves its ultimate purpose of paving the way for a truly single market for franchisors after 1992 by removing much of the bureaucracy and paper shuffling that is necessitated by notification to the Commission and application for individual exemption under Article 85(3) of the Treaty of Rome.

Although individual Member State's domestic law may continue for some time to come to create particular legal problems, the block exemption undoubtedly sets a precedent for the acceptance of franchising and the avoidance of over-involved regulatory machinery such as that seen in the United States.

Structure

When a franchisor is considering entering other EC Member States, the structure adopted is vital to success. Direct franchising, using a non-UK subsidiary joint venture and appointing an area developer all have their particular advantages and disadvantages, and for a full discussion of these options the reader is directed to the previous chapter on international franchising. EEIG's add still further options in the EC.

Language

Franchisors, like all other European businessmen, must seriously consider the linguistic differences between Member States and how they impact upon their franchise networks. It is not possible to ride on the back of the English language universally.

The Manual, for example, will have to be carefully translated and updated in each Member State language. The monitoring of advertisements will be impossible without the appropriate linguistic knowledge. Training courses in English alone will not be sufficient, whilst records and accounts will obviously be kept in the language of each Member State.

None of these is a new problem for businesses working abroad. What is new, however, is that language will become the key to the single market and will impact upon franchises probably more than any other business medium. It will affect more than just external procedures such as monitoring franchisees, etc, and these will take on a proximity and importance previously unknown to international franchisors.

Conclusion

The single market affords all EC Member State businesses a tremendous opportunity to expand. Franchises are no exception. Exactly how much of a truly single market there will be by December 31st 1992 is not yet certain, nevertheless the removal of physical, technical and fiscal barriers is a reality.

Franchisors are well positioned to take advantage of this harmonisation but they will have to adopt new approaches in many areas. The main strength of franchising, – the ability rapidly to expand a network – may well mean that it becomes the best way for small and medium sized businesses to tackle the single market, and protect themselves from the threat of being taken over by corporations from other Member States seeking to enter the United Kingdom.

Appendix 1
BRITISH FRANCHISE ASSOCIATION MEMBERS

Accounting Centre (The)
Alan Paul Hairdressing PLC
Alfred Marks (Franchise) Limited
Alpine Soft Drinks PLC
ANC Holdings Limited
Anicare Group Services (Veterinary)
    Limited
Apautela
Appollo Window Blinds Limited
Avis Rent-a-Car Limited
Badgeman Limited – Sketchley
    Business Service Group
Bally Group (UK) Limited
Balmforth & Partners (Franchises)
Bath Doctor (The)
Body and Face Place
Britannia Business Sales Limited
British Damp Proofing
Budget Rent-a-Car International Inc.
Burger King (UK) Limited
Circle 'C' Stores Limited
Circle K (UK) Limited
City Link Transport Holdings Limited
Clarks Shoes Limited
Coca Cola Export Corporation (The)
Colour Counsellors Limited
Command Performance International
Computa Tune
Computerland Europe Sarl
Country Rose Management
    (Franchise) Limited
Crown Eyeglass PLC
Dampcure/Woodcure 30
Don Miller's Hot Bread Kitchens
Dyno-Services Limited
EDS Drycleaning Systems Limited
    Euroclean Centre
Euroclean
Everett Masson & Furby Limited
Exchange Travel (Franchises) Limited

Fast Frame Franchises Limited
Fersina International
Francesco Group
Garden Building Centres
Global Cleaning Contracts Limited
Global Franchise Services
Great Adventure Game (The)
Gun-Point Limited
Holiday Inns (UK) Limited
Holland & Barrett Franchising Limited
Home Tune Limited
In-Toto Limited
Interlink Express Parcels Limited
Kall-Kwik Printing (UK) Limited
Keith Hall Hairdressing
Kentucky Fried Chicken (GB) Limited
Knobs & Knockers Franchising
    Limited
Kwik Strip (UK) Limited
Late Late Supershop (UK) Limited
    (The)
Master Thatchers Limited
Metro-Rod PLC
Midas (Great Britain) Limited
Mixamate Holdings Limited
Mobiletuning Limited
Molly Maid (UK)
Motabitz (Franchising) Limited
Nationwide Investigations Group
    Limited
Northern Dairies Limited
Oasis Trading
Olivers (UK) Limited
Pancake Place Limited (The)
Pass & Co
PDC Copyprint (Franchise) Limited
Perfect Pizza (The)
PIP (UK) Limited
Pizza Express Limited
Poppies (UK) Limited

110

Practical Used Car Rental Limited
Prontaprint
Pronuptia De Paris (Young's Franchise Limited)
Rodier Paris
Safeclean International
Servicemaster Limited
Silver Shield Screens Limited
Singer SDL Limited
Sketchley Recognition Express Limited
Snap-On-Tools Limited
Snips in Fashion
Spud-U-Like Limited

Strachan Studio
Swinton Insurance
The Late Late Supershop (UK) Limited
J W Thornton Limited (Thorntons)
Tie Rack Limited
TNT (UK) Limited
Unigate Dairies Limited
Uticolor (Great Britain) Limited
Wetherby Training Services
Wimpy International Limited
Young's Formal Wear (Young's Franchise Limited)
Yves Rocher (London) Limited

Associates

A1 Damproofing
Alpine Double Glazing
Autosheen Car Valeting Services (UK) Limited
Banson Tool Hire
Bellina Limited
Berni Restaurants
Blinkers
Britannia Business Sales Limited
Cico Chimney Linings Limited
Coffeeman Management Limited
Computa Tune
Countryside Garden Maintenance Services
Curtain Dream PLC
Dash Limited
Direct Salon Services
Fires & Things Limited
Garden Building Centres Limited

House of Colour
J. Evershed & Son Limited – Eversheds Community Stores
Knobs & Knockers Franchising Limited
M & B Marquees
Mainly Marines Franchising Limited
Morley's (Fast Foods) Limited
Mr Lift Limited
Original Artshops Limited
Professional Appearance Services Limited
Re-Nu Limited
Snappy Snaps UK Limited
Stained Glass Overlay
Team Audio Limited
Trust Parts Limited
Ventrolla Limited
Weigh & Save

Appendix 2
ARTICLES 85 AND 86 OF
THE TREATY OF ROME

Article 85

1. The following shall be prohibited as *incompatible with the common market:*
All agreements between undertakings, decisions by associations of under-takings and concerted practices which may affect trade *between Member States* and which have as their *object or effect* the *prevention, restriction or distortion of competition* within the common market, and in particular those which:

(a) directly or indirectly fix purchase or selling prices or any other trading conditions;

(b) limit or control production, markets, technical development, or investment;

(c) share markets or sources of supply;

(d) apply dissimilar conditions to equivalent transactions with other trading parties, thereby placing them at a competitive disadvantage; and

(e) make the conclusion of contracts subject to acceptance by the other parties of supplementary obligations which, by their nature or according to commercial usage, have no connection with the subject of such contracts.

2. Any agreements or decisions prohibited pursuant to this Article shall be *automatically void.*

3. The provisions of para 1 may, however, be declared inapplicable in the case of:

(a) any agreement or category of agreements between undertakings;

(b) any decision or category of decisions by associations of undertakings;

(c) any concerted practice or category of concerted practices

which *contributes to improving the production or distribution of goods or to promoting technical or economic progress,* while allowing consumers a fair share of the resulting benefit, and which does not:

(a) impose on the undertakings concerned restrictions which are not indispensable to the attainment of these objectives;

(b) afford such undertakings the possibility of eliminating competition in respect of a substantial part of the products in question.

Article 86

"Any abuse by one or more undertakings of a dominant position within the common market or in a substantial part of it shall be prohibited as incompatible with the common market in so far as it may affect trade between Member States. Such abuse may, in particular, consist in:

(a) directly or indirectly imposing unfair purchase or selling prices or other unfair trading conditions;

(b) limiting production, markets or technical development to the prejudice of consumers;

(c) applying dissimilar conditions to equivalent transactions with other trading parties, thereby placing them at a competitive disadvantage;

(d) making the conclusion of contracts subject to acceptance by the other parties of supplementary obligations which, by their nature or according to commercial usage, have no connection with the subject of such contracts."

Appendix 3
PRONUPTIA JUDGMENT

PRONUPTIA DE PARIS Gmbh v. PRONUPTIA DE PARIS IRMGARD
SCHILLGALLIS (Case 161/84)

BEFORE THE COURT OF JUSTICE OF THE EUROPEAN COMMUNITIES

(*Presiding*, Lord Mackenzie Stuart C.J.; Everling, Bahlmann and Joliet PP.C.;
Koopmans, Due and Galmot JJ.)
Mr. Pieter VerLoren van Themaat, *Advocate General*.

29 January 1986

Reference from Germany by the Bundesgerichtschof (Federal Supreme Court)
under **Article 177** EEC.

Restrictive practices. Franchising. There are at least three distinct types of
franchising agreement, each of which should be treated separately for the
purposes of EEC restrictive practices law: (a) service franchise agreements; (b)
production franchise agreements; and (c) distribution franchise agreements. [13]

Restrictive practices. Franchising. Distribution. Distribution franchising agreements do not *per se* infringe **Article 85** EEC, but may do so depending on their
content. [14]–[15]

Restrictive practices. Franchising. Distribution. Know-how. One of the two
essential conditions for the operation of a distribution franchise system is the
ability of the franchisor to communicate his know-how to the franchisees and
provide them with the necessary assistance in putting his methods into effect
without aiding his competitors. Clauses essential to achieve this are permissible
under **Article 85(1)** EEC and include: (a) prohibition on the franchisee opening
a shop in an area where he could be in competition with another franchisee, for
the duration of the franchise and a reasonable time thereafter; (b) obligation on
the franchisee not to alienate his shop without the prior approval of the
franchisor. [16]

Restrictive practices. Franchising. Distribution. Reputation. The second
essential condition for the operation of a distribution franchise system is the
ability of the franchisor to preserve the identity and reputation of the network.
Clauses which provide a basis for essential control to that end do not restrict
competition under **Article 85(1)** EEC and include an obligation on the franchisee:
(a) to apply the commercial methods developed by the franchisor and to utilise
his know-how; (b) to sell contract goods only in premises arranged and decorated
according to the franchisor's specifications so as to guarantee a uniform image;
(c) not to move his shop to another location without the franchisor's approval;
(d) not to assign the contract without the franchisor's approval; (e) to accept the

franchisor's control over the selection of goods offered in the shop; (f) to submit all advertising to the franchisor. [17]–[22]

Restrictive practices. Franchising. Distribution. The following clauses in a distribution franchising agreement are not essential for the operation of such a system, are restrictive of competition and thus infringe **Article 85(1)** EEC: clauses which partition markets between the franchisor and franchisee or between franchisees *inter se,* including an obligation on the franchisee to sell the contract goods only at the location designated in the contract. [23]–[24]

Restrictive practices. Franchising. Distribution. Prices. Clauses in a distribution franchising agreement which restrict the franchisee's ability to fix his own prices freely restrict competition contrary to **Article 85(1)** EEC. However, for the franchisor merely to recommend prices is acceptable. [25]

Restrictive practices. Franchising. Distribution. Inter-State trade. Market partitioning. Distribution franchising agreements which contain clauses partitioning markets between franchisor and franchisee or between franchisees *inter se* are *per se* capable of affecting inter-State trade even if they are concluded between enterprises established in the same member-State, in so far as they prevent franchisees setting themselves up in another member-State. [26]

Restrictive practices. Franchising. Distribution. Group exemption. Regulation 67/67 does not apply to typical distribution franchising agreements. [34]

The Court *interpreted* **Article 85(1)** EEC and Regulation 67/67 *in the context of* an international franchising system for the distribution and sale of wedding apparel, the Germany subsidiary of the French parent running its own shops as well as licensing franchisees in specific territories in Germany to run shops under its supervision, *to the effect that* franchising agreements for the distribution of goods are not *per se* anticompetitive, *that* whether they are or not depends on their clauses, *that* those clauses necessary for the proper use of the franchisor's know-how and for protection of the identity and reputation of the franchisor's mark are acceptable under **Article 85(1),** *that* clauses which partition markets within the franchise system (intra-brand) are anti-competitive, *and that* Regulation 67/67 does not apply to such distribution franchising agreements.

Dr. Rainer Bechtold, of the Stuttgart Bar, for the plaintiff.
Dr. Eberhard Kolonko, for the defendant.
S. C. de Margerie, for the French Government as *amicus curiae.*
Dr. Norbert Koch, Legal Adviser to the E.C. Commission for the Commission as *amicus curiae.*

The following case was referred to by the Court in its judgment:

1. ETABLISSEMENTS CONSTEN SA AND GRUNDIG-VERKAUFS-GmbH *v.* EEC COMMISSION (56 & 58/64), 13 July 1966: [1966] E.C.R. 299, [1966] C.M.L.R. 418. Gaz: 56/64

The following further cases were referred to by the Advocate General:

2. S.V.P.N.A.S. *v.* BILLY, 19 June 1973 (Trinbunal de Grande Instance, Bressuire).

3. MAJE DISTRIBUTION, 4 March 1974 (Tribunal Correctionnel, Paris).
4. MORVAN *v.* INTERCONTINENTS, 28 April 1978 (Cour d'Appel, Paris).
5. TELEFLEURS *v.* INTERFLORA, 10 May 1978 (Cour d'Appel de Paris): Cahiers de Droit de l'Enterprise No. 6-78.
6. Judgment of 22 April 1982 (Cour d'Appel, Douai): [1982] *Gazette du Palais* (Doctrine) 565.
7. FELICITAS *v.* GEORGES, 19 June 1982 (Cour d'Appel, Colmar): [1982] Dalloz Jur. 553.
8. MEIEREI-ZENTRALE, 23 March 1982 (Bundesgerichtshof): [1982] WuW 781.
9. GTE. SYLVANIA INC. *v.* CONSUMERS UNION OF THE UNITED STATES INC.: 441 U.S. 942.
10. ITALY *v.* EEC COUNCIL AND COMMISSION (32/65), 13 July 1966: [1966] E.C.R. 389, [1969] C.M.L.R. 39. Gaz: 32/65
11. LA TECHNIQUE MINIERE *v.* MASCHINENBAU ULM GmbH (56/65), 30 June 1966: [1966] E.C.R. 235, [1966] C.M.L.R. 357. Gaz: 56/65
12. BRASSERIE DE HAECHT SA *v.* WILKIN (No. 1) (23/67), 12 December 1967: [1967] E.C.R. 407, [1968] C.M.L.R. 26. Gaz: 23/67
13. BRAUEREI A. BILGER SÖHNE GmbH *v.* JEHLE (43/69), 18 March 1970: [1970] E.C.R. 127, [1974] 1 C.M.L.R. 382. Gaz: 43/69
14. DE NORRE *v.* NV BROUWERIJ CONCORDIA (47/76), 1 February 1977: [1977] E.C.R. 65, [1977] 1 C.M.L.R. 378. Gaz: 47/76
15. SA FONDERIES ROUBAIX-WATTRELOS *v.* SOC. NOUVELLE DES FONDERIES A. ROUX (63/75), 3 February 1976: [1976] E.C.R. 111, [1976] 1 C.M.L.R. 538. Gaz: 63/75
16. METRO-SB-GROßMÄRKTE GmbH & CO. KG *v.* E.C. COMMISSION (26/76), 25 October 1977: [1977] E.C.R. 1875, [1978] 2 C.M.L.R. 1. Gaz: 26/76
17. L'OREAL NV & L'OREAL SA *v.* DE NIEUWE A.M.C.K. PVba (31/80), 11 December 1980: [1980] E.C.R. 3775, [1981] 2 C.M.L.R. 235, Gaz: 31/80
18. SA LANCOME AND COSPARFRANCE NEDERLAND BV *v.* ETOS BV AND ALBERT HEIJN SUPERMART BV (99/79), 10 July 1980: [1980] E.C.R. 2511, [1981] 2 C.M.L.R. 164. Gaz:99/79
19. HASSELBLAD (GB) LTD. *v.* E.C. COMMISSION (86/82), 21 February 1984: [1984] E.C.R. 883, [1984] 1 C.M.L.R. 559. Gaz: 86/82
20. L.C. NUNGESSER KG AND KURT EISELE *v.* E.C. COMMISSION (258/78), 8 June 1982: [1982] E.C.R. 2015, [1983] 1 C.M.L.R. 278. Gaz: 258/78
21. CODITEL SA *v.* CINE-VOG FILMS SA (No. 2) (262/81), 6 October 1982: [1982] E.C.R. 3381, [1983] 1 C.M.L.R. 49. Gaz: 262/81

Table of Proceedings

Opinion of VerLoren van Themaat A.G., 19 June 1985
Judgment of the European Court of Justice, 28 January 1986
Urteil of the European Court of Justice, 28 January 1986
Language of the proceedings: German

Opinion of the Advocate General (Mr. Pieter Verloren van Themaat)

1. *Introduction*

1.1 *The questions referred by the Bundesgerichtshof*
In a dispute with its French franchisor over the payment of arrears of royalties, a German franchisee successfully pleaded in the appeal court that the franchise agreement in question was void under EEC competition law. According to the appeal court **Article 85** of the EEC Treaty prohibits franchise agreements of the kind at issue in the proceedings, inasmuch as they contain restrictions of competition which are not exempted, under **Article 85(3)** and Regulation 67/67 of 22 March 1967, from the prohibition laid down in **Article 85(1)** of the Treaty.

The plaintiff in the main proceedings appealed against that judgement to the Bundesgerichtshof. The Bundesgerichtshof considered that the judgment of the appeal court raised questions of Community law, and therefore, by an order of 15 May 1984, referred a number of questions to the Court of Justice.

According to writers on the subject, distribution systems involving franchise agreements did not gain currency in the member-States until the early 1970s. Systems of that kind developed very quickly, however, and now constitute a significant proportion of distribution systems. Even if, in answering the questions referred, the Court restricts itself to franchise agreements having the characteristics of the agreements at issue, its answers will therefore have repercussions for the validity of tens of thousands of contracts. Furthermore, the importance of the Court's answers to the questions referred is reinforced by the fact that according to the written and oral observations which it presented in these proceedings the Commission has not yet adopted a clear policy in the matter.

The questions referred by the Bundesgerichtshof are as follows:
1. Is **Article 85(1)** of the EEC Treaty applicable to franchise agreements such as the contracts between the parties, which have as their object the establishment of a special distribution system whereby the franchisor provides to the franchisee, in addition to goods, certain trade names, trade marks, merchandising material and services?
2. If the first question is answered in the affirmative: Is Commission Regulation 67/67 of 22 March 1967 on the application of **Article 85(3)** of the Treaty to certain categories of exclusive dealing agreements (block exemption) applicable to such contracts?
3. If the second question is answered in the affirmative:
   (a) Is Regulation 67/67 still applicable if several undertakings which, though legally independent, are bound together by commercial ties and form a single economic entity for the purposes of the contract participate on one side of the agreement?
   (b) Does Regulation 67/67, and in particular Article 2(2)(c) thereof, apply to an obligation on the part of the franchisee to advertise solely with the prior agreement of the franchisor and in a manner that is in keeping with the latter's advertising, using the publicity material supplied by him, and in general to use the same business methods? Is it relevant in this connection that the franchisor's publicity material contains price recommendations which are not binding?
   (c) Does Regulation 67/67, and in particular Articles 1(1)(b), 2(1)(a) and 2(2)(b) thereof, apply to an obligation on the part of the franchisee to confine the sale of the contract goods exclusively or at least for the most

117

part to particular business premises specially adapted for the purpose?

(d) Does Regulation 67/67, and in particular Article 1(1)(b) thereof, apply to an obligation on the part of the franchisee − who is bound to purchase most of his supplies from the franchisor − to make the rest of his purchases of goods covered by the contract solely from suppliers approved by the franchisor?

(e) Does Regulation 67/67 sanction an obligation on the franchisor to give the franchisee commercial, advertising and professional support?

1.2   *The main provisions of the contracts entered into by the franchisee concerned.*

As appears from the three contracts between the parties in the main proceedings, which were submitted to the Court at its request after the hearing, the franchisor binds itself:

Not to grant to any third party the right to use the trade mark 'Pronuptia de Paris' in the contract territory concerned (Hamburg, Oldenburg and Hannover respectively) (clause 1(1));

Not to open any other Pronuptia shops in the contract territory (clause 1(2));

Not to provide goods or services to third parties in the contract territory (clause 1(2);

To provide commercial assistance to the defendant in advertising, in establishing and stocking her shop, in training staff and with regard to sales techniques, fashions and products, purchasing and marketing and, very generally, to help the defendant to incrfease her turnover and profits (clause 3(1)).

The franchisee (who according to clause 3(5) remains the sole proprietor of her business, bear the risks of the business herself and her sole enjoyment of the profits) is obliged *inter alia:*

To sell the products covered by the agreement, using the trade name and trade mark Pronuptia de Paris, only in the shop referred to in clause 1, which must be equipped mainly for the sale of bridal fashions, in accordance with the brand image of Pronuptia de Paris (clauses 3(3) and 4(1));

To purchase from the franchisor 80 per cent. of wedding dresses and accessories, together with a proportion of cocktail and evening dress to be set by the defendant (clause 3(6)):

To purchase the remaining wedding dresses and accessories and cocktail and evening dress exclusively from suppliers approved by the franchisor (clause 3(6)).

To pay to the franchisor a royalty of 10 per cent. on all sales (including sales of articles not supplied by Pronuptia) during the validity of the contract (clause 5(1));

To refrain, during the period of validity of the contract and for one year after its termination, from competing in any way with a Pronuptia shop and in particular from engaging in the specialised sale of wedding dresses and

accessories in the Federal Republic of German, in West Berlin or in an area where Pronuptia is already represented (clauses 6(6) and 9);

To make the sale of the goods covered by the contract her main objective (clause 6(6));

To carry on business in a specified location and to equip the premises primarily for the sale of bridal wear, in accordance with the image of Pronuptia de Paris and following its instructions (clauses 1(3), 3(3) and 4(1));

To carry on business, and in particular to sell products covered by the contract, under the trade mark and trade name Pronuptia de Paris, only in those premises (clause 3(3) and 4(1));

To use the trade mark Pronuptia de Paris in her advertising only with the prior approval of the franchisor; to harmonise her advertising with that of Pronuptia, using the advertising material made available by Pronuptia with the recommended prices included therein (clause 1(1) and 6(1));

To advertise, to distribute advertising material to the best of her abilities and in general to apply the business methods of the franchisor (clause 6(5));

Strictly to respect all industrial and commercial property rights of Pronuptia and to inform Pronuptia immediately of any infringements of those rights by third parties of which she might become aware (claus 14).

Pursuant to clause 6(1), Pronuptia is to recommend to the franchise appropriate standard prices; both parties are to regard these standard prices as guidelines for retail sale (without prejudice to the franchisee's liberty to set prices herself).

1.3 *Plan of discussion*

As I have already pointed out, the answer to be given by the Court to the questions referred may have repercussions on the validity of other franchise agreements, and on the approach to be adopted by the Commission in this field. In the second part of this opinion I shall therefore make a number of general remarks regarding this system of distribution, which is relatively new to the Community. In particular, I shall examine to what extent a sufficient degree of certainty with regard to the content and legal nature of franchise agreements for the sale of products already exists in legislation, judicial decisions and academic literature, and especially within the trade organisations concerned, so as to enable the Court to deliver a more general ruling. I do not think that the wording of the questions referred by the Bundesgerichtshof prevents that. It precludes the Court only from ruling with regard to franchise agreements which have been current in the Community for a longer period (for example, in the hotel, café and restaurant sector) in relation to the provision of services or to manufacturing.

In the third part of my opinion I shall investigate the similarities and differences between franchise agreements, in particular franchise agreements such as that now at issue, and other distribution systems already current in Community legal practice, especially those which have been discussed in judgments of the Court, such as agency agreements, exclusive distribution or purchasing contracts, selective distribution systems, brewery contracts, and licensing agreements.

I shall also discuss what conclusions may be drawn in this case from previous decisions of the Court.

In the fourth part of my opinion I shall state how, in my view, the questions referred in this case should be answered.

2. *General remarks regarding franchise agreements for the distribution of products*

2.1 *The development of the franchise system as a new distribution system*

It appears from the already quite extensive literature on the subject, that the franchise system, based on earlier American experience, was introducecd into the EEC in the early 1970s. Its subsequent development has however been rapid. In 1969 there were only a few franchise systems in the distribution sector in the Federal Republic of Germany. By 1978 the total number of franchise systems (including arrangements for the provision of services) had risen to 85 (with 11,000 franchisees); in May 1982 there were 200 such systems, with 120,000 franchisees and a total turnover of 100 thousand million DM, of which 65 to 75 thousand million DM was in the retail sector. In France (where franchising also began to develop in the early 1970s) there were more than 300 franchise systems in 1981 and 500 in 1985 (with 25,000 participating shops and 8 per cent. of total retail sales). In the Netherlands there were 280 franchise systems in 1983. Similar development took place after 1970 in other member-States.

2.2 *Legal characteristics of the franchise system according to academic opinion*

It appears from the literature, and was confirmed by the Commission at the hearing, that none of the member-States have specific legislative provisions regarding franchise agreements. Furthermore, no precise definition of franchise agreements in general, or of franchise agreements for the distribution of products in particular, can be drawn from the case law that exists or from the relevant academic writing. The main elements of franchise systems for the distribution of products in all the member-States examined seem however to be the following:

(1) althbough they remain independent and bear their own risks, franchisees are integrated to a considerable extent in the franchisor's distribution network;

(2) marketing strategy is based on a chain effect, brought about by the use, in return for payment, of a common business name, trade mark, sign or symbol, and – in many cases – uniform arrangement of shop premises;

(3) exclusive rights are granted to the franchisee within a defined area and for defined products, and exclusive rights that vary in scope are granted to the franchisor with regard to the supply or selection of the products to be sold by the franchisee. The writers on the subject also seem to be agreed that the term 'franchise agreement', as it is used in Europe, must be understood in a much more restricted sense than the original American term, which applied to many more distribution systems. As will appear from my remarks below, however, recent American literature also uses the term in a more restricted sense.

On the basis of a comparative legal study, Mr. E.M. Kneppers-Heynert, in a recent article in the *Bijblad Industriële Eigendom*,[1] arrived at the following general description, which seems to me to be reasonably representative:

Franchising is a contractually governed form of commercial co-operation between independent undertakings, whereby one party, the franchisor, gives one or more other parties, the franchisees, the right to use his trade name or mark and other distinguishing features, in the sale of products or of services. The sale takes place on the basis of an exclusive marketing concept (system or formula) developed by the franchisor; in return, the franchisor receives royalties. The use of those rights by the franchisee is supervised by the franchisor in order to ensure uniform presentation to the public and uniform quality of the goods or services.

The European Code of Ethics for Franchising, drawn up by the European Franchising Federation and the eight national associations of which it is composed (six of them from EEC member-States), was submitted to the Court at the hearing. It refers *inter alia* to the following six characteristics of a franchise agreement:[2]

1. 'Ownership [by the franchising firm (the Franchisor)] of a Company Name, a Trade Name, Initials or Symbols (possibly a Trade Mark) of a business or a service, *and* Know-how, which is made available to the franchised firm(s) – the Franchisee(s)... [and its] control of a range of Products and/or Services presented in a distinctive and original format, and which must be adopted and used by the franchisee(s), the format being based on a set of specific business techniques which have been previously tested, and which are continually developed and checked as regards their value and efficiency'.

2. 'Implicit in any Franchising Agreement is that there shall be a payment made in one form or another by the Franchisee to the Franchisor in recognition of the service supplied by the Franchisor in providing his name, format, technology and know-how.'

3. 'Franchising is therefore something more than a Sales Agreement or a Concession Agreement of a Licence Contract in that both parties accept important obligations to one another, over and above those established in a conventional trading relationship.'

4. 'The Franchisor will guarantee the validity of its rights over the brand, sign, initials, slogan, etc. and will grant the franchised firms unimpaired enjoyment of any of these which it makes available to them.'

5. 'The Franchisor will select and accept only those franchise candidates who possess the qualifications required by the franchise. All discrimination on the grounds of politics, race, language, religion or sex, will be excluded from the qualifications.'

6. 'The Franchise Contract will specify in particular the points set out below, it being understood that the provisions adopted will be consistent with national or community law.

The method and conditions of payment of fees and royalties.

The duration of the Contract and the basis for renewal; the time and duration of notice.

The rights of the Franchisor prior to assignment by the Franchisee.

The definition of "open territorial rights" granted to the Franchisee, including options (if granted) on adjoining territories.

Basis for distribution of the assets affected by the contract, if the Contract is terminated.

Distribution arrangements relative to supply of goods, including responsibility for transport and transport charges.

Terms of payment.

Services provided by the Franchisor: Marketing assistance, Promotion, Advertising: Technology & Know-how: Managerial Administrative & Business Advice: Financial & Taxation Advice: Conditions under which these services to be provided and relevant charges: Training.

Obligations of the Franchisee: To provide Accounts & Operating Data: To receive Training and to accept Inspection Procedures.'

With regard to training and assistance the Code of Ethics also contains a large number of specific guidelines, of which only the following seem relevant to the assessment of franchise agreements of the kind referred to in the Code of Ethics in the light of **Article 85** of the EEC Treaty:

The Franchisor will assist the Franchisee by providing guidance as to the operating costs and margins that he should be achieving at any given time in his business.

Any non-concurrence [sic] clause applicable after breach or termination of the contract, must be precisely stated and defined in the contract as regards its duration and territorial extent.

2.3 *Case law*

Only in France have the definitions formulated by the trade organisations been more or less adopted by the courts: see Tribunal de Grande Instance de Bressuire, 19 June 1973 (S.V.P.N.A.S. *v.* BILLY); Tribunal Correctionnel de Paris, 4 March 1974 (MAJE DISTRIBUTION); Cour d'Appel de Paris (Fifth Chamber), 28 April 1978 (MORVAN v. INTERCONTINENTS); Cour d'Appel de Paris, 10 May 1978 (TELEFLEURS V. INTERFLORA[3]); Cour d'Appel de Douai, 22 April 1982[4]; Cour d'Appel de Colmar (First Civil Chamber), 9 June 1982 (FELICITAS *v.* GEORGES[5]). In those judgments it is striking that exclusive rights are not always regarded as essential (Cour d'Appel de Colmar and Cour d'Appel de Douai), but permission to use a trade name, signs and symbols and the application of uniform sales methods are so considered. In the absence of legislative definitions, moreover, franchise agreements are assessed exclusively on the basis of the provisions of the agreement at issue.

Within the Community it is only in the judgment of the Bundesgerichtshof of 23 March 1982 (MEIEREI-ZENTRALE[6]) that I have been able to find a judicial ruling on the competition law aspects of franchise agreements. In that judgment the prohibition of resale price maintenance laid down in section 15 of the Gesetz gegen Wettbewerbsbeschränkungen (German Restraint of Competition Act)[7] was considered applicable to a franchise agreement in which resale prices were fixed. In its 1981 report *Full-line Forcing and Tie-In-Sales*, however, the British Monopolies and Mergers Commission did take the view that exclusive supply obligations could in certain circumstances be significant from the point of view of competition law.

As I have already pointed out, in the United States the term franchise agreement was initially used in a very wide sense. According to the more recent restricted use of the term (which served as a model for the European development) a franchise is defined as a licence from the owner of a trade mark or trade name permitting another to sell a product or service under that mark or name.[8]

In the United States, as in the United Kingdom, exclusive purchase obligations contained in franchise agreements are not automatically regarded as 'tying arrangements' prohibited by competition law. In appropriate market conditions they may however fall under that prohibition. Since the 1977 SYLVANIA[9] judgment the 'rule of reason' has been applied to vertical territorial restriction clauses in order to ascertain whether there is restriction of competition (in particular horizontal restriction). **Contract provisions regarding resale prices are regarded as prohibited *per se* where it appears that the franchisor, not content with mere price recommendations, is attempting one way or another to force the franchisee to apply his suggestions or recommendations.** In the SYLVANIA judgment the 'rule of reason' was applied to territorial restrictions, in particular restrictions on premises, such as those at issue in the Pronuptia case, notwithstanding the resulting restrictions on competition between retailers of Sylvania products. Despite the concomitant restrictions on 'intra-brand' competition, vertical restrictions on competition such as those at issue in the SYLVANIA case were regarded as beneficial for 'inter-brand' competition. Only in certain cases and on the basis of their actual economic consequences may such vertical restrictions of competition be held to be caught by the *per se* prohibition contained in American antitrust legislation. Having regard to the later American legal practice the decisive question seems to be whether or not there is effective competition with other products on the relevant market. In speaking of the American practice I should point out that in the United States the problem peculiar to the EEC of separate national markets with prices which are often widely divergent does not exist. A single internal market was achieved long ago in the United States, so that the problem of obstacles to parallel imports does not arise.

2.4 Conclusions

On the basis of academic opinion and case law in the Community, on the basis of the views of the European Franchising Federation and on the basis of the most recent American definitions of franchise agreements of the type at issue, I think, that the significant distinguishing features of a franchise agreement for the sale of products are the independence of the undertakings involved, the existence of a licence for the use of a company name, trade name, emblem or other symbols, and for know-how in a broad sense, together with a uniform manner of presentation, the usual consideration being the payment of a royalty by the franchisee for the licences granted. In the American case law it seems that the market position of the undertakings concerned and the distinction between the vertical relationship between franchisor and franchisee and the horizontal relationship between each of the franchisees and their competitors are of particular importance in assessing such agreements from the point of view of competition law. Except in extraordinary market conditions, it seems that inter-branch competition is considered more important for the maintenance of effective competition than intra-brand competition. **In the United States the imposition of fixed prices by franchisors seems to be regarded as automatically contrary to the prohibition of price agreements, just as it is in the Federal Republic of Germany.** For the rest, the judicial practice in the United States and in three of the large member-States of the EEC seems to be to judge each agreement on its own merits, taking into account its specific provisions and, in so far as competition aspects are to be dealt with, the specific circumstances of the relevant market. The last-mentioned factor is particularly relevant with regard to the various exclusivity clauses to be found in franchise agreements.

3.   *Similarities and differences between franchise agreements and other distribution systems considered in previous judgments of the Court*

3.1   *Exclusive agents*

Since in the literature and the case law on franchise agreements the fact that the franchisee is an independent undertaking or that he deals in his own name and at his own risk is considered to be an essential characteristic of such agreements, I think, contrary to Pronuptia's contention, that comparison of his new type of agreement with agency agreements as referred to in the Commission communication of 24 December 1962[10] is not relevant to the questions referred by the Bundesgerichtshof. As appears from clause 3(5) of the agreements at issue, they do not differ in that respect from the general picture.

3.2   *Exclusive distribution agreements*

The contracts in question are similar in more respects to exclusive distribution agreements. In particular the franchisee's exclusive purchase rights laid down in clause 1(1) and (2), and the franchisor's (restricted) exclusive supply rights laid down in clause 3(6) are clearly similar, at first sight, to the characteristics which determine the applicability of Regulation 67/67 of 22 March 1967 on the application of **Article 85(3)** of the Treaty to certain categories of exclusive dealing agreements. It is not surprising, therefore, that in this case the national court raised separate questions on the issue of the applicability of that regulation.

With regard to the first question referred by the national court, regarding the applicability in principle of **Article 85** to franchise agreements, I think a particularly relevant analogy may be made with the Court's statement of the problem in its judgment of 13 July 1966 in Case 32/65 (ITALY *v.* EEC COMMISSION[11]). In particular the third paragraph on page 407 of the Reports[12] may, subject to the differences which I shall discuss later between franchise agreements and 'classical' exclusive distribution agreements, be applied by analogy in answering the first question put by the national court.

In that paragraph it is stated:

It is not possible either to argue that **Article 85** can never apply to an exclusive dealing agreement on the ground that the grantor and the grantee thereof do

124

not compete with each other. For the competition mentioned in **Article 85(1)** means not only any possible competition between the parties to the agreement, but also any possible competition between one of them and third parties. This must all the more be the case since the parties to such an agreement could attempt, by preventing or limiting the competition of third parties in the product, to set up or preserve to their gain an unjustified advantage detrimental to the consumer or the user, contrary to the general objectives of **Article 85**. Therefore even if it does not involve an abuse of a dominant position, an agreement between businesses operating at different levels may affect trade between member-States and at the same time have as its object or effect the prevention, restriction or distortion of competition and thus fall under the prohibition in **Article 85(1)**. Thus each of **Articles 85** and **86** has its own objective and so soon as the particular features of either of them are present they apply indifferently to various types of agreements.

In the following paragraph the Court refuses to compare exclusive distribution systems with agency agreements and other forms of integration in which a single undertaking incorporates its distribution network into its own organisation (and there is thus no question of agreements between several independent undertakings).
I think the particular importance of the passage quoted lies in the fact that it seems valid *mutatis mutandis* for all bilateral vertical agreements. Furthermore, like the American case law, it appears to treat possible restrictions on horizontal competition as decisive for the application of Article 85(1), rather than the mutual restrictions on their commercial freedom agreed to by the parties to a vertical relationship.
That conclusion is not affected by the Court's statement in the GRUNDIG-CONSTEN judgment (Joined Cases 56 and 58/84, CONSTEN AND GRUNDIG *v.* EEC COMMISSION [13]) (with regard to the argument that the agreement in question had increased competition between similar products of different brands) that 'although competition between producers is generally more noticeable than that between distributors of products of the same make, it does not thereby follow that an agreement tending to restrict the latter kind of competition should escape the prohibition of **Article 85(1)** merely because it might increase the former'. The Court went on to state that 'for the purpose of applying **Article 85(1)**, there is no need to take account of the concrete effects of an agreement once it appears that it has as its object the prevention, restriction or distortion of competition'.
Closer examination of the GRUNDIG-CONSTEN judgment as a whole shows, I think, that there too the Court was particularly concerned with restrictions of competition between the exclusive distributor and third parties (in that case, parallel importers of products of the same brand), that is, intentional restrictions on horizontal competition. In that respect I refer in particular to the Court's remarks at the bottom of page 342 and the top of page 343 of the Reports. [14] Greater importance is however ascribed also to horizontal 'intra-brand competition', especially where national markets are protected against parallel imports, than is the case in recent American judgements.
The necessary details were set out by the Court in a preliminary ruling of 30 June 1966 in Case 56/65 (SOCIETE TECHNIQUE MINIERE *v.* MASCHINENBAU ULM [15]), where it held that "in order to decide whether an agreement containing a clause "granting an exclusive right of sale" is to be considedred as prohibited by reason of its object or of its effect, it is appropriate to take into account in particular the nature and

quantity, limited or otherwise, of the products covered by the agreement, the position and importance of the grantor and the concessionnaire on the market for the products concerned, the isolated nature of the disputed agreement or, alternatively, its position in a series of agreements, the severity of the clauses intended to protect the exclusive dealership or, alternatively, the opportunities allowed for other commercial competitors in the same products by way of parallel re-exportation and importation'.

3.3 *Brewery contracts*

The exclusive distribution agreements which the Court has been called upon to consider mainly concerned exclusive importers, and according to statements made by the Commission at the hearing that was also generally true of exclusive distribution agreements notified to it. In particular they did not directly concern large numbers of retailers, as is the case here. In that respect the Court's judgments regarding brewery contracts may however be relevant. Building on a passage from the MASCHINENBAU ULM judgment cited above, in the first HAECHT judgment (Case 23/67[16]) the Court held with regard to brewery contracts of the kind in question (involving the obligation to purchase from one brewery only) that:

> ... in order to examine whether it is caught by Article 85(1) an agreement cannot be examined in isolation from the ... context, that is, from the factual or legal circumstances causing it to prevent, restrict or distort competition. The existence of similar contracts may be taken into consideration for this objective to the extent to which the general body of contracts of this type is capable of restricting the freedom of trade.

If that paragraph, together with the paragraph which follows it, is applied by analogy to franchise agreements, I think it can be inferred that **Article 85(1)** is applicable where a franchisor from one member-State has such a market position in a second member-State that through his subsidiaries, if any, and by means of a number of franchise agreements with independent traders he significantly impedes the access to the market of other producers or wholesalers in that second member-State.

It appears from paragraph 5 of the judgment of the Court in Case 43/69 (BILGER *v.* JEHLE[17]) that in taking into account other comparable contracts not only contracts concluded by a large number of retailers with the same producer (or wholesaler) should be considered but also similar exclusive supply contracts concluded with other producers from the *same State.* In the case of brewery contracts the combined effects of such contracts between retailers and producers in the same member-State may indeed result in partitioning of the market. As far as I have been able to ascertain the Court has until now only had to deal with brewery contracts between a brewery and its commercial clients in a single member-State. I think, however, that in principle the partitioning of markets (or other forms of restriction on horizontal competition) may come about as a result of the combined effect of franchise agreements for similar products independently of the place where the producer or wholesaler is established.

On the subject of brewery contracts, I think that the judgment of the Court of 1 February 1977 in Case 47/76 (DE NORRE *v.* BROUWERIJ CONCORDIA[18]) is also of some relevance to the second question referred by the Bundesgerichtshof in the present case. In that judgment the Court held that in spite of certain differences, recognised by the Court, between such agreements and traditional exclusive distribution agreements, for which Regulation 67/67 was originally enacted, the regulation also applies to brewery contracts, that is, 'agreements to which only two undertakings from one member-State only are party, under which one party agrees with the other to purchase only from that other certain goods for resale and which do not display the features set out in Article 3 of Regulation 67/67 of the Commission ... if, failing exemption, they would fall under the prohibition contained in **Article 85(1)** of the EEC Treaty'. That ruling was based in particular on a finding that 'agreements such as that in question fulfil the conditions laid down in Article 1(1) (b) of Regulation 67/67', as appears from paragraph 13, and on the previous judgment in the ROUBAIX-WATTRELOS case (Case 63/75[19]), as appears from paragraphs 16 to 33.

Again with reference to that judgment, I think that in deciding whether or not it is possible to apply it by analogy in the present case the fact that the judgment is restricted to agreements to which only two undertakings from the same member-State are party is not of vital significance. There is nothing in the judgment to indicate that the Court would not have considered Regulation 67/67 to be applicable to a brewery contract between a retailer in one member-State and a brewery in another member-State.

However, the judgment naturally leaves entirely open the question whether other characteristics of franchise agreements of the kind at issue in these proceedings do indeed militate against the applicability of Regulation 67/67. As I shall argue in more detail in the following part of my opinion, I think that is indeed the case

3.4 Selective distribution systems

In these proceedings Pronuptia has also relied on the judgment of the Court in Case 26/76 (METRO *v.* COMMISSION[20]). In paragraph 20 of that judgment the Court held that:

> In the sector covering the production of high quality and technically advanced consumer durables, where a relatively small number of large- and medium-scale producers offer a varied range of items which, or so consumers may consider, are readily interchangeable, the structure of the market does not preclude the existence of a variety of channels of distribution adapted to the peculiar characteristics of the various producecrs and to the requirements of the various categories of consumers.
>
> On this view the Commission was justified in recognising that selective distribution systems constituted, together with others, an aspect of competition which accords with **Article 85(1)**, provided that resellers are chosen on the basis of objective criteria of a qualitative nature relating to the technical qualifications of the reseller and his staff and the suitability of his trading premises and that such conditions are laid down uniformly for all potential resellers and are not applied in a discriminatory fashion.

The mere fact that the franchise agreements in question contain not only qualitative but strict quantitative criteria means, in my view, that this last sentence is not applicable by analogy in this case.

The preceding sentence of paragraph 20 is indeed of some indirect relevance to this case, as is the second last sentence of paragraph 21, which reads as follows:

> For specialist wholesalers and retailers the desire to maintain a certain price level,

which corresponds to the desire to preserve, in the interests of consumers, the possibility of the continued existence of this channel of distribution in conjunction with new methods of distribution based on a different type of competition policy, forms one of the objectives which may be pursued without necessarily falling under the prohibition contained in **Article 85(1)**, and, if it does fall thereunder, either wholly or in part, coming within the framework of **Article 85(3)**.

The second sentence of paragraph 22 also seems to me to be of some relevance to the present case. It states that:

the Commission must ensure that this structural rigidity [of prices, referred to in the preceding sentence] is not reinforced, as might happen if there were an increase in the number of selective distribution networks for marketing the same product.

Finally, paragraph 24 states which provisions were not considered by the Commission to be restrictive of competition.

In its judgment in Case 31/80 (L'ORÉAL v. DE NIEUWE AMCK[21]) the Court held in paragraph 17 that:

When admission to a selective distribution network is made subject to conditions which go beyond simple objective selection of a qualitative nature and, in particular, when it is based on quantitative criteria, the distribution system falls in principle within the prohibition in Article 85(1), provided that, as the Court observed in its judgment of 30 June 1966 (SOCIETE TECHNIQUE MINIERE v. MASCHINENBAU ULM GmbH), the agreement fulfils certain conditions depending less on its legal nature than on its effects first on 'trade between member-States' and secondly on 'competition'.

The following two paragraphs define those conditions in further detail (according to paragraph 18, regard must be had in particular to the consequences of the agreement in question for the possibility of parallel imports, while paragraph 19 refers *inter alia* to the paragraphs of the first HAECHT judgment quoted above). In the LANCOME case (Case 99/79[22]) the Court had already taken the same position as that expressed in paragraph 17. The paragraphs referred to are also of some relevance to the present case.

With regard to the prohibited nature of a 'premises clause' such as that contained in clause 4 of the agreements at issue, the Commission has also relied on paragraph 51 of the judgment of the Court of 21 February 1984 in Case 86/82 (HASSELBLAD v. E.C. COMMISSION[23]). After confirming that quantitative selection criteria are prohibited, that paragraph states that 'Clause 28 of the dealer agreement allowed the applicant in fact to restrict the freedom of dealers, even authorised dealers, to establish their business in a location in which the applicant considers their presence capable of influencing competition between dealers'. Paragraph 52 goes on to confirm that that clause, among others, is prohibited.

3.5 Licence agreements

Since licences also play a key rôle in franchise agreements, the judgments of the Court in NUNGESSER (Case 258/78[24]) and CODITEL II (Case 262/81[23]) are also relevant to this case. In paragraph 58 of the NUNGESSER judgment the Court concluded that 'having regard to the specific nature of the products in question ... in a case such as the present, the grant of an *open* exclusive licence, that is to say a licence which does not affect the position of third parties such as parallel importers and licencees for other territories, is not in itself incompatible with Article 85(1) **of the Treaty'.** In paragraph 61 of the same judgment the Court pointed out that it had consistently held 'that absolute territorial protection granted to a licensee in order to enable parallel imports to be controlled and prevented results in the artificial maintenance of separate national markets, contrary to the Treaty'. The key importance of that statement is confirmed in paragraph 78.

In the CODITEL II case the Court held that: 'A contract whereby the owner of the copyright for a film grants an exclusive right to exhibit that film for a specific period in the territory of a member-State is not, as such, subject to the prohibitions contained in **Article 85** of the Treaty. It is, however, where appropriate, for the national court to ascertain whether, in a given case, the manner in which the exclusive right conferred by that contract is exercised is subject to a situation in the economic or legal sphere the object or effect of which is to prevent or restrict the distribution of films or to distort competition on the cinematographic market, regard being had to the specific characteristics of that market.' However, it is stated in paragraph 19 of that judgment, that the exercise of the exclusive right to exhibit a cinematographic film must not give rise *inter alia* to 'the possibility of charging fees which exceed a fair return on investment, or an exclusivity the duration of which is disproportionate ...'. That paragraph in particular is relevant to the present case, since the basic issue concerns the royalties.

4. *Proposed replies to the questions referred*

4.1 *General remarks*

All the judgments referred to contain, I think, elements which should be borne in mind in answering the questions referred.

The type of franchise agreement referred to in the questions corresponds, in my view, to the description of franchise agreements contained in the literature and case law reviewed above, inasmuch as the right to the use of the company name and the mark or sign 'Pronuptia de Paris', the provision of know-how in a broad sense and the obligation to arrange the premises in accordance with the image of the franchisor and according to its instructions are central to those agreements (clauses 1(3), 3(1) and (3), 4(1) and 14). The fundamental importance of those factors is confirmed by the licence royalties agreed upon, in the amount of 10 per cent. of the franchisee's total turnover (clause 5(1)). Under clause 3(5) of the agreement, however, the franchisee alone bears the risks of his business. From an economic point of view I think it is above all these characteristics which make franchise agreements extraordinarily attractive to franchisors as a new distribution method. To outside observers a shop set up and run in accordance with the contract resembles a subsidiary. Contrary to the case of a subsidiary, however, the franchisor does not have to carry any investment costs. Nor need he conduct any market studies in the place where the shop is to be established, since in the event of inadequate sales (in particular where costs are high and profits low) he bears no risk whatsoever, but is still entitled to the substantial royalty of 10 per cent. of total turnover.

It would appear from the rapid development of the new system that it also has advantages for the franchisee; the main advantage is probably the fact that it gives him (usually exclusive) access to products of high quality the market for which is already established. The market for such products may in particular be established where, as in this case and in other franchise systems mentioned by the franchisee, the franchisor already has subsidiaries in other parts of the member-State concerned, and the franchise system thus constitutes an extention of a system of subsidiaries which has already stood the test of the market.

For consumers, finally, the presence of a franchise system alongside other distribution systems may have some appeal for the same reasons, but also under the same conditions, as those set out in paragraph 20 of the METRO judgment with regard to selective distribution systems. In so far as the admission of franchisees to the system is made subject to quantitative restrictions (for example, by accepting only one franchisee in a defined area, as in this case), I consider, on the basis of the L'OREAL, LANCOME and HASSELBLAD judgments, that **Article 85(1)** must be held to be applicable in principle to the agreement in question, if the general conditions developed in the Court's judgments in Cases 32/65, 56 and 58/64, 56/65, 23/67, 43/69, 47/76, 26/76 and 258/78 (cited above) are fulfilled.

I think the following criteria relevant to the assessment of franchise agreements such as those at issue can be drawn from the judgments referred to:

(a) **Since the important point for the application of Article 85(1) is, according to all the judgments referred to, the horizontal effects of vertical agreements (for instance the exclusion of certain competitors, such as parallel importers),** it seems to me that the question whether or not a franchise agreement results in a fair division of costs and benefits as between franchisor and franchisee is not in itself relevant to the question whether **Article 85(1)** is applicable. The same is true in principle of specific obligations of the franchisee, such as the obligation of specialisation (clauses 3(3), 4(1) and 6(6)), the obligation to advertise (clauses 1(1) and 6(4) and (5)) and the obligation to set up and run the shop in a particular manner (clauses 3(3) and 4(1)). **With regard to such vertical obligations I think Article 85(1) can only apply when it can be shown in a particular case that they cause injury to third parties (competitors, suppliers or purchasers), which will seldom be the case where there are adequate alternative chains of distribution for similar products.**

(b) If the main issue is thus the 'horizontal' effects, or more correctly the results of the agreement for third parties, then, according to the judgments of the Court, particular attention must be paid to the questions whether (i) parallel imports remain possible (see for example the GRUNDIG-CONSTEN, BILGER and NUNGESSER judgments), (ii) whether, having regard to the market position of the suppliers concerned, access to the market for other suppliers or dealers is restricted (see the quotations from Cases 56/65, 23/67, 43/69, 26/76 and 31/80) and (iii) whether the agreement results in price increases (METRO and CODITEL II) or involves price-fixing by means of contractual obligations or concerted practices on the part of the franchisor, its subdiaries and its various franchisees.

With regard to this last criterion I am of the view, contrary to the American and German case law referred to, that the Court's judgments regarding resale price maintenance and other forms of price agreement need only be applied in a case where a party is in a position of economic strength on the local markets concerned, or where price maintenance is also applied by competitors. In the light of paragraphs

21 and 22 of the METRO judgment I think, too, that the strong upward influence on prices which will almost certainly be exerted by the royalty provision in the agreement at issue should only be regarded as a ground for applying **Article 85(1)** where a franchisor from one member-State plays a rôle of price leader or otherwise occupies a position of economic strength in a significant number of local markets in a second member-State.

On the basis of those criteria I think it possible to give a sufficiently clear answer to the first question referred by the national court to enable that court to reach a decision on the facts of this case. I think a more concrete answer than that proposed by the Commission is desirable.

Since, the reasons which I shall discuss, I am of the view that Regulation 67/67 is not applicable to franchise agreements such as those here at issue. Question 3 in the order for reference does not as such require an answer. **In its judgment the Court might, however, wish to make it clear that obligations such as those referred to in subparagraphs (b), (d) and (e) of Question 3 cannot, except in unusual circumstances, be regarded as restrictions of competition within the meaning of Article 85(1).**

4.2 Answer to the first question

In the light of the criteria which I have deduced from the judgments of the Court and summarised above, I think clauses 1(1) and (2), 3(3), 4(1), 5(1) and 6(1) and (6) of the agreements are of particular importance for the answer to the first questioin. Since according to the existing literature and case law, the nature of franchise agreements remains undefined, I would go so far as to suggest that the Court should restrict its answer to the first question asked by the Bundesgerichtshof to franchise agreements with the same content as those concluded between the parties in this case. It would of course be very useful for practitioners if the Court included a summary of those agreements in its judgment. The answer to the first question could in my view be as follows:

Article 85(1) of the EEC Treaty is applicable to franchise agreements such as those concluded between the parties in this case in so far as *inter alia:*

(a)   **they are concluded between a franchisor from one member-State, or its subsidiary as referred to in Question 3(a), and one or more franchisees in one or more other member-States, and**

(b)   **by way of its subsidiaries and franchisees in one or more of those other member-States or in a significant part of their territory the franchisor has a substantial share of the market for the relevant product; and either**

(c)   **the agreements prevent or restrict, or are intended to prevent or restrict, parallel imports of the products covered by the contract into the contract territory or exports of those products by the franchisee to other member-States.**

or

(d)   **the agreements result – in particular through the establishment of local or regional monopolies for the products covered by the contract, through royalty provisions and contractual provisions or concerted practices with regard to the setting of prices and on account of the absence of effective competition from similar products – in the setting of unreasonably high retail prices, that is to say, prices which could not be charged if effective** competition existed, even allowing for the superior quality of the products covered by the contract.

In the wording of this answer I have made it clear that criteria (c) and (d) are to be regarded as alternative criteria. In accordance with the judgments of the Court, criterion (c) places the emphasis on the absolute territorial protection of national markets, which cannot fail to result in significant restriction of horizontal competition unless the market shares involved are negligible. In criterion (d), on the other hand, the accent is placed on the prevention of monopolistic price increases, which as a rule will only be possible where the party concerned has a substantial share of the relevant local or regional markets and where there is no downward influence on prices as a result of other means of distribution for similar products.

4.3 *Answer to the second and third questions*

I agree with the Commission and the French. Government that block exemption for franchise agreements is desirable. I consider it particularly desirable having regard to the frequency with which they now occur and their generally beneficial nature; **as a rule, it is only in particular market circumstances (in particular, the absence of competing distribution systems) or where they are applied in a particular manner that the intentional or unintentional restriction of competition associated with them may stand in the way of exemption under** Article 85(3) **of the EEC Treaty.**
As a rule franchise agreements will presumably benefit consumers by improving the distribution of products, since they make possible the rapid penetration of new products or products with particular qualities onto discrete local retail markets. It is the task of the Commission first to acquire the necessary experience by adopting a number of individual decisions in representative cases, and then, in a block-exemption regulation in accordance with the four conditions of **Article 85(3)**, to lay down the conditions in which the positive effects of franchise agreements can be attributed a greater weight then the restrictions on competition which may be considered essential to their positive effect.
Like the Commission and the French Government I am also of the view, however, that Regulation 67/67 cannot be considered applicable to franchise agreements such as those now at issue. For me the following considerations were decisive in arriving at that conclusion:
In the first place, it is clear that when Regulation 67/67 was adopted franchise agreements for the distribution of products within the Community were still extremely rare; during the preparation of the regulation, therefore, no consideration could be given to the specific problems which they raise. The problems to which consideration was given in preparing that regulation, and in regard to which sufficient experience had been gained, as required by the fourth recital in the preamble to Regulation 19/65, related in fact only to exclusive importers. Similarly, according to the Commission's answer to a question which I posed at the hearing, during the preparation of the recent block exemptions for exclusive distribution and exclusive purchasing agreements their application to franchise agreements was not advocated by interested parties or by government experts.
Secondly, on the basis of the literature and case law referred to and the views of the franchising organisations mentioned above, I think that franchise

agreements are predominantly characterised by the effort, by means of licences for trade names, trade marks, signs or symbols and know-how in a broad sense and by other provisions, to assimulate the commercial practices of the franchisee as closely as possible to those of the franchisor or its subsidiaries. The franchisee, for his part, is entirely responsible for the risks of his business and must pay a royalty, in this case a substantial one, to the franchisor. Exclusive supply and purchase obligations play only a subordinate rôle, and from the point of view of competition policy they can only be assessed in the context of the objective pursued, namely the thorough integration of franchisees in the franchisor's network of uniformly managed retail outlets. In Regulation 67/67, on the other hand, it is licensing agreements which are subordinate in nature.

Thirdly, franchise agreements with the characteristics of those in question also differ substantially from brewery contracts (to which the Court has held Regulation 67/67 to be applicable) inasmuch as they result in the formation of rigid local or regional monopolies for the products concerned. In that regard I refer in particular to clause 1 of the agreements which were submitted. Furthermore, the difference referred to in the previous paragraph between those agreements and exclusive distribution agreement also exists in relation to brewery contracts.

Fourthly, I think that the application of Regulation 67/67 is excluded by Article 3(b) of that regulation. Franchise agreements such as those here at issue give the franchisee absolute territorial protection and make it difficult for dealers to obtain supplies of the products covered by the contract from other dealers within the Common Market. In addition to clause 1, which I have already mentioned, I refer in that regard to clauses 3(3) and (6) and 4(1) of the agreements.

For those four reasons I propose that the Court should answer the second question asked by the national court in the following manner:

Regulation 67/67 on the application of **Article 85(3)** of the Treaty to certain categories of exclusive dealing agreements is not applicable to franchise agreements with a content similar to those concluded between the parties in this case.

It would not then be necessary to reply to the third question referred by the national court. However, the answer which I propose to the first question may, perhaps in combination with remarks which the Court may wish to make in its judgment regarding clauses of the agreement which do not restrict competition, enable the national court to decide which of the provisions of the agreement referred to in the third question must be considered relevant for the application of **Article 85(1).**

JUDGMENT

[1] By order dated 15 May 1984, received by the Court on the 25 June following, the Bundesgerichtshof, in accordance with **Article 177** of the EEC Treaty, asked a number of questions relating to the interpretation of **Article 85** EEC and of Commission Regulation 67/67 of 22 March 1967 concerning the application of **Article 85(3)** to categories of exclusive dealing agreements, [26] so that it should be determined whether these provisions apply to franchise agreements.

[2] These questions have arisen in the course of proceedings between the firm Pronuptia de Paris GmbH of Frankfurt am Main (hereinafter called the 'franchisor'), a subsidiary of a French company of the same name, and Mrs. Schillgallis of Hamburg who runs a business under the name Pronuptia de Paris (hereinafter called the 'franchisee'). The litigation concerns the obligation of the franchisee to pay the franchisor arrears of fees based on its sales figures for 1978 to 1980.

[3] The French parent company of the franchisor distributes under the name 'Pronuptia de Paris' wedding dresses and other clothes worn at weddings. Distribution of these products in the Federal Republic of Germany is carried out in part through shops run directly by its subsidiary and in part through shops belonging to independent retailers tied to the subsidiary by franchise agreements, executed in its name by the subsidiary acting both on behalf of the parent company and on its own behalf.

[4] By three agreements signed on 24 February 1980 the franchisee obtained a franchise for three separate areas. Hamburg, Oldenburg and Hanover. The terms of these three agreements are for practical purposes identical. More precisely, they include the following provisions:

[5] The franchisor:

– grants to the franchisee the exclusive right to use the mark 'Pronuptia de Paris' for sale of its products and services for a particular territory outlined in a map attached to the agreement, as well as the right to advertise in that territory;

– agrees not to open another Pronuptia shop in the territory in question and not to provide any product or service to third parties in that territory;

– agrees to assist the franchisee in the commercial and promotional aspects of his business, in the setting up and designing of the shop, in the training of personnel, sales techniques, in fashion and product advice, sales, marketing, and generally in all respects in which, in the experience of the franchisor, it could contribute towards the improvement of the turnover and profitability of the franchisee.

[6] The franchisee, who remains the sole proprietor of its business and bears the associated risks, is required:

– to use the name Pronuptia de Paris and sell merchandise under that name only in the shop specified in the agreement. The shop must be arranged and decorated principally for sale of wedding-related products, according to the directions of the franchisor, with the purpose of protecting the worth of the mark used by the Pronuptia distribution chain. The shop may not be transferred to another site or redesigned without the franchisor's approval.

– to purchase from the franchisor 80 per cent. of its requirements of wedding dresses and accessories as well as a proportion to be determined by the franchisor himself of cocktail dresses and formal wear and to obtain the remainder only from suppliers approved by the franchisor;

– to pay to the franchisor, in consideration of the benefits provided, an initial payment for the contract territory of 15,000 DM and, for the duration of the contract, a royalty equalling 10 per cent. of the turnover realised by the sale of both Pronuptia products and all other merchandise; evening dresses purchased from suppliers other than Pronuptia are not, however, included in this figure;

- to take account, without prejudice to its freedom to fix its own retail prices, of the recommended resale prices proposed by the franchisor;

- to advertise in the licensed territory only with the consent of the franchisor and in any case to make such advertising conform to that carried out on a national or international level by the franchisor, to disseminate as conscientiously as possible the catalogues and other promotional aids supsplied by the franchisor, and generally to use the commercial methods communicated by the franchisor to the franchisee;

- to make its principal objective the sale of wedding articles;

- to refrain from any act of competition with a Pronuptia business, and in particular not to open any business with an identical or similar purpose to that covered by the agreement nor to participate, directly or indirectly, in such a business in the territory of the Federal Republic of Germany inclusive of West Berlin or in any territory where Pronuptia is represented in any way whatsoever, for the duration of the agreement and for one year following termination;

- not to transfer to third parties the rights and obligations arising out of the contract nor to sell the business without prior agreement of the franchisor, it being understood that the franchisor will grant his approval if the transfer is required for health reasons and the new contracting party can establish that he is solvent and prove that he is not in any form whatsoever a competitor of the franchisor.

[7] The first instance court ruled that the franchisee must pay 158,502 DM arrears of royalties due on its turnover in the years 1978-1980. The franchisee appealed against this judgment to the Oberlandesgericht, Frankfurt am Main, claiming it was not required to pay the arrears because the agreement infringed **Article 85(1)** of the Treaty and did not benefit from the group exemption for exclusive dealing agreements provided by Regulation 67/67. In a judgment of 2 December 1982, the Oberlandesgericht accepted the franchisee's arguments. It found that the reciprocal obligations of exclusivity constituted restrictions on competition within the Common Market, since the franchisor could not supply any other business in the contract territory and the franchisee could only purchase and resell other merchandise from other member-States in a very limited way. Since no exemption under **Article 85(3)** applied to them, held the Oberlandesgericht, these agreements must be considered void under **Article 85(2)**. With respect to the issue of exemption, the Oberlandesgericht considered in particular that it was not necessary for it to decide if franchise agreements are in principle excluded from the application of Regulation 67/67. In fact, according to the Oberlandesgericht, the agreements at issue in any event involved undertakings going beyond the scope of Article 1 of the regulation and constituted restrictions on competition not covered by Article 2.

[8] The franchisor applied for review of this judgment to the Bundesgerichtshof, requesting reinstatement of the first instance court's judgment. The Bundesgerichtshof concluded that its judgment on the application depended on an interpretation of Community law. It requested,

therefore, that the Court issue a preliminary ruling on the following questions:

1. Is **Article 85(1)** of the EEC Treaty applicable to franchise agreements such as the contracts between the parties, which have as their object the establishment of a special distribution system whereby the franchisor provides to the franchisee, in addition to goods, certain trade names, trade marks, merchandising material and services?

2. If the first question is answered in the affirmative: Is Regulation no. 67/67/EEC of the Commission of 22 March 1967 on the application of **Article 85(3)** of the Treaty to certain categories of exclusive dealing agreements (block exemption) applicable to such contracts?

3. If the second question is answered in the affirmative:
(a) Is Regulation no. 67/67/EEC still applicable if several undertakings which, though legally independent, are bound together by commercial ties and form a single economic entity for the purposes of the contract participate on one side of the agreement?

(b) Does Regulation no. 67/67/EEC, and in particular Article 2(2)(c) thereof, apply to an obligation on the part of the franchisee to advertise solely with the prior agreement of the franchisor and in a manner that is in keeping with the latter's advertising, using the publicity material supplied by him, and in general to use the same business methods? Is it relevant in this connection that the franchisor's publicity material contains price recommendations which are not binding?

(c) Does Regulation no. 67/67/EEC, and in particular Articles 1(1)(b), 2(1)(a) and 2(b) thereof, apply to an obligation on the part of the franchisee to confine the sale of the contract goods exclusively or at least for the most part to particular business premises specially adapted for the purpose?

(d) Does Regulation 67/67/EEC, and in particular Article 1(1)(b) thereof, apply to an obligation on the part of a franchisee—who is bound to purchase most of his supplies from the franchisor—to make the rest of his purchases of goods covered by the contract solely from suppliers approved by the franchisor?

(e) Does Regulation No. 67/67/EEC sanction an obligation on the franchisor to give the franchisee commercial, advertising and professional support?

On the first question
[9] The firm Pronuptia de Paris GmbH of Frankfurt am Main, the franchisor, has argued that a system of franchise agreements makes it possible to combine the advantages of a form of distribution which presents a homogeneous face to the public (like that of subsidiaries) with distribution by independent retailers themselves bearing the risks of sale. This system, made up of a network of vertical agreements intended to guarantee a uniform image to the outside world, reinforces the franchisor's ability to compete on the horizontal plane, that is to say in relation

to other forms of distribution. The system thus makes it possible for an enterprise that otherwise would not have the necessary financial means at its disposal to create a supra-regional distribution network, a network comprising, as franchisees, small enterprises which keep their autonomy. In view of these advantages **Article 85(1)** cannot apply unless the franchise agreements involve restrictions on the freedom of the contracting parties which go beyond those demanded by the nature of a franchise system. Exclusive supply and stocking provisions, to the degree that they aim to ensure a uniform range of goods, obligations to use uniform promotional materials, uniform layout of the business premises and the prohibition on selling in other shops the products delivered under the agreement are inherent in the very nature of the franchise agreement and are thus outwith the scope of **Article 85(1)**.

[10] Mrs. Schillgallis, the franchisee, proposes that the first question should be answered in the affirmative. The contracts in question are characterised by territorial protection given to the franchisee. They cannot be assimilated to agreements with commercial agents, given that unlike the latter franchisees act in their own name and on their own account and shoulder the marketing risks. The system of franchise agreements in question involves noticeable restrictions on competition, given the fact that Pronuptia is, as it itself proclaims, the French world leader in the wedding dress and accessory market.

[11] The French government, for its part, contends that **Article 85(1)** can be applied to franchise agreements which are contracts concerning distribution of a product concluded with independent businessmen, but that it does not necessarily apply, given the positive aspects of such agreements.

[12] The Commission maintains that the scope of **Article 85(1)** is not limited to specific types of contracts. When its conditions are met, therefore, **Article 85(1)** applies equally to those agreements which, apart from delivery of merchandise, have as their object the licensing of a trade name and trade mark, whether registerted or not, or of the provision of services.

[13] We should begin by noting that franchise agreements, whose legality has not hitherto been considered by this Court, present enormous diversity. From the arguments before the Court, it is necessary to distinguish between different types of franchise, particularly: service franchise agreements, by which the franchisee offers services under the sign and the trade name, or indeed the trade mark, of the franchisor and complies with the franchisor's directives; production franchise agreements by which the franchisee himself manufactures, according to the instructions of the franchisor, products which he sells under the franchisor's trade mark; and finally, distribution franchise agreements by which the franchisee restricts himself to the sale of certain products in a shop carrying the mark of the franchisor. The Court will only consider this third type of agreement which conforms to that expressly referred to in the question from the national court.

[14] It should next be observed that the compatibility of distribution franchise agreements with **Article 85(1)** cannot be assessed in the abstract but depends on the clauses contained in such contracts. In order to give a fully useful response to the national court this Court will consider those contracts which have a content similar to that described above.

[15] In a distribution franchise system such as this, an enterprise which has established itself as a distributor in a market and which has thus been able to perfect a range of commercial methods gives independent businessmen the chance, at a price, of establishing themselves in other markets by using its mark and the commercial methods that created the franchisor's success. More than just a method of distribution, this is a manner of exploiting financially a body of knowledge,

without investing the franchisor's own capital. At the same time this system gives businessmen who lack the necessary experience access to methods which they could otherwise only acquire after prolonged effort and research and allows them also to profit from the reputation of the mark. Distribution franchise agreements are thus different from either dealership agreements or those binding approved resellers appointed under a system of selective distribhution which involve neither use of a single mark nor application of uniform commercial methods nor payment of royalties in consideration of the advantages thus conferred. Such a system, which permits the franchisor to take advantage of his success, is not by itself restrictive of competition. For it to function two conditions must be satisfied.

[16] First, the franchisor must be able to communicate his know-how to the franchisees and provide them with the necessary assistance in putting his methods into effect, without running the risk that this know-how and assistance will aid his competitors, even indirectly. **It thus follows that those clauses which are essential to prevent this risk do *not* constitute restrictions of competition in the sense of Article 85(1). These include the prohibition on the franchisee opening, for the duration of the franchise or for a reasonable period after its termination, a shop with an identical or similar purpose in an area where he could be in competiotion with one of the members of the network. The same applies to the obligation on the franchisee not to sell his shop without the prior approval of the franchisor: this clause serves to ensure that the benefit of the know-how and assistance provided does not go indirectly to a competitor.**

[17] **Secondly, the franchisor must be able to take appropriate measures to preserve the identity and reputation of the network which is symbolised by the mark. It thus follows that those clauses which provide a basis for such control as is indispensable for this purpose also do *not* constitute restrictions of competition in the sense of** Article 85(1).

[18] This covers then the obligation on the franchisee to apply the commercial methods developed by the franchisor and to utilise the know-how provided.

[19] This is also the case with the franchisee's obligation only to sell the merchandise covered by the agreement in premises set up and decorated according to the franchisor's specifications, which have as their purpose to guarantee a uniform image corresponding to specified requirements. **The same requirements apply to the location of the shop the choice of which is apt to affect the reputation of the network. This explains why the franchisee cannot transfer his shop to another location without the consent of the franchisor.**

[20] **The prohibition on the franchisee assigning the rights and obligations under the contract without the assent of the franchisor safeguards the franchisor's right freely to choose its franchisees, whose qualifications as traders are essential for establishing and preserving the reputation of the network.**

[21] Thanks to the control exercised by the franchisor over the selection of goods offered by the franchisee, the public can find at each franchisee's shop merchandise of the same quality. It can be impractical in certain cases, such as the field of fashion goods, to formulate objective quality specifications. Enforcing such specifications can also, because of the large number of franchisees, impose too great a cost on the franchisor. A clause prescribing that the franchisee can *only* sell products provided by the franchisor or by suppliers selected by him must, in these circumstances, be considered *necessary* for the *protection* of the *reputation* of the *network*. It must not however, operate to prevent the franchisee from obtaining the products from other franchisees.

[22] Finally, since advertising contributes to defining the image which the public

has of the mark, which symbolises the network, a clause which requires all advertising by the franchisee to be submitted for the approval of the franchisor is likewise essential for the preservation of the identity of the network, provided that the approval only relates to the nature of the advertising.

[23] It should on the other hand be stressed that, far from being necessary for the protection of the know-how provided or for the preservation of the identity and reputation of the network, certain clauses *do restrict competition between its members.* That is the case with clauses which effect a division of markets between the franchisor and franchisees or between franchisees or which prevent price competition between them.

[24] The attention of the national court should, in this regard, be drawn to the clause which requires the franchisee to sell the merchandise covered by the agreement *only* at the location designated in the contract. This clause prohibits the franchisee from opening a second shop. Its real significance emerges if one juxtaposes it to the undertaking by the franchisor to the franchisee, to ensure to him exclusivity of use of the licensed mark in a given territory. In order to honour the promise thus made to a franchisee the franchisor must not only refrain from establishing itself in the territory but must also secure undertakings from the other franchisees not to open another shop outside their own. The jutaxposition of clauses of this type results in a kind of market partitioning between the franchisor and the franchisees or among the franchisees and thus restricts competition within the network. As follows from the judgment in CONSTEN AND GRUNDIG v. EEC COMMISSION, [28] this type of restriction constitutes a restriction on competition in the sense of Article 85(1), since it concerns a mark that is already widely known. It is certainly possible that a prospective franchisee may not want to take the risk of joining the chain and making his investment, paying a relatively high entry fee and agreeing to pay a considerable annual fee, if he were not in a position to hope that his business would be profitable thanks to a certain amount of protection from competition by the franchisor and other franchisees. This consideration can, however, be significant only in the context of an examination of the agreement in the light of the conditions of **Article 85(3).**

[25] Although the clauses which restrict the franchisee's ability to fix his own prices in complete freedom are restrictive of competition, it is not so where the franchisor has merely communicated to the franchisees recommended prices, on condition however that there is no concerted practice between the franchisor and the franchisee or between franchisees with a view to the actual application of such prices. It is for the national court to determine whether this condition has been satisfied.

[26] Finally, it should be said that distribution franchise agreements which contain clauses effecting a partitioning of markets between franchisor and franchisees or between franchisees are *per se* capable of affecting trade between member-States, even if they are concluded between enterprises established in the same member-State, to the extent that they prevent the franchisees from setting themselves up in another member-State.

[27] In view of the above considerations, the first question must be answered as follows:
1.   The compatibility of distribution franchise agreements with **Article 85(1)** depends on the clauses contained in the agreements and on the economic context in which they are included;
2.   **The clauses that are indispensable to prevent the know-how and assistance provided by the franchisor from benefiting competitors do not constitute**

restrictions of competition within the meaning of **Article 85(1)**;

3. The clauses which implement the control essential for the preservation of the identity and the reputation of the organisation represented by the trade mark also do not constitute restrictions on competition within the meaning of **Article 85(1)**;

4. The clauses which effect a partitioning of markets between franchisor and franchisee or between franchisees constitute restrictions of competition within the meaning of **Article 85(1)**;

5. The fact that the franchisor has communicated suggested prices to the franchisees does not constitute a restriction on competition, on condition that there has not been a concerted practice between franchisor and franchisees or between franchisees with a view to effective application of these prices;

6. Distribution franchise agreements which contain clauses effecting a partitioning of markets between franchisor and franchisee or between franchisees are capable of affecting trade between member-States.

On the second question

[28] The second question, which was only asked in the event of an affirmative reply to the first, deals with the question whether Commission Regulation 67/67 of 22 March 1967 on the application of **Article 85(3)** of the Treaty to certain categories of exclusive dealing agreements comes into play in distribution franchise agreements. In light of the considerations set out above regarding those clauses which effect a partitioning of the market between franchisor and franchisees and between franchisees, this question retains some relevance and we should therefore consider it.

[29] The firm Pronuptia de Paris, the franchisor, urges the Court to answer the second question in the affirmative. Regulations 67/67 should apply to exclusive distribution and supply undertakings regardless of whether such undertakings occur in agreements which also license a trade mark or other distinctive marks of the enterprise. In a franchise agreement, the exclusive purchase and distribution obligations offer the very advantages set out in the sixth recital of Regulation 67/67. Clauses other than those envisaged by Article 2 of Regulation 67/67 would present no obstacle to application of the exemption, since they did not restrain competition within the meaning of **Article 85(1)**.

[30] Mrs. Schillgallis, the franchisee, argues that Regulation 67/67 does not apply to franchise agreements. First, this regulation was devised by the Commission on the basis of its experience in the period before its adoption, experience which was limited to dealership agreements. Second, the franchisor has clearly more powers over the franchisee than the grantor of a dealership over his distributor. Third, the restriction on competition inherent in franchise agreements also occurs on the horizontal level, since the franchisor itself generally operates its own subsidiaries which function at the same stage of the economic process as the franchisees.

[31] The French government confines itself to stating that Regulation 67/67 does not appear to be applicable to this type of contract.

[32] The Commission admits that it does not have sufficient experience to define the concept of a franchise agreement. It adds that the purpose of Regulation 67/67 was not to exempt restrictions on competition contained in agreements licensing trade marks, trade names or symbols, licences which, with the communication of know-how and commercial assistance, appear to it to be the essential element in

a franchise agreement. However, if licensing agreements of this sort contain accords on the supply of goods for resale, and if these supply accords can be severed from the licensing accords, Regulation 67/67 could apply to supply agreements, insofar as its conditions are met. In this respect the exclusive dealer cannot, in that capacity, submit to restrictions on competition other than those specified in Article 1(1) or Article 2(1) of the regulation. In the agreements the subject of the Bundesgerichts-hof's questions, the location clause contained in the franchise agreement establishes such a close relationship between the elements of exclusive distribution and of licensing in the franchise agreement that these elements constitute an indivisible whole, making the group exemption inapplicable even to that part of the contract relating to the grant of exclusive selling rights.

[33] It is appropriate in this regard to note several elements in the text of Regulation 67/67. First, the category of agreements benefiting from the group exemption is defined by reference to reciprocal (or non-reciprocal) undertakings for distribution and purchase and not by reference to elements such as the use of a common mark, the application of uniform commercial methods and the payments of royalties in consideration of the benefits granted, which are characteristic of distribution franchise agreements. Second, the very terms of Article 2 expressly deal only with exclusive sales agreements, the nature of which, as set out above, is different from that of a distribution franchise agreement. Third, the same Article lists the restrictions and obligations which can be imposed on an exclusive distributor without referring to those which can be stipulated as obligations of the other contracting party; while in the case of a distribution franchise agreement the obligations assumed by the franchisor, especially the obligations to communicate know-how and to assist the franchisee, assume a very special importance. Fourth, the list of obligations burdening an exclusive distributor set out in Article 2(2) permits inclusion of neither the obligation to pay royalties nor the clauses which set up the control system indispensable for preserving the identity and reputation of the network.

[34] We may conclude therefore that Regulation 67/67 is not applicable to distribution franchise agreements such as those examined in the course of these proceedings.

On the third question

[35] In view of the answers provided to the national court's second question, the third question has become irrelevant.

Costs

[36] The costs incurred by the French Government and by the Commission of the European Commun ities, which have submitted observations to the Court, are not recoverable. As these proceedings are, in so far as the parties to the main action are concerned, in the nature of a setp in the action pending before the national court, the decision as to costs is a matter for that court.

On these grounds, THE COURT, in answer to the questions referred to it by the Bundesgerichtshof, by order dated 15 May 1984,

HEREBY RULES:

1.(a) The compatibility of distribution franchise agreements with **Article 85(1)** depends on the clauses contained in the contracts and on the economic context in which they have been included;

(b) Clauses that are indispensable to prevent the know-how and assistance provided to the franchisee by the franchisor from benefiting the franchisor's competitors do not constitute restrictions of competition within the meaning of **Article 85(1)**;

(c) Clauses which implement the control indispensable for preservation of the identity and the reputation of the system symbolised by the trade mark also do not constitute restrictions of competition within the meaning of **Article 85(1)**;

(d) Clauses which effect a division of markets between franchisor and franchisee or between franchisees constitute restrictions of competition within the meaning of **Article 85(1)**;

(e) The fact that the franchisor has transmitted suggested prices to the franchisees does not constitute a restriction of competition, on condition that there has not been a concerted practice between franchisor and franchisees or between franchisees regarding putting these prices into effect;

(f) Distribution franchise agreements which contain clauses effecting a division of markets between franchisor and franchisee or between franchisees are capable of affecting trade between member-States.

2. Regulation 67/67 is not applicable to distribution franchise agreements such as those which have been considered in this proceeding.

1   [1984] B.I.E. 251.
2   *Translator's note:* What follows is taken from the published English version.
3   *Cahiers de Droit de l'Entreprise* no. 6-78.
4   [1982] Gaz. Pal. (Doctrine) 565.
5   [1982] Dall. Jur. 553.
6   [1982] WuW 781.
7   For an English translation of the Restraint of Competition Act see [1982] 1 *Commercial Laws of Europe* 1.
8   Black's Law Dictionary, 5th Edition, 1979; von Kalinowski, *Antitrust Laws and Trade Regulation*, Vol. 2, paragraph 6H.01/1981 supplement.
9   441 U.S. 942.
10 J.O. 2921/62.
11 [1966] E.C.R. 389, [1969] C.M.L.R. 39.
12 Page 63 (C.M.L.R.).
13 [1966] E.C.R. 299 at 342, [1966] C.M.L.R. 418 at 473.
14 Page 473 (C.M.L.R.)
15 [1966] E.C.R. 235 at 250, [1966] C.M.L.R. 357 at 375-376.
16 [1967] E.C.R. 407 at 415, [1968] C.M.L.R. 26 at 40.
17 [1970] E.C.R. 127, [1974] 1 C.M.L.R. 382.
18 [1977] E.C.R. 65, [1977] 1 C.M.L.R. 378.
19 [1976] E.C.R. 111, [1976] 1 C.M.L.R. 538.
20 [1977] E.C.R. 1875, [1978] 2 C.M.L.R. 1.
21 [1980] E.C.R. 3775, [1981] 2 C.M.L.R. 235.
22 [1980] E.C.R. 2511, [1981] 2 C.M.L.R. 164.
23 [1984] E.C.R. 883, [1984] 1 C.M.L.R. 559.
24 [1982] E.C.R. 2015, [1983] 1 C.M.L.R. 278.
25 [1982] E.C.R. 3381, [1983] 1 C.M.L.R. 49.
26 J.O. 849/67, [1967] O.J. Spec. Ed. 10.
27 Cases 56 and 58/64, [1966] E.C.R. 299, [1966] C.M.L.R. 418.

Appendix 4
DE MINIMIS NOTICE

Commission notice of 3 September 1986 on agreements of minor importance which do not fall under Article 85(1) of the Treaty establishing the European Economic Community (^{1})

(86/C 231/02)

I

1. The Commission considers it important to facilitate cooperation between undertakings where such cooperation is economically desirable without presenting difficulties from the point of view of competition policy, which is particularly true of cooperation between small and medium-sized undertakings. To this end it published the 'Notice concerning agreements, decisions and concerted practices in the field of cooperation between undertakings' (^{2}) listing a number of agreements that by their nature cannot be regarded as restraints of competition. Furthermore, in the Notice concerning its assessment of certain subcontracting agreements (^{3}) the Commission considered that this type of contract which offers opportunities for development, in particular, to small and medium-sized undertakings is not in itself caught by the prohibition in Article 85 (1). By issuing the present Notice, the Commission is taking a further step towards defining the field of application of Article 85 (1), in order to facilitate cooperation between small and medium-sized undertakings.

2. In the Commission's opinion, agreements whose effects on trade between Member States or on competition are negligible do not fall under the ban on restrictive agreements contained in Article 85 (1). Only those agreements are prohibited which have an appreciable impact on market conditions, in that they appreciably alter the market position, in other words the sales or supply possibilities, of third undertakings and of users.

3. In the present Notice the Commission, by setting quantitative criteria and by explaining their application, has given a sufficiently concrete meaning to the concept 'appreciable' for undertakings to be able to judge for themselves whether the agreements they have concluded with other undertakings, being of minor importance, do not fall under Article 85 (1). The quantitative definition of 'appreciable' given by the Commission is, however, no absolute yardstick; in fact, in individual cases even agreements between undertakings which exceed these limits may still have only a negligible effect on trade between Member States or on competition, and are therefore not caught by Article 85 (1).

4. As a result of this Notice, there should no longer be any point in undertakings obtaining negative clearance, as defined by Article 2 of Council Regulation No 17 (^{4}), for the agreements covered, nor should it be necessary to have the legal

143

position established through Commission decisions in individual cases: notification with this end in view will no longer be necessary for such agreements. However, if it is doubtful whether in an individual case an agreement appreciably affects trade between Member States or competition, the undertakings are free to apply for negative clearance or to notify the agreement.

5.   In cases covered by the present Notice the Commission, as a general rule, will not open proceedings under Regulation No 17, either upon application or upon its own initiative. Where, due to exceptional circumstances, an agreement which is covered by the present Notice nevertheless falls under Article 85 (1), the Commission will not impose fines. Where undertakings have failed to notify an agreement falling under Article 85 (1) because they wrongly assumed, owing to a mistake in calculating their market share or aggregate turnover, that the agreement was covered by the present Notice, the Commission will not consider imposing fines unless the mistake was due to negligence.

6.   This Notice is without prejudice to the competence of national courts to apply Article 85 (1) on the basis of their own jurisdiction, although it constitutes a factor which such courts may take into account when deciding a pending case. It is also without prejudice to any interpretation which may be given by the Court of Justice of the European Communities.

II

7.   The Commission holds the view that agreements between undertakings engaged in the production or distribution of goods or in the provision of services generally do not fall under the prohibition of Article 85 (1) if:

– the goods or services which are the subject of the agreement (hereinafter referrred to as 'the contracts products') together with the participating undertakings' other goods or services which are considered by users to be equivalent in view of their characteristics, price and intended use, do not represent more than 5% of the total market for such goods or services (hereinafter referred to as 'products') in the area of the common market affected by the agreement and

– the aggregate annual turnover of the participating undertakings does not exceed 200 million ECU.

8.   The Commission also holds the view that the said agreements do not fall under the prohibition of Article 85 (1) if the abovementioned market share or turnover is exceeded by not more than one tenth during two successive financial years.

9.   For the purposes of this Notice, participating undertakings are:

(a)   undertakings party to the agreement;

(b)   undertakings in which a party to the agreement, directly or indirectly,

– owns more than half the capital or business assets or

- has the power to exercise more than half the voting rights, or

- has the power to appoint more than half the members of the supervisory board, board of management or bodies legally representing the undertakings, or

- has the right to manage the affairs;

(c) undertakings which directly or indirectly have in or over a party to the agreement the rights or powers listed in (b).

(d) undertakings in or over which an undertaking referred to in (c) directly or indirectly has the rights or powers listed in (b).

Undertakings in which several undertakings as referred to in (a) to (d) jointly have, directly or indirectly, the rights or powers set out in (b) shall also be considered to be participating undertakings.

10. In order to calculate the market share, it is necessary to determine the relevant market. This implies the definitionof the relevant product market and the relevant geographical market.

11. The relevant products market includes besides the contract products any other products which are identical or equivalent to them. This rule applies to the products of the participating undertakings as well as to the market for such products. The products in question must be interchangeable. Whether or not this is the case must be judged from the vantage point of the user, normally taking the characteristics, price and intended use of the goods together. In certain cases, however, products can form a separate market on the basis of their charcteristics, their price or their intended use alone. This is true especially where consumer preferences have developed.

12. Where the contract products are components which are incorporated into another product by the participating undertakings, reference should be made to the market for the latter product, provided that the components represent a significant part of it. Where the contract products are components which are sold to third undertakings, reference should be made to the market for the components. In cases where both conditions apply, both markets should be considered separately.

13. The relevant geographical market is the area within the Community in which the agreement produces in effects. This area will be the whole common market where the contract products are regularly bought and sold in all Member States. Where the contract products cannot be bought and sold in a part of the common market, or are bought and sold only in limited quantitities or at irregular intervals in such a part, that part should be disregarded.

14. The relevant geographical market will be narrower than the whole common market in particular where:

- the nature and characteristics of the contract product, e.g. high transport costs in relation to the value of the product, restrict its mobility; or

– movement of the contract product within the common market is hindered by barriers to entry to national markets resulting from State intervention, such as quantitative restrictions, severe taxation differentials and non-tariff barriers, e.g. type approvals or safety standard certification. In such cases the national territory may have to be considered as the relevant geographical market. However, this will only be justified if the existing barriers to entry cannot be overcome by reasonable effort and at an acceptable cost.

15.   Aggregate turnover includes the turnover in all goods and services, excludings tax, achieved during the last financial year by the participating undertaking. In cases where an undertaking has concluded similar agreements with various other undertakings in the relevant market, the turnover of all participating undertakings should be taken together. The aggregate turnover shall not include dealings between participating undertakings.

16.   The present Notice shall not apply where in a relevant market competition is restricted by the cumulative effects of parallel networks of similar agreements established by several manufacturers or dealers.

17.   The present Notice is likewise applicable to decisions by associations of undertakings and to concerted practices.

---

1   The present Notice replaces the Commission Notice of 19 December 1977, OJ No C 313, 29.12.1977, p.3
2   OJ No C 75, 29. 7. 1968, p.3, corrected by OJ No C 84, 28.8. 1968, p.14.
3   OJ No C 1, 3. 1. 1979, p.2.
4   OJ No 13, 21. 2. 1962, p. 204/62.

Appendix 5
FORM A/B

Note: This form must be accompanied by an Annex containing the information specified in the attached Complementary Note.

The form and Annex must be supplied in 13 copies (one for the Commission and one for each Member State). Supply three copies of any relevant agreement and one copy of other supporting documents.

Please do not forget to complete the Acknowledgement of Receipt annexed.

If space is insufficient, please use extra pages, specifying to which items on the form they ralate.

FORM A/B

TO THE COMMISSION OF THE EUROPEAN COMMUNITIES

Directorate-General for Competition,
Rue de la Loi, 200,
B-1049 Brussels.

A. Application for negative clearance pursuant to Article 2 of Council Regulation No 17 of 6 February 1962 relating to implementation of Article 85 (1) or of Article 86 of the Treaty establishing the European Economic Community.

B. Notification of an agreement, decision or concerted practice under Article 4 (or 5) of Council Regulation No 17 of 6 February 1962 with a view to obtaining exemption under Article 85 (3) of the Treaty establishing the European Economic Community, including notifications claiming benefit of an oppositon procedure.

Identity of the parties

1. *Identity of applicant/notifier*

    Full name and address, telephone, telex and facsimile numbers, and brief description (^{1}) of the undertaking(s) or association(s) of undertakings submitting the application or notification.

    For partnerships, sole traders or any other unincorporated body trading under a business name, give, also, the name, forename(s) and address of the proprietor(s) or partner(s).

    Where an application or notification is submitted on behalf of some other person (or is submitted by more than one person) the name, address and position of the representative (or joint representative) must be given, together with proof of his authority to act. Where an application or notification is submitted by or on behalf of more than one person they should appoint a joint representative (Article 1(2) and (3) of Commission Regulation No 27)

(^{1}) E.g. 'Motor vehicle manufacturer', 'Computer service bureau', 'Conglomerate'.

2. *Identity of any other parties*

Full name and address and brief description of any other parties to the
agreement, decision or concerted
practice (hereinafter referred to as 'the
arrangements').

State what steps have been taken to
inform these other parties of this
application or notification.

(This information is not necessary in
respect of standard contracts which an
undertaking submitting the application
or notification has concluded or intends
to conclude with a number of parties
(e.g. a contract appointing dealers.)

Purpose of this application/notification
(see Complementary Note)

*(Please answer yes or no
to the questions)*

Are you asking for negative clearance alone? (See Complementary
Note – Section IV, end of first paragraph – for the consequence of
such a request.)

Are you applying for negative clearance, and also notifying the
arrangements to obtain an exemption in case the Commission does
not grant negative clearance?

Are you only notifying the arrangements in order to obtain an
exemption?

Do you claim that this application may benefit from an oppositon
procedure? (See Complementary Note – Sections III, IV, VI and VII
and Annex 2). If you answer 'yes', please specify the Regulation and
Article number on which you are relying.

Would you be satisfied with a comfort letter? (See the end of Section
VII of the Complementary Note.)

The undersigned declare that the information given above and in the . . . pages annexed
hereto is correct to the best of their knowledge and belief, that all estimates are identified as
such and are their best estimates of the underlying facts and that all the opinions expressed
are sincere.

They are aware of the provisions of Article 15(1) (a) of Regulation No 17 (see attached
Complementary Note).

Place and date: ....

Signatures: ....

....

....

Write nothing in this margin

Form A/B

Directorate-General for Competition

> To

ACKNOWLEDGEMENT OF RECEIPT

(This form will be returned to the address inserted above if the top half is completed in a single copy by the person lodging it)

Your application for negative clearance dated: ....

Your notification dated: ....

concerning: ....

Your reference: ....

Parties:

1. ....

2. .... and others

(There is no need to name the other undertakings party to the arrangement)

(To be completed by the Commission.)

was received on: ....

and registered under no IV/: ....

Please quote the above number in all correspondence

Provisional address:
Rue de la Loi 200
B-1049 Brussels

Telephone:
Direct line: 235 ....
Telephone exchange: 235 11 11

Telex:
COMEU B 21877

Telegraphic address:
COMEUR Brussels

149

Appendix 6
FORM C2/76 (RTPA)

Form RTP(C) **Restrictive Trade Practices Act 1976**

Certificate

I certify that to the best of my knowledge
the documents I enclose with this form give:

tick box(es)

★ All the terms of an agreement subject to registration under the Restrictive Trade Practices Act 1976

☐

★ Full details of the changes to the agreements(s)

☐

☐

★ full details of the ending of the agreement(s)

Office of Fair Trading reference(s);

**The documents are listed on the other side of this form.
I have signed one copy of each document and/or memorandum.**

Signed

Name in BLOCK CAPITALS

on behalf of

(a party to the above agreement)

Status and address of person signing

Dated

Please turn over

150

List of documents and/or memoranda

Please enclose **two** copies of each document and/or memorandum, **one** of which should be signed.

Printed in England for H.M.S.O. Dd 8119032

Appendix 7
REGULATION 4087/88:
THE FRANCHISE BLOCK EXEMPTION

THE COMMISSION OF THE EUROPEAN COMMUNITIES, Having regard to the Treaty establishing the European Economic Community, Having regard to Council Regulation No 19/65/EEC of 2 March 1965 on the application of Article 85 (3) of the Treaty to certain categories of agreements and concerted practices (^{1}), as last amended by the Act of Accession of Spain and Portugal, and in particular Article 1 thereof, Having published a draft of this Regulation (^{2}), Having consulted the Advisory Committee on Restrictive Practices and Dominant Positions, Whereas:

(1) Regulation No 19/65/EEC empowers the Commission to apply Article 85 (3) of the Treaty by Regulation to certain categories of bilateral exclusive agreements falling within the scope of Article 85 (1) which either have as their object the exclusive distribution or exclusive purchase of goods, or include restrictions imposed in relation to the assignment or use of industrial property rights.

(2) Franchise agreements consist essentially of licences of industrial or intellectual property rights relating to trade marks or signs and know-how, which can be combined with restrictions relating to supply or purchase of goods.

(3) Several types of franchise can be distinguished according to their object: industrial franchise concerns the manufacturing of goods, distribution franchise concerns the sale of goods, and service franchise concerns the supply of services.

(4) It is possible on the basis of the experience of the Commission to define categories of franchise agreements which fall under Article 85 (1) but can normally be regarded as satisfying the conditions laid down in Article 85 (3). This is the case for franchise agreements whereby one of the parties supplies goods or provides services to end users. On the other hand, industrial franchise agreements should not be covered by this Regulation. Such agreements, which usually govern relationship between producers, present different characteristics than the other types of franchise. They consist of manufacturing licences based on patents and/or technical know-how, combined with trade-mark licences. Some of them may benefit from other block exemptions if they fulfil the necessary conditions.

(5) This Regulation covers franchise agreements between two undertakings, the franchisor and the franchisee, for the retailing of goods or the provision of services to end users, or a combination of these activities, such as the

152

processing or adaptation of goods to fit specific needs of their customers. It also covers cases where the relationship between franchisor and franchisees is made through a third undertaking, the master franchisee. It does not cover wholesale franchise agreements because of the lack of experience of the Commission in that field.

(6)   Franchise agreements as defined in this Regulation can fall under Article 85 (1). They may in particular affect intra-Community trade where they are concluded between undertakings from different Member States or where they form the basis of a network which extends beyond this boundaries of a single Member State.

(7)   Franchise agreements as defined in this Regulation normally improve the distribution of goods and/or the provision of services as they give franchisors the possibility of establishing a uniform network with limited investments, which may assist the entry of new competitors on the market, particularly in the case of small and medium-sized undertakings, thus increasing interbrand competition. They also allow independent traders to set up outlets more rapidly and with higher chance of success than if they had to do so without the franchisor's experience and assistance. They have therefore the possibilities of competing more efficiently with large distribution undertakings.

(8)   As a rule, franchise agreements also allow consumers and other end users a fair share of the resulting benefit, as they combine the advantage of a uniform network with the existence of traders personally interested in the efficient operation of their business. The homogeneity of the network and the constant cooperation between the franchisor and the franchisees ensures a constant quality of the products and services. The favourable effect of franchising on interbrand competion and the fact that consumers are free to deal with any franchisee in the network guarantees that a reasonable part of the resulting benefits will be passed on to the consumers.

(9)   This Regulation must define the obligations restrictive of competition which may be included in franchise agreements. This is the case in particular for the granting of an exclusive territory to the franchisees combined with the prohibition on actively seeking customers outside that territory, which allows them to concentrate their efforts on their allotted territory. The same applies to the granting of an exclusive territory to a master franchisee combined with the obligation nor to conclude franchise agreements with third parties outside that territory. Where the franchisees sell or use in the process of providing services, goods manufactured by the franchisor or according to its instructions and or bearing its trade mark, an obligation on the franchisees not to sell, or use in the process of the provision of services, competing goods, makes it possible to establish a coherent network which is identified with the franchised goods. However, this obligation should only be accepted with respect to the goods which form the essential subject-matter of the franchise. It should notably not relate to accessories or spare parts for these goods.

(10)   The obligations referred to above thus do not impose restrictions which are

not necessary for the attainment of the abovementioned objectives. In particular, the limited territorial protection granted to the franchisees is indispensable to protect their investment.

(11)   It is desirable to list in the Regulation a number of obligations that are commonly found in franchise agreements and are normally not restrictive of competition and to provide that if, because of the particular economic or legal circumstances, they fall under Article 85 (1), they are also covered by the exemption. This list, which is not exhaustive, includes in particular clauses which are essential either to preserve the common identity and reputation of the network or to prevent the know-how made available and the assistance given by the franchisor from benefiting competitors.

(12)   The Regulation must specify the conditions which must be satisfied for the exemption to apply. To guarantee that competition is not eliminated for a substantial part of the goods which are the subject of the franchise, it is necessary that parallel imports remain possible. Therefore, cross deliveries between franchisees should always be possible. Furthermore, where a franchise network is combined with another distribution system, franchisees should be free to obtain supplies from authorized distributors. To better inform consumers, thereby helping to ensure that they receive a fair share of the resulting benefits, it must be provided that the franchisee shall be obliged to indicate its status as an independent undertaking, by any appropriate means which does not jeopardize the common identity of the franchised network. Furthermore, where the franchisees have to honour guarantees for the franchisor's goods, this obligation should also apply to goods supplied by the franchisor, other franchisees or other agreed dealers.

(13)   The Regulation must also specify restrictions which may not be included in franchise agreements if these are to benefit from the exemption granted by the Regulation, by virtue of the fact that such provisions are restrictions falling under Article 85 (1) for which there is no general presumption that they will lead to the positive effects required by Article 85 (3). This applies in particular to market sharing between competing manufacturers, to clauses unduly limiting the franchisee's choice of suppliers or customers, and to cases where the franchisee is restricted in determining its prices. However, the franchisor should be free to recommend prices to the franchisees, where it is not prohibited by national laws and to the extent that it does not lead to concerted practices for the effective application of these prices.

(14)   Agreements which are not automatically covered by the exemption because they contain provisions that are not expressly exempted by the Regulation and not expressly excluded from exemption may nonetheless generally be presumed to be eligible for application of Article 85 (3). It will be possible for the Commission rapidly to establish whether this is the case for a particular agreement. Such agreements should therefore be deemed to be covered by the exemption provided for in this Regulation where they are notified to the Commission and the Commission does not oppose the application of the exemption within a specified period of time.

(15) If individual agreements exempted by this Regulation nevertheless have effects which are incompatible with Article 85 (3), in particular as interpreted by the administrative practice of the Commission and the case law of the Court of Justice, the Commnission may withdraw the benefit of the block exemption. This applies in particular where competition is significantly restricted because of the structure of the relevant market.

(16) Agreements which are automatically exempted pursuant to this Regulation need not be notified. Undertakings may nevertheless in a particular case request a decision pursuant to Council Regulation No 17 (¹) as last amended by the Act of Accession of Spain and Portugal.

(17) Agreements may benefit from the provisions either of this Regulation or of another Regulation, according to their particular nature and provided that they fulfil the necessary conditions of application. They may not benefit from a combination of the provisions of this Regulation with those of another block exemption Regulation.

HAS ADOPTED THIS REGULATION:

Article 1

1. Pursuant to Article 85 (3) of the Treaty and subject to the provisions of this Regulation, it is hereby declared that Article 85 (1) of the Treaty shall not apply to franchise agreements to which two undertakings are party, which include one or more of the restrictions listed in Article 2.

2. The exemption provided for in paragraph 1 shall also apply to master franchise agreements to which two undertakings are party. Where applicable, the provisions of this Regulation concerning the relationship between franchisor and franchisee shall apply *mutatis mutandis* to the relationship between franchisor and master franchisee and between master franchisee and franchisee.

3. For the purpose of this Regulation

(a) 'franchise' means a package of industrial or intellectual property rights relating to trade marks, trade names, shop signs, utility models, designs, copyrights, know-how or patents, to be exploited for the resale of goods or the provision of services to end users;

(b) 'franchise agreement' means an agreement whereby one undertaking, the franchisor, grants the other, the franchisee, in exchange for direct or indirect financial consideration, the right to exploit a franchise for the purposes of marketing specified types of goods and/or services; it includes at least obligations relating to:

   – the use of a common name or shop sign and a uniform presentation of contract premises and/or means of transport.

   – the communication by the franchisor to the franchisee of know-how.

   – the continuing provision by the franchisor to the franchisee of commercial or technical assitance during the life of the agreements;

155

(c) 'master franchise agreement' means an agreement whereby one undertaking, the franchisor, grants the other, the master franchise, in exchange of direct or indirect financial consideration, the right to exploit a franchise for the purposes of concluding franchise agreements with third parties, the franchisees;

(d) 'franchisor's goods' means goods produced by the franchisor or according to its instructions, and/or bearing the franchisor's name or trade mark;

(e) 'contract premises' means the premises used for the exploitation of the franchise or, when the franchise is exploited outside those premises, the base from which the franchisee operates the means of transport used for the exploitation of the franchise (contract means of transport);

(f) 'know-how' means a package of non-patented practical information, resulting from experience and testing by the franchisor, which as secret, substantial and identified;

(g) 'secret' means that the know-how, as a body or in the precise configuration and assembly of its components, is not generally known or easily accessible, it is not limited in the narrow sense that the individual component of the know-how should be totally unknown or unobtainable outside the franchisor's business;

(h) 'substantial' means that the know-how includes information which is of importance for the sale of goods or the provision of services to end users, and in particular for the presentation of goods for sale, the processing of goods in connection which the provision of services, methods of dealing with customers, and administration and financial management; the know-how must be useful for the franchisee by being capable, at the date of conclusion of the agreement, of improving the competitive position of the franchisee, in particular by improving the franchisee's performance or helping it to enter a new market;

(i) 'identified' means that the know-how must be described in a sufficiently comprehensive manner so as to make it possible to verify that it fulfils the criteria of secrecy and substantiality; the description of the know-how can either be set out in the franchise agreement or in a separate document or recorded in any other appropriate form.

Article 2

The exemption provided for in Article 1 shall apply to the following restrictions of competition:

(a) an obligation on the franchisor, in a defined area of the common market, the contract territory, not to:

- grant the right to exploit all or part of the franchise to third parties.

- itself exploit the franchise, or itself market the goods or services which are the subject-matter of the franchise under a similar formula.

- itself supply the franchisor's goods to third parties;

(b) an obligation on the master franchisee not to conclude franchise agreement with third parties outside its contract territory;

(c)   an obligation on the franchisee to exploit the franchise only from the contract premises;

(d)   an obligation on the franchisee to refrain, outside the contract territory, from seeking customers for the goods or the services which are the subject-matter of the franchise.

(e)   an obligation on the franchisee not to manufacture, sell or use in the course of the provision of services, goods competing with the franchisor's goods which are the subject-matter of the franchise, where the subject-matter of the franchise is the sale or use in the course of the provision of services both certain types of goods and spare parts or accessories therefor, that obligation may not be imposed in respect of these spare parts or accessories.

Article 3

1.   Article 3 shall apply notwithstanding the presence of any of the following obligations on the franchisee, in so far as they are necessary to protect the franchisor's industrial or intellectual property rights or to maintain the common identity and reputation of the franchised network:

(a)   to sell, or use in the course of the provision of services, exclusively goods matching minimum objective qualaity specifications laid down by the franchisor;

(b)   to sell, or use in the course of the provision of services, goods which are manufactured only by the franchisor or by third parties designated by it, where it is impracticable, owing to the nature of the goods which are the subject-matter of the franchise, to apply objective quality specifications;

(c)   **not to engage, directly or indirectly, in any similar business in a territory where it would compete with a member of the franchised network, including the franchisor; the franchisee may be held to this obligation after termination of the agreement, for a reasonable period which may not exceed one year, in the territory where it has exploited the franchise;**

(d)   not to acquire financial interests in the capital of a competing undertaking, which would give the franchisee the power to influence the economic conduct of such undertaking;

(e)   to sell the goods which are the subject-matter of the franchise only to end users, to other franchisees and to resellers within other channels of distribution supplied by the manufacturer of these goods or with its consent;

(f)   to use its best endeavours to sell the goods or provide the services that are the subject-matter of the franchise; to offer for sale a minimum range of goods, achieve a minimum turnover, plan its orders in advance, keep minimum stocks and provide customer and warranty services;

(g)   to pay to the franchisor a specified proportion of its revenue for advertising and itself carry out advertising for the nature of which it shall obtain the franchisor's approval.

2.   Article 1 shall apply notwithstanding the presence of any of the following obligations on the franchisee:

(a)   not to disclose to third parties the know-how provided by the franchisor; the franchisee may be held to this obligation after termination of the agreement.

(b)   to communicate to the franchisor any experience gained in exploiting the franchise and other franchisees, non-exclusives know-how resulting from that experience.

(c)   to inform the franchisor of infringements of licensed industrial or intellectual property rights, to take legal action agaisnt infringers or to assist the franchisor in any legal actions against infringers;

(d)   not to use know-how licensed by the franchisor for purposes other than the exploitation of the franchise; the franchisee may be held to this obligation after termination of the agreement;

(e)   to attend or have its staff attend training courses arranged by the franchisor;

(f)   to apply the commercial methods devised by the franchisor, including any subsequent modification thereof, and use the licensed industrial or intellectual property rights;

(g)   to comply with the franchisor's standards for the equipments and presenttion of the contract premises and/or means of transport;

(h)   to allow the franchisor to carry out checks of the contract premises and/or means of transport, including the goods sold and the services provided, and the inventory and accounts of the franchisee;

(i)   not without the franchisor's consent to change the location of the contract premises;

(j)   not without the franchisor's consent to assign the rights and obligations under the franchise agreement.

3.   In the event that, because of particular circumstances, obligations referred to in paragraph 2 fall within the scope of Article 85 (1), they shall also be exempted even if they are not accompanied by any of the obligations exempted by Article 1.

Article 4

The exemption provided for in Article 1 shall apply on condition that:

(a)   the franchisee is free to obtain the goods that are the subject-matter of the franchise from other franchisees; where such goods are also distributed through another network of authorized distributors, the franchisee must be free to obtain the goods from the latter.

(b)   where the franchisor obliges the franchisee to honour guarantees for the franchisor's goods, that obligation shall apply in respect of such goods supplied by any member of the franchised network or other distributors which give a similar guarantee, in the common market.

(c)   the franchisee is obliged to indicate its status as an independent undertaking; this indication shall however not interfere with the common identity of the franchised network resulting in particular from the common name or shop sign and uniform appearance of the contract premises and/or means of transport.

Article 5

The exemption granted by Article 1 shall not apply where:

(a) undertakings producing goods or providing services which are identical or are considered by users as equivalent in view of their characteristics, price and intended use, enter into franchise agreements in respect of such goods or services;

(b) without prejudice to Article 2 (e) and Article 3 (1)(b), the franchisee is prevented from obtaining supplies of goods of a quality equivalent to those offered by the franchisor;

(c) without prejudice to Article 2(e), the franchisee is obliged to sell, or use in the process of providing services, goods manufactured by the franchisor or third parties designated by the franchisor and the franchisor refuses, for reasons other than protecting the franchisor's industrial or intellectual property rights, or maintaining the common identity and reputation of the franchised network, to designate as authorized manufacturers third parties proposed by the franchisee;

(d) the franchisee is prevented from continuing to use the licensed know-how after termination of the agreement where the know-how has become generally known or easily accessible, other than by breach of an obligation by the franchisee;

(e) the franchisee is restricted by the franchisor, directly or indirectly, in the determination of sale prices for the goods or services which are the subject-matter of the franchise, without prejudice to the possibility for the franchisor of recommending sale prices;

(f) the franchisor prohibits the franchisee from challenging the validity of the industrial or intellectual property rights which form part of the franchise, without prejudice to the possibility for the franchisor of terminating the agreement in such a case;

(g) **franchisees are obliged not to supply within the common market the goods or services which are the subject-matter of the franchise to end users because of their place of residence.**

Article 6

1. The exemption provided for in Article 1 shall also apply to franchise agreements whichll fulfil the conditions laid down in Article 4 and include obligations restrictive of competition which are not covered by Articles 2 and 3 (3) and do not fall within the scope of Article 5, on condition that the agreements in question are notified to the Commission in accordance with the provisions of Commission Regulation No 27(¹) and that the Commission does not oppose such exemption within a period or six months.

2. The period of six months shall run from the date on which the notification is received by the Commission. Where, however, the notification is made by registered post, the period shall run from the date shown on the postmark of the place of posting.

3. Paragraph 1 shall apply only if:

(a)   express reference is made to this Article in the notification or in a communication accompanying it; and

(b)   the information furnished with the notification is complete and in accordance with the facts.

4.   The benefit of paragraph 1 can be claimed for agreements notified before the entry into force of this Regulation by submitting a communication to the Commission referring expressly to this Article and to this notification. Paragraphs 2 and 3(b) shall apply *mutatis mutandis*.

5.   The Commission may oppose exemption. It shall oppose exemption if it receives a request to do so from a Member State within three months of the forwarding to the Member State of the notification referred to in paragraph 1 or the communication referred to in paragraph 4. This request must be justified on the basis of considerations relating to the competition rules of the Treaty.

6.   The Commission may withdraw its opposition to the exemption at any time. However, where that opposition was raised at the request of a Member State, it may be withdrawn only after consultation of the advisory Committee on Restrictive Practices and Dominant Positions.

7.   If the opposition is withdrawn because the undertakings concerned have shown that the conditions of Article 85 (3) are fulfilled, the exemption shall apply from the date of the notification.

8.   If the opposition is withdrawn because the undertakings concerned have amended the agreement so that the conditions of Article 85 (3) are fulfilled, the exemption shall apply from the date on which the amendments take effect.

9.   If the Commission opposes exemption and its opposition is not withdrawn, the effects of the notification shall be governed by the provisions of Regulation No. 17.

Article 7

1.   Information acquired pursuant to Article 6 shall be used only for the purposes of this Regulation.

2.   The Commission and the authorities of the Member States, their officials and other servants shall not disclose information acquired by them pursuant to this Regulation of a kind that is covered by the obligation of professional secrecy.

3.   Paragraphs 1 and 2 shall not prevent publication of general information or surveys which do not contain information relating to particular undertakings or associations of undertakings.

Article 8

The Commission may withdraw the benefit of this Regulation, pursuant to Article

7 of Regulation No 19/65/EEC, where it finds in a particular cases that an agreement exempted by this Regulation nevertheless has certain effects which are incompatible with the conditions laid down in Article 85 (3) of the EEC Treaty, and in particular where territorial protection is awarded to the franchisee and:

(a)   access to the relevant market or competition therein is significantly restricted by the cumulative effect of parallel networks of similar agreements established by competing manufacturers or distributors;

(b)   the goods or services which are the subject-matter of the franchise do not face, in a substantial part of the common market, effective competition from goods or services which are identical or considered by users as equivalent in view of their characteristics, price and intended use;

(c)   the parties, or one of them, prevent end users, because of their place of residence, from obtaining, directly or through intermediaries, the goods or services which are the subject-matter of the franchise within the common market, or use differences in specifications concerning those goods or services in different Member States, to isolate markets;

(d)   franchisees engage in concerted practices relating to the sale prices of the goods or services which are the subject-matter of the franchise;

(e)   the franchisor uses its right to check the contract premises and means of transport, or refused its agreement, to requests by the franchisee to move the contract premises or assign its rights and obligations under the franchise agreement, for reasons other than protecting the franchisor's industrial or intellectual property rights, maintaining the common identity and reputation of the franchised network or verifying that the franchisee abides by its obligations under the agreement.

Article 9

This Regulation shall enter into force on 1 February, 1989.

It shall remain in force until 31 December 1999.

Appendix 8
CLAUSES OF FRANCHISE AGREEMENTS AFFECTED BY THE FRANCHISING BLOCK EXEMPTION – COMMISSION REGULATION (EEC) NO. 4087/88

The block exemption details what provisions must, can and cannot be incorporated into franchise agreements.

The table below details these in what is hopefully an easily understandable form and gives examples of relevant clauses which might commonly be founded in franchise agreements. (It should be borne in mind that these clauses are only examples and that every franchise will have different requirements and hence slightly different provisions in its agreement.) The clauses given in Article 5 are examples of *prohibited* clauses.

1. Article 2
Exempted restrictions

The Franchisor

The franchisor can agree with the franchisee not to do any of the following in the contract Territory:-

Not to grant the franchise to another franchisee.

Not to compete with the franchisee.

Not itself to supply competing goods to any third parties.

The franchisor hereby grants to the franchisee the exclusive right to carry on the business in the Territory for the duration of this agreement and agrees not to compete with the franchisee in any way nor to supply directly the Goods to third parties in the Territory during the duration of this Agreement.

The Master Franchisee

The master franchisee/area developer may agree not to grant franchises outside of the contract Territory:-

The master franchisee shall have the right to operate the services within the Territory through wholly owned limited liability companies or through franchising the business to third parties within the Territory. The master franchisee shall not be permitted to actively carry on the business outside of the Territory through wholly owned limited liability companies or through sub-franchises granted to third parties.

The Franchisee

A franchisee may agree:

(a) Only to run the franchise from named premises.

The franchisee shall operate the business only from the Premises.

(b) Not to solicit custom from outside the contract territory.

The franchisee shall not solicit customers for the franchise from without the Territory, although nothing shall prevent him from meeting the orders of unsolicited customers from outside of the Territory.

(c) Not to manufacture, sell or use in the course of providing services competing Goods (although spare parts are not covered by this exemption).

The franchisor shall at no time during the continuance of this Agreement and any extension and/or variation thereof engage in or seek to engage in the manufacture sale or use of goods which compete with the Goods, (save that this shall not apply to any provision of spare parts for repair of the Goods).

2. ARTICLE 3.1

Conditionally permitted obligations of franchisees

The following obligations can be imposed upon the franchisees, only in so far as is necessary to protect the franchisor's industrial/intellectual property rights or maintain the common identity and reputation of the franchise network.

Comply with quality specifications laid down for goods used/sold.

The franchisee shall only use such Goods in the carrying out of the services as shall meet the minimum technical specifications laid out in schedule I hereto.

To tie in goods manufactured by the franchisor or by third parties where quality specifications are not possible due to the nature of the goods.

In order to maintain the high standards of reliability and uniformity of business and to enable the franchisees and other franchisees to enjoy the benefit of bulk purchase supply to the franchisees, during the term of this Agreement the franchisee shall purchase the Goods specified in Schedule I hereto from the franchisor, other franchisees and such third parties as are indicated in Schedule II.

Non-competition clauses during and post-term against both franchisor and any other franchisees (the post-term restrictions can last for up to one year).

The franchisee shall not be engaged, interested or concerned in any business in the Territory which may compete with the services or any part of them and during the term or up to one year after the termination of the Agreement including any financial interest in such business which may enable it to influence such business' conduct.

Not to hold any financial interest in a competitor that would enable it to influence the economic conduct of such an undertaking.

The franchisee shall not be engaged, interested or concerned in any business in the Territory which may compete with the services or any part of them and during the term or up to one year after the termination of the Agreement, including any financial interest in such business which may enable it to influence such business' conduct.

Only to re-sell to end-users, other franchisees and other re-sellers supplied by the manufacturer or with his consent.

The franchisee shall sell the Goods only to other franchisees and end-users. It shall at no time sell the goods to wholesalers.

Use best endeavours to sell the Goods/ provide the Services and offer a minimum range of goods for sale; achieve minimum turnover; plan orders in advance; keep minimum stocks and provide the customer with warranty services.

The franchisee shall during the first year of this Agreement achieve a minimum turnover of £60,000 and thereafter a minimum turnover of £100,000 for the second year which will thereafter increase each subsequent year pro rata with any increase in the retail price index published in the United Kingdom or any index shall at any time replace the said retail price index. In any event the franchisee shall use its best endeavours to promote the services in the Territory and shall at all times maintain a minimum stock of the Goods so as to enable it to properly meet such demand and carry out appropriate guarantee and warranty work.

Pay a fixed proportion of revenue as an advertising fee and ensure that all advertising has prior approval of the franchisor.

The franchisee will pay to the franchisor on the first day of every month an Advertising Fee equivalent to 5% of the previous month's gross turnover which monies the franchisor shall use for its national Advertising Budget. In addition to the Advertising Fee, the franchisee shall undertake such local advertising/ promotion described in the manual as the franchisor in its reasonable discretion deems necessary in order to properly market the services in the franchisee's locality. All such advertising and promotions must have the prior written consent of the franchisor. In no circumstances will the franchisee undertake any national advertising.

3 ARTICLE 3.2

Unconditionally permitted obligations of the franchisee

The following obligations can be imposed on the franchisee:-

Confidentiality of know-how, during and after the term of the Agreement.

The franchisee will not furnish any information as to the know-how the methods of operation, publicity, profits, financial affairs, present or future plans or policies of the franchisor or any other information relating to the operation of the franchisor either during the term of the Agreement or at any time after its termination.

The non-exclusive licensing back of any improvements that the franchisee may make.

The franchisee will immediately notify the franchisor of any improvements in the Goods which it makes and upon the request of the franchisor shall grant the franchisor a non-exclusive licence without cost which licence will enable the franchisor to sub-licence the improvements to third parties.

To inform the franchisor of any intellectual property right infringements and take any action against infringers or assist the franchisor to do so.

The franchisee shall immediately inform the franchisor of any infringement of the marks as soon as it shall become aware of the same and the expense of taking any such steps as may be necessary against the infringers to preserve the franchisor's rights shall be taken by the franchisee as directed by the franchisor, and the costs of doing so shall be borne entirely by the franchisor.

Only to use the know-how licensed under the Agreement in the exploitation of the franchise during the term of the Agreement and following the termination not to use it in any way at all.

The franchisor shall, at all times during the currency of the Agreement, use the know-how licensed to it by the franchisor hereunder only in order to carry out the services in accordance with this Agreement, and after the expiration of the Term or any earlier termination thereof not to use the know-how.

Attend or have staff attend training courses arranged by the franchisor.

The franchisor shall, from time to time at the expense of the franchisee, provide the franchisee and his senior staff with such training as the franchisor thinks fit at such place or places in the United Kingdom as the franchisor may require. The franchisee shall ensure that it and his relevant staff attend such training sessions as and when required.

To apply the commercial methods (and any modification thereof) and the licensed industrial/intellectual property rights.

The franchisee shall carry out the Business using the Marks at all times in a manner deemed appropriate by the franchisor.

The franchisee shall carry on the Business in strict accordance with the contents of the Manual as amended from time to time.

Comply with franchisor's standards for Equipment, Transport and Premises.

The franchisee shall ensure that all transport and equipment used by it, in connection with the Business, shall be in such mechanical condition and decorated in such manner as the franchisor shall, from time to time, require.

The franchisee shall ensure that the Premises are, at all times, decorated in such manner and by such signs, insignees and marks as the franchisor shall, from time to time, require.

Allow the franchisor to carry out spot checks of the Premises/Transport including inventory and Accounts.

The franchisee shall, at all times, permit the franchisor and any person authorised by the franchisor to visit the Premises and inspect the Equipment and Goods to ensure that they are in fit state of repair and condition.

The franchisee shall permit the franchisor and any person authorised by it to enter at all reasonable times and upon reasonable notice upon the Premises and inspect all books of account, vouchers and other supporting documentation and correspondence.

Not to change location of Premises without the franchisor's consent.

The franchisee shall carry out the Business from the Premises and shall not change the location of the Premises or assign all or part of them to a third party without the prior written consent of the franchisor.

Not to assign the rights and obligations under the Franchise Agreement without the franchisor's consent.

The franchisee shall not have the right to assign his rights or obligations under this Agreement but shall have the right at any time to sell the Business with the prior written consent of the franchisor and subject to the conditions listed below...

These conditionally and unconditionally permitted obligations will be exempted from 85(1) even if the Agreement does not contain any of the restrictions exempted under Article 2.

4. ARTICLE 4

Compulsory conditions

These provisions must be contained in any agreement that seeks to take advantage of the Block Exemption.

The franchisee must be able to obtain its goods from other franchisees and any other authorised distributors.

In order to maintain the high standards of reliability and uniformity of business and to enable the franchisees and other franchisees to enjoy the benefit of bulk purchase supply to the franchisees, during the term of this Agreement the franchisee shall purchase the Goods specified in Schedule I hereto from the franchisor, other franchisees and such third parties as are indicated in Schedule II.

If there are guarantees to be honoured, the franchisee must honour guarantees on all goods distributed by any franchisee or any distributor which may give a similar guarantee in the Common Market.

The franchisee shall honour all current guarantees on Goods in the Territory regardless of the Goods' origin.

The franchisee must indicate its independent status.

The franchisee shall clearly indicate on all literature and correspondence and by way of a prominently displayed notice board at the Premises the fact that it is an independent franchisee of the franchisor and is in no other way connected with it.

5. ARTICLE 5

Prohibited conditions

These provisions must not be contained in any agreement that seeks to take advantage of the Block Exemption. The clauses below are examples of prohibited provisions.

Agreements between competing manufacturers/suppliers of identical or similar services.	Non-applicable.
Prohibtions on alternative sourcing of supplies (without prejudice) to Article 3.1 above.	The franchisee shall source the Goods only from the franchisor regardless of the quality, availability and pricing policy of alternate supplies.
If only approved suppliers are permitted in order to preserve quality, reputation, etc. of the franchise *and* the franchisor refuses for reasons other than protecting intellectual property rights, etc.	The franchisee will source the Goods directly from the franchisor or such other parties as the franchisor shall in its complete discretion without limitation, approve. (NB. It is not the clause but the franchisor's actions under it that are prohibited.)
Prohibition of the franchisee using know-how of the franchisor after the termination of the franchise agreement when such know-how has come into the public domain by means other than the franchisee's breach.	The franchisee undertakes not at any time after the termination of this Agreement by whatever means to use the know-how regardless of whether or not it might reasonably be deemed to be within the public domain.
The franchisee is not free to determine its own sales prices (although the franchisor can recommend prices).	The franchise shall ensure that at all times it does not charge less than the minimum sale price detailed in Schedule I hereto.

Prevent the franchisee challenging the intellectual/industrial property rights of the franchisor (without prejudice to the franchisor's ability to terminate in such a case).	The franchisee shall at no time seek to challenge the franchisor's rights to the property in the marks.
Discriminating against the supply to end-users on the basis of their place of residence.	The franchisee shall undertake not to supply the Goods to purchasers the place of residence of which lies outside of the Territory.

It should be noted that:-

(1)   Any agreement that fulfils the conditions of of Article 4 can take advantage of the Block Exemption even though it contains restrictions on competion which are not covered by Articles 2 and 3 but do not come within Article 5, provided they are notified and not opposed within 6 months of such notification.

(2)   Under Article 8 the Commission can withdraw the benefit of the Block Exemption if an agreement, although ostensibly complying with it, has effects incompatible with Article 85(3).

Appendix 9
TRADE MARKS

Classification of goods for the purpose of registration of trade marks

The following headings give a general indication of the types of goods falling within the respective classes under Schedule IV of the Trade Mark Rules, 1938 (as amended). Parts of an article or apparatus are classified with the actual article or apparatus, except where such parts constitute articles included in other classes.

1. Chemical products used in industry, science, photography, agriculture, horticulture, forestry; artificial and synthetic resins; plastics in the form of powders, liquids or pastes, for industrial use; manures (natural and artificial); fire extinguishing compositions; tempering substances and chemical preparations for soldering; chemical substances for preserving foodstuffs; tanning substances; adhesive substances used in industry.

2. Paints, varnishes, lacquers; preservatives against rust and against deterioration of wood; colouring matters, dyestuffs; mordants; natural resins; metals in foil and powder form for painters and decorators.

3. Bleaching preparations and other substances for laundry use; cleaning, polishing, scouring and abrasive preparations; soaps; perfumery; essential oils, cosmetics, hair lotions; dentifrices.

4. Industrial oils and greases (other than edible oils and fats and essential oils); lubricants; dust laying and absorbing compositions; fuels (including motor spirit) and illuminants; candles, tapers, nightlights and wicks.

5. Pharmaceutical, veterinary and sanitary substances; infants' and invalids' foods; plasters; materials for bandaging; material for stopping teeth, dental wax; disinfectants; preparations for killing weeds and destroying vermin.

6. Unwrought and partly wrought common metals and their alloys, anchors, anvils, bells, rolled and cast building materials; rails and other metallic materials for railway tracks; chains (except driving chains for vehicles); cables and wires (non-electric); locksmiths' work; metallic pipes and tubes; safes and cashboxes; steel balls; horse-shoes; nails and screws and other goods in non-precious metal not included in other classes; ores.

7. Machines and machine tools; motors (except for land vehicles); machine couplings and belting (except for land vehicles); large size agricultural implements; incubators.

8. Hand tools and instruments; cutlery, forks and spoons; side arms.

9. Scientific, nautical, surveying and electrical apparatus and instruments (including wireless), photographic, cinematographic, optical, weighing, measuring, signalling, checking (supervision), life-saving and teaching apparatus and instruments; coins and counter-feed apparatus; talking machines; cash registers, calculating machines; fire-extinguishing apparatus.

10. Surgical, medical, dental and veterinary instruments and apparatus (including artificial limbs, eyes and teeth).

11. Installations for lighting, heating, steam generating, cooking, refrigerating, drying, ventilating, water supply and sanitary purposes.

12. Vehicles; apparatus for locomotion by land, air or water.

13. Firearms; ammunition and projectiles, explosive substances; fireworks.

14. Precious metals and their alloys and goods in precious metals or coated therewith (except cutlery, forks and spoons); jewellery; precious stones; horological and other chronometric instruments.

15. Musical instruments (other than talking machines and wireless apparatus).

16. Paper, cardboard, articles of paper or of cardboard (not included in other classes); printed matter; newspapers and periodicals, books; book-binding materials; photographs; stationery, adhesive materials (stationery); artists' materials; paint brushes; typewriters and office requisites (other than furniture); instructional and teaching material (other than apparatus); playing cards; printers' type and clinches (stereotype).

17. Gutta percha, india rubber, balata and substitutes, articles made from these substances and not included in other classes; plastics in the form of sheets, blocks, rods and tubes, being for use in manufactures; materials for packing, stopping or insulating, asbestos, mica and their products; hose pipes (non-metallic).

18. Leather and imitations of leather, and articles made from these materials, and not included in other classes; skins, hides; trunks and travelling bags; umbrellas, parasols and walking sticks; whips, harness and saddlery.

19. Building materials, natural and artificial stone, cement, lime mortar, plaster and gravel; pipes of earthenware or cement; road-making materials; asphalt, pitch and bitumen, portable buildings; stone monuments; chimney pots.

20. Furniture, mirrors, picture frames; articles (not included in other classes) of wood, cork, reeds, cane, wicker, horn, bone, ivory, whalebone, shell, amber, mother-of-pearl, meerschaum, celluloid, susstitutes for all these materials or of plastics.

21. Small domestic utensils and containers (not of precious metals, or coated

therewith); combs and sponges; brushes (other than paint brushes); brush-making materials; instruments and materials for cleaning products; steel wool; unworked or semi-worked glass (excluding glass used in building); glassware, porcelain and earthenware, not included in other classes.

22 Ropes, string, nets, tents, awnings, tarpaulins, sails, sacks; padding and stuffing materials (hair, kapoc, feathers, seaweed, etc); raw fibrous textile materials.

23. Yarns, threads.

24. Tissues (piece goods); bed and table covers; textile articles not included in other classes.

25. Clothing, including boots, shoes and slippers.

26. Lace and embroidery, ribbons and braid; buttons, press buttons, hooks and eyes, pins and needles; artificial flowers.

27. Carpets, rugs, mats and matting; linoleums and other materials for covering existing floors; wall hangings (non-textile).

28. Games and playthings; gymnastic and sporting articles (except clothing); ornaments and decorations for Christmas trees.

29. Meat, fish, poultry and game, meat extracts; preserved, dried and cooked fruits and vegetables; jellies, jams; eggs, milk and other dairy products; edible oils and fats; preserves, pickles.

30. Coffee, tea, cocoa, sugar, rice, tapioca, sago, coffee substitutes; flour, and preparations made from cereals; bread, biscuits, cakes; pastry and confectionery, ices; honey, treacle; yeast, baking powder; salt, mustard; pepper; vinegar, sauces; spices, ice.

31. Agricultural, horticultural and forestry products and grains not included in other classes; living animals; fresh fruit and vegetables; seeds; live plants and flowers; food-stuffs for animals, malt.

32. Beer, ale and porter; mineral and aerated waters and other non-alcoholic drinks, syrups and other preparations for making beverages.

33. Wines, spirits and liqueurs.

34. Tobacco, raw and manufactured; smokers' articles and matches.

35.1. Accounting, auditing, book-keeping, copying of documents, statistics, valuations, pay-lists, transcribing of messages, hire of office machinery, office management, stenography, shorthand, typing agencies, analysis, duplications

2. Advertising of all kinds, publicity, news agencies, directories, information; addresses; bill-posting, window dressing

3. Fire and burglar alarms

4. Radio and television commercial advertising, sound & video recordings, commercial communications, message sending

5. Agencies, assessments, business consultants, business direction, business enquiries, business research, business supervision, employment consulting, management valuations

36.1. Housing agents, house rentals, real estate

2. Assurance, broking, credit, financing, guarantees, insurance, investment, leasing, loans, lotteries, monetary transactions, pawn broking, securities, stock broking, underwriting

3. Safe deposits, deposits of valuables

37.1. Maintenance and repair services: whatever the product check the appropriate goods class, eg baggage, navigational, watches, buildings

3. Hire services: whatever the products being hired check the goods class concerned, eg motor cars

4. Construction Service: whatever the service is concerned with check the products class, eg asphalting

5. Boiler-making

6. Painting and decorating

7. Housing and office buildings

8. Cleaners, dry cleaning, laundries, washing, swimming pools, cleaners, polishing

9. Disinfecting, pest control

38. Communication: Broadcasting, message sending, radio and tv programmes, telex service, telephony, telegraphy, postal services

39.1. Transportation: freight, hire, etc, where service relates to any form of transport, eg cars, ships, aeroplanes

2. Storage, warehousing: depending on the product being stored, eg fruit

40. Material treatment: depending on the material to be treated, check the product class concerned, eg embroidery, fire proofing of textiles

40.1. Education, eg beauty schools

2. Schools, academies, teaching, training

3.   Entertainment, hire of cinema films

4.   Amusement parks, pleasure grounds: depending on the type of entertainment, search the relevant goods and service classes

42.1.Miscellaneous. Depending on the type of product with which the service is connected, search the relevant product class and service class

2.   Decoration: if the specification lists a particular type of decoration service, eg glass decoration, check the class into which the product falls, ie glass = 2(IV)

Procedure for Registration of a Mark

(a)   Registrar's preliminary advice

It is often helpful to obtain the registrar's advice on the registrability of a proposed mark prior to making an application for registration, if there is some doubt about its distinctiveness, non-deceptiveness, or uniqueness.

(b)   Searches

On payment of the prescribed fee, a search amongst the classified representations and indexes of marks for goods in all classes at the Trade Marks Branch of the Patent Office, may be made. The indexes include a classified index of devices, and alphabetical indexes of words occurring as trade marks or parts of trade marks arranged according to their beginnings and endings. The indexes also include pending applications as well as those marks already protected by registration.

(c)   Official objections

If the examiner considering the application raises objections to a mark, for whatever reason, the applicant may put forward arguments in support of the mark in writing or apply for an oral hearing before a senior officer of the registry. Significant prior use of the mark may be of assistance in establishing distinctiveness and evidence of this use may be submitted for consideration. Otherwise, in some cases, an objection may be overcome by a slight amendment of a mark of the services claimed in an application. If objections are maintained, a written statement of the reasons for refusal of an application may be sought and an appeal made to the court or the Secretary of State.

(d)   Advertisement

Once an application has passed the examiner it is advertised in the weekly Trade Marks Journal, to enable anybody with a just cause to oppose registration of any application. One month is allowed from the date of advertisement within which opposition may be lodged.

(d)   Opposition to registration

Notice of intention to oppose the registration of a mark (for which a fee is payable) must be given within one month from the date of advertisement of the mark in the Trade Marks Journal, or such further time as the registrar may, on application, allow. The notice must state the grounds of opposition, and the opponent's address for service in Great Britain or Northern Ireland, and must be accompanied by an unstamped duplicate, which will be forwarded to the applicant by the registrar.

Failure to give the applicant notice by letter before making the formal opposition will be taken into account in considering any application by an opponent for an order for costs if the opposition is not contested by the applicant.

After the filing of the applicant's counter-statement, the opponent's and the applicant's evidence, and the opponent's evidence in reply, the registrar will appoint a time for hearing the parties.

(e) Registration

When:

(i) an application has been advertised in the Trade Mark Journal;

(ii) either the prescribed or extended period has elapsed without opposition, or such an opposition has proved unsuccessful; and

(iii) all the other conditions have been complied with

the mark will be entered on the register on payment of the registration fee and filing of Form TM-No 10. A certificate of registration will then be issued to the applicant without request. The effective date of registration is the *date of receipt of the application*.

Appendix 10
NATIONAL FRANCHISE ASSOCIATIONS

European Franchising Federation

Avenue de Broqueville 5
B 1150 Brussels
BELGIUM

Tel (02) 7366464

European National Associations

Belgian Franchise Association
Rue St Bernard 60
1060 Bruxelles
BELGIUM

Tel 600730 3060

British Franchise Association
Thames View
Newtown Road
Henley-on-Thames
Oxon
RG9 1HG

Tel (0491) 578050

Danish Franchise Association
Sjaelsmarkvej 1 B
DK 2970 Hoersholm
DENMARK

Tel. (45) 02 76 5064

Irish Franchise Association
13 Frankfield Terrace
Summerhill South
Cork
Ireland

Tel 021-270859/50

Swiss Franchise Association
c/o Gesplan
5 Rue Toepffer
Geneva
SWITZERLAND

Tel 010 41 2 2283636

Dutch Franchise Association
Arubalaan 4
1213 Vg Hilversum
THE NETHERLANDS

Tel 035 83 39 34

French Franchise Association
9 Bd des Italiens
75002 Paris
FRANCE

Tel (1) 42 60 0022-42 610396

German Franchise Association
St Paul Strasse 9
8000 Munchen 2
WEST GERMANY

Tel (089) 53 50 27

Italian Franchise Association
20121 Milano
C so di Porta Nuova 3
ITALY

Tel 02-6507 79

Norwegian Franchise Association
c/o Mr. Torleif Karlsen
Astveitskogen 41
5084 Tertnes
NORWAY

Swedish Franchise Association
P O Box 26002, S-100 41
Stockholm
Sweden

Tel 08 723 05 33

Non-European Associations

International Franchise Assn.
1350 New York Avenue NW
Suite 900
Washington DC 2005
USA

Tel (202) 628 8000

Association of Canadian
Franchisors
Suite 1050
595 Bay Street
Toronto
Ontario
M5G 2C2
CANADA

Japanese Franchise Association
Elsa Building 602
3-13-12 Roppongi
Minato-Ku
Tokyo
JAPAN

Tel 03 408 1796

South African Franchise Assn
c/o Johannesburg Chamber of
Commerce
Private Bag 34
Auckland Park 2006
SOUTH AFRICA

Tel 726 5300

Franchisors Association of Australia
Suit 2, 6a Post Office St
Pymbel NSW 2073
AUSTRALIA

Tel (02) 449 5311 Officer

Appendix 11
BANKING AFFILIATES OF THE BFA

Bank of Scotland PLC
57-60 Haymarket
London SW1Y 4QY

(01-925 0499)

John Perkins
Senior Manager
Franchise and Licensing
Barclays Bank PLC
Corporate Marketing Department
168 Fenchurch Street
London EC3P 3HP

(01-626 1567)

Glen Strachan
Business Development Manager
Clydesdale Bank PLC
P O Box 43
30 St. Vincent Place
Glasgow G1 2HL

(041-248 7070)

Christopher Walker
Franchise Manager
Lloyds Bank PLC
Small Business Services
71 Lombard Street
London EC3P 3BS

(01-626 1500)

Dai Rees
Franchise Manager
Midland Bank PLC
Small & Medium Enterprise Unit
Market Department
P O Box 2
41 Silver Street
Sheffield S1 3GG

(0742-529037)

Peter Stern
Senior Franchise Manager
National Westminister Bank PLC
Commercial Banking Services
75 Cornhill
London EC3V 3NN

(01-280 4477)

Ron Campbell/Tim Bowyer
Manager
Franchise and Licensing Department
The Royal Bank of Scotland PLC
Regent House
42 Islington High Street
London N1 8XL

(01 833 2121)

TSB Scotland PLC
Henry Duncan House
P O Box 177
120 George Street
Edinburgh EH2 4TS

(031-225 4555)

Appendix 12
CHARTERED ACCOUNTANT AFFILIATES OF THE BFA

BDO Binder Hamlyn

Ernst and Young

KPMG Peat Marwick McLintock

Kidsons

Levy Gee Consultant Limited

Neville Russell

Price Waterhouse

Touche Ross

Appendix 13
FRANCHISE CONSULTANT AFFILIATES OF THE BFA

Caledonian Franchise Consultant

Caltain Associates

Corporate Franchising & Licensing

Ernst and Young

Franchise & Marketing Management

Saffery Champness Consultancy Services Limited

Stoy Hayward Franchising Services

Appendix 14
BFA CODE OF ETHICS

1. The BFA's Code of Advertising Practice shall be based on that established by the Advertising Standards Association and shall be modified from time to time in accordance with alterations notifed by the ASA.

    The BFA will subscribe fully to the ASA Code unless, on some specific issue, it is resolved by a full meeting of the Council of the BFA that the ASA is acting against the best interests of the public and of franchising business in general on that specific issue, in this case the BFA will be required to notify formally the ASA, setting out the grounds for disagrement.

2. No member shall sell, offer for sale, or distribute any product or render any service, or promote the sale or distribution thereof, under any representation or condition (including the use of the name of a 'celebrity') which has the tendency, or effect of misleading or deceiving pruchasers or prospective purchasers.

3. No member shall imitate the trademark, trade name, corporate identity, slogan, or other mark or identification of another franchisor in any manner of form that would have the tendency or capacity to mislead or deceive.

4. Full and accurate written disclosure of all information material to the franchise relationship shall be given to prospective franchiseees within a reasonable time prior to the execution of any binding document.

5. The franchise agreement shall set forth clearly the respective obligations and responsibilities of the parties and all other terms of the relationship, and be free from ambiguity.

6. The franchise agreement and all matters basic and material to the arrangement and relationship thereby created, shall be in writing and executed copies thereof given to the franchisee.

7. A franchisor shall select and accept only those franchisees who, upon reasonable investigation, possess the basic skills, education, personal qualities, and adequate capital to succeed. There shall be no discrimiantion based on race, colour, religion, national origin or sex.

8. A franchisor shall exercise reasonable surveillance over the activities of his franchisees to the end that the contractual obligations of both parties are observed and the public interest safeguarded.

9. Fairness shall characterise all dealings between a franchisor and its fran-

chisees. A franchisor shall give notice to its franchisee of any contractual breach and grant reasonable time to remedy default.

10. A franchisor shall make every effort to resolve complaints, grievances and disputes with its franchisees with good faith and goodwill through fair and reasonable direct communication and negotiation.

Appendix 15
CONSUMER CREDIT ACT 1974

CC1/88
Consumer Credit Act 1974

Application for a standard licence

This is the form specified by the Director General under section 6 of the Act
as the application form for a standard licence referred to in General Notice No 31

Please use black ink (BLOCK LETTERS) or typescript

1 Give the **full** name of applicant (the name of the partnership,
company etc or, if a sole trader, title, all forenames and surname, in
that order, of the individual)

2 Give the name or names under which the business is to be carried
on (if different from that given in section 1) ie list all trading names

3 Give the full address of the applicant's principal or prospective
principal place of business in the United Kingdom

No. road or street

Village or district

Post town or city

County and postcode

4 If a body corporate (eg a limited company) registered in the United
Kingdom give the Registered Office address. If a company
incorporated outside the United Kingdom, give the full name(s)
and address(es) of all persons within the United Kingdom
authorised to accept documents

Please indicate whether the address is of

a) the Registered Office

b) authorised persons

Put **X** in box

No. road or street

Village or district

Post town or city

County and postcode

5 Indicate which business activities you would like your licence to
cover.

Consumer credit
If you want to lend your own money or offer credit which you will
finance from your own resources, you need a licence for this category.
Please note how this differs from credit brokerage (see C below)   **A**

Consumer hire   **B**

Credit brokerage
If you wish to introduce customers to a source of credit or finance
your own sales by offering credit facilities financed by a finance
house, bank or third party, you need a licence for this category.   **C**

Debt adjusting and debt counselling   **D**

Debt collecting   **E**

Credit reference agency   **F**

Canvassing off trade premises
Authority to canvass off trade premises debtor-creditor-supplier
agreements or regulated consumer hire agreements   **Z**
Please read Note 3

Continued

185

CC1/86 *continued*

6 Is the applicant either: Put X in box

a) a sole trader? | yes |

| no | If **yes** to **b**, give title, all forenames and
                   surname (in that order) of each partner

b) a partnership? | yes |

| no | _____

                  _____

                  _____

                  _____

c) a body corporate registered in the United Kingdom?   If **yes** to **c**, give title, all forenames and
(eg a limited company, co-operative, credit union) | yes | surname (in that order) of all directors
                                                               and the secretary
                                                    | no |

_____

_____

_____

_____

_____

d) any other type of organisation?
(eg an unincorporated body or a company incorporated outside the | yes | If **yes** to **d**, specify which type of organis-
United Kingdom)   ation, and give all forenames and
                                                                  | no | surname (in that order) of everyone
                                                                            responsible for managing its affairs

_____

_____

_____

_____

7 Give the adress to which correspondence about this application   No. road or street
should be sent (if different from 3)

                                                                    _____

                                                                    Village or district

                                                                    _____

                                                                    Post town or city

                                                                    _____

                                                                    County and postcode

8 **Declaration**   I/We hereby apply for the standard
Please read this section carefully before completing and signing it   licence shown covering the business
                                                                    activities specified in section 5
WARNING   Signed *Please read Note 4*
You may not engage in any business activities for which a licence under
the Act is required unless and until you have been granted a licence which   _____
covers those activities.
                                                                    Name in BLOCK LETTERS of person signing
The Consumer Credit Act provides that a person who, in connection with
any application, knowingly or recklessly gives information to the Director   _____
General, which, in a material particular, is false or misleading, commits a
criminal offence. It is the responsibility of the applicant to ensure that the   Position or authority
information given is correct.
                                                                    _____

                                                                    Telephone number

                                                                    _____

                                                                    Date

Total fee payable   and enclose the specified fee of £
                                                                    (by cheque/postal order/money order,
                 No. of categories applied for in Section 5   crossed and made payable to THE OFFICE
                                                                    OF FAIR TRADING for consideration of the

	1	2	3	4	5	6	7
Sole trader	£80	£90	£100	£110	£120	£130	£140
All other cases	£150	£160	£170	£180	£190	£200	£210

application.

Please read Note 5

CC2/86

Consumer Credit Act 1974

Information in support of an application for a standard licence

Please use black ink (BLOCK LETTERS) or typescript

1 Give the **full** name of applicant as shown in section 1 on **Form CC1/86.**

2 If the applicant is a body registered with a Registrar of Companies or the Registrar of Friendly Societies, give the registration number and supply a copy of the Certificate of Incorporation. (If constituted under any other Act or authority not referred to above, give the title of the Act or authority concerned and the registration number where appropriate.)

3 Give the title, all forenames and surname (in that order) and address of anyone (eg business associate, senior employee, associate, or close relative) not named on the application who can direct or influence the way in which the business is run. *Please read Note 6.*

No. road or street

Village or district

Post town or city

County and postcode

4 If the applicant is a body corporate, give the title, all forenames and surname (in that order) and address of anyone not named in section 3 on whose instructions the directors act. *Pleae read Note. 7.*

No. road or street

Village or district

Post town or city

County and postcode

5 If the applicant is a body corporate, give the title, all forenames and surname (in that norder) and address of anyhone who, either alone or with a relative or associate, can control one-third or more of the voting power at a general meeting. *Please read Note 7.*

No. road or street

Village or district

Post town or city

County and postcode

6 If the applicant is a body corporate which is the subsidiary of another body corporate, give the name and address of the holding company. (In the case of a complicated company structure, please attach a 'family tree' if possible.) *Please read Note 7.*

No. road or street

Village or district

Post town or city

County and postcode

7 If the holding company shown in section 6 has a licence under the Consumer Credit Act 1974, give its number. If no licence is held, give the title, all forenames and surname (in that order) of its directors and secretary.

8 If any of the persons named on this form or **Form CC1/86** have changed their names by deed poll, marriage, use or other means, or have used other names, give full details in the order – title, all forenames, surname.

9 Give the reference number of any previous application made or any licence held under the Consumer Credit Act by the applicant or anyone named on this form or **Form CC1/86**, or by any partnership or body corporate in which the applicant or anyone named on this form or **Form CC1/86** was or is a partner, director or controller.

Continued overleaf

CC2/86 *continued*

10 Give the type of business(es) to be carried on by the
applicant, eg finance house, motor dealer, TV rental, etc.

11 Give the approximate number of branches or outlets of the business.

12 Has the applicant or, to your knowledge, anyone else named
on this form or **Form CC1/86**

a) been convicted of any offence involving fraud or other
dishonesty or violence? *Please read Note 8.*

[yes]
[no]

If **yes** to **a**, please read *Note 9* and give full details

b) been convicted under any of the Acts listed in *Note 15* or
under orders or regulations made under any of those Acts?

[yes]
[no]

If **yes** to **b**, please read *Note 9* and give full details

13 Has the applicant, if an individual or a partnership, or
anyone named on this form or Form CC1/86 been adjudged
bankrupt or, in Scotland, had their estate sequestrated
during the last ten years?

[yes]
[no]

If **yes**, please read *Note 10* and give full details

14 Has the applicant, if a body corporate or an unincorporated
body of persons, or any body of persons named on this form
or **Form CC1/86**, had a liquidator, receiver or manager
appointed; had a winding-up petition presented to the court
or passed a resolution for voluntary winding-up within the
last three years?

[yes]
[no]

If **yes**, please read *Note 11* and give full details

15 Has anyone named on this form or **Form CC1/86** been an
officer of a body to which question **14** applies?

[yes]
[no]

If **yes**, please read *Note 12* and give full details

16 Has the applicant or, to your knowledge, anyone else named
on this form or **Form CC1/86** ever applied for authorisation
under the:
a) Banking Act 1979?
b) Credit Unions Act 1979?
c) Insurance Brokers Registration Act 1977?
d) Prevention of Fraud Act 1958?

[yes]
[no]

If **yes** to **a, b, c, or d,** please read *Note 13* and give full details

17 Have any county court judgments been recorded against the
applicant or, to your knowledge, anyone else named on this
form or **Form CC1/86,** within the last three years?

[yes]
[no]

If **yes**, please read *Note 14* and give full details

18 Declaration

Please read this section carefully before completing and signing it

WARNING

The Consumer Credit Act provides that a person who, in
connection with any application, knowingly or recklessly gives
information to the Director General which, in a material particular,
is false or misleading, commits a criminal offence. It is the
responsibility of the applicant to ensure that the information given
is correct.

Signed

Name in BLOCK LETTERS of person signing

Position or authority

Telephone number

Date

Appendix 16
CASE STUDIES

THE KALL-KWIK PRINTING STORY

Kwik Kopy Corporation, a quick service printing operation was established in Houston, Texas in 1965. By 1978 it had 350 outlets in the USA. In 1988 it has over 1,000 units located in the USA, Canada, Australia, UK, Israel and South Africa. In the UK, the *Kall-Kwik Printing* franchise system (as it was re-named) did not take the traditional route. Moshe Gerstenhaber, the founder of the UK operation, decided he wanted to be in franchising; attracted by the theoretical synergy of interests between franchisor and franchisee. To Gerstenhaber's mind there was very little to fault in the concept of franchising. The franchisor develops a business system and by trial and error, through the operation of a pilot scheme, finds the correct balance and market niche to allow the business to make good profits. The franchisee, who has a burning ambition to succeed in business and earn a great deal more money than he does in his current employment, is prepared to lease the proven system [hence 'system leasing' as an alternative name to franchising – see page 8 above] and pay the franchisor an on-going fee for support services and a rental fee for the use of the system. It is the fusing of the interests of natural allies. Gerstenhaber therefore obtained the master licence for the UK (with further rights for Europe) in 1978.

The fact that *Kall-Kwik* in the UK is both a franchisee as well as a franchisor adds a further dimension to the complex relationship. The acquisition of the rights and the access to the then 13 years' experience of *Kwik-Copy* in the USA allowed *Kall-Kwik* background information against which to judge its actual experience in the UK.

The *Kall-Kwik* system was established in the UK in late October 1978. Based on a business plan, *3i* [then ICFC] subscribed to 18% of the equity and advanced a 7 year loan to the company. Two pilot units were converted to the *Kall-Kwik* colours late in 1978 and the first franchised centre was launched in May 1979. In fact, 2 franchised outlets were opened during May 1979 and one of the original owners is still there, recognised as being one of the 'founding fathers' of the system.

The following 10 years were full of intense hard work and continuing progress. The company had in May 1989 some 170 outlets with system sales in the tens of millions of pounds. In terms of number of outlets and system sales it is amongst the top 5 franchises in the UK (possibly number 3). It has recorded the fastest growth from amongst all the franchisors in the UK which commenced operation in 1978 or later.

In 1989 *Kall-Kwik* received the British Franchise Association's Franchisor of the Year Award, just 10 years after its first unit was opened.

The main practical lessons which Gerstenhaber claims the company learned over the 10 year period are as follows:

1. Franchising is all about people. The relationship between franchisee and franchisor is an extremely complex one and requires a great deal of on-going investment to keep it moving in the right direction.

2. Franchising does not always eliminate the need for the head office overheads and management layers. For the franchisees to be successful and maintain their level of commitment they need a great deal of guidance and support from the franchisor. This on-going investment reduces the margins and the rewards which the franchisor gains from the system. It can be said, therefore, that if the business which is franchised is expected to yield only a small franchise system it might be more profitable and less complicated to establish a few 'company owned stores' operation instead.

3. Building a franchise company is a long term affair; the franchisor expecting to make a quick return is likely to be disappointed. The build up of the system is demanding and the return is likely to be seen in the medium to long term time span.

4. Even a good system with a substantial support team cannot force a franchisee to succeess. The personal motivation of the individual has to be there. There is a need for a deep sense of commitment by the franchisee and a burning desire to succeed. It is important that the franchisee takes advantage of the proven methods and system and does not try continually to re-invent the wheel.

Franchising is an entrepreneural concept. Most franchise companies develop from modest beginnings, often starting with a one-man retail or service operation which the entrepreneur commences without an inkling that a system will develop from it in the distant future. What happens in reality is that the entrepreneur finds himself [or herself] running a successful unit, expands it to one or two more and discovers that it is getting increasingly difficult to keep control over the business, motivates staff and managers and opts, therefore for the franchising method in which the business can capitalise on the investment and energies of the franchisee.

Kall-Kwik claims that its main achievement is that many of its franchisees are very successful and earning an excellent income. They enjoy the pleasure of recognition within their community and the material rewards of a successful business.

The attraction of the *Kall-Kwik* system has motivated 6 members of the same family to take up 3 separate units. It also permitted the build-up of a substantial group of franchisees with multiple unit ownership and the purchase of centres by corporate head office staff. A measure of the company's success is that, during a period of 6 months recently, 3 members of the head office team have resigned and acquired their own *Kall-Kwik* units.

ALAN PAUL PLC

Introduction

The Group operates two retail businesses:

- Alan Paul Hairdressing, which provides a range of modern hairdressing services; and

- The Body & Face Place, which manufacturers and sells natural beauty products that are both environmentally safe and non-animal tested.
Each business both owns and franchises outlets. By franchising the Group has been able to expand rapidly into 112 locations.
A particular feature of the Alan Paul Hairdressing franchise programme is the ability to motivate salon staff with the opportunity of running their own business while remaining associated with Alan Paul.
At least 70 per cent, of the products retailed by The Body & Face Place are manufactured by the Company at its unit in St Cyrus, Angus, Scotland, and are distributed nationally from a new purpose-built warehouse on the Wirral near the Company's head office.

History

Alan Paul Hairdressing was established by Alan Moss, the present Chairman, in 1970 and initially traded from one salon in Bromborough, the Wirral. The number of salons operated by the Company increased over the years and in 1980, in response to the desire of senior managers to run their own outlets, the Company was amongst the first to franchise hairdressing salons. By 1985 the Company had expanded into 11 salons in the Merseyside area of which 2 were franchised and in 1986 it became a member of the British Franchise Association.

To accelerate the rate of growth it was already enjoying, in January 1986 Alan Paul issued an Offer for Subscription which was sponsored by Capital Ventures Limited to raise £400,000 under the Business Expansion Scheme. The issue was fully subscribed.

Recognising the growing market for non-animal tested natural beauty products, in 1987 the Comapny purchased the long established business of Edinburgh Aromatics and certain of its assets. This business manufactured a small range of such products and retailed them under the name of "The Body & Face Place" through 11 franchised outlets located mainly in Scotland, the first of which had been opened in 1976. Following the acquisition of this business, the Company has widened the range of natural beauty products manufactured and, through the application of its franchising expertise, has increased the nujmber of retail outlets to 52 situated in central shopping locations in the United Kingdom.

In November 1988 the Company raised £557,000 by means of a rights issue underwitten by Arbuthnot Latham Bank Limited to finance the purchase of a further 7 hairdressing salons in the London area.

Alan Paul Hairdressing currently operates 60 salons of which 42 are franchised and The Body & Face Place operates 52 retail outlets of which 45 are franchised.

Alan Paul PLC was floated on the USM on 1st June 1989 through a placing which valued it at £12.19 million. Placed at 140p the shares opened on their first day at over 190p (a 35 per cent premium) and settled back to 157-162p.

At the time of publication the company is about to open both an Alan Paul Hairdressing and a Body & Face Place outlet in the IMP complex in Osaka, Japan, advised by the author.

Business

Alan Paul Hairdressing

Alan Paul Hairdressing provides modern well equipped salons located mainly in the high street. All the salons are uniformly designed and fitted out in bright colours to reflect Alan Paul's exciting corporate image. Initially the salons are owned and operated by the Company and will be considered for franchising when a satisfactory level of clientele has been secured. This method of establishing new franchises ensures that the requisite high level of service is offered from the outset, and that all staff and the franchisees are fully trained and well versed in the operation of an Alan Paul salon.

As part of the franchise arrangements, the Company provides an ongoing training programme to its managers through its regional training staff. Each salon, whether Company owned or franchised, is required to have one training night per week to pass on this training to junior staff. In the case of franchises, the cost of this training is built into the fee structure of the franchise and the franchisee's continued participation in the training programme is a requirement of the franchise agreement. The Company prepares all the operating and accounting records for each franchised salon, makes all VAT and PAYE returns and provides administrative services so that the same information is obtained for both franchised and Company owned salons. This control over training and administration enables the quality of service and the financial information to be monitored closely to maximise performance.

In September 1988, the Company introduced a range of high quality, environmentally safe hair care products manufactured by the Group at St Cyrus which are sold through the salon network under the 'Alan Paul' name.

The Body & Face Place

The Body & Face Place creates, proudces and retails a range of non-animal tested, environmentally safe natural beauty products. The retail outlets, which are located in central shopping areas, are fitted in natural colours and materials in keeping with the image of the products. These outlets can be franchised immediately without the establishment of an initial customer base.

The Body & Face Place identifies suitable locations for new outlets and, upon receipt of an initial payment from the prosepctive franchisee, negotiates the acquisition of the site and fits it out in the corporate style on behalf of the franchisee. Advertising and promotional costs are provided for in the franchise fee; additional charges are made for specific promotions.

Approximately 70 per cent of the products retailed through The Body & Face Place shops are manufactured by the Company with the balance being primarily sourced and distributed by the Group. Research and development of new products is carried out at St Cyrus and the Company currently continues to create new products as well as improving and updating the existing range to enhance its position as a retailer of an individual range of beauty products. The products currently manufactured include cleansers, toners, moisturiser, creams, shampoos, conditioners, cosmetics and suncare lotions.

The franchise training programme and its requirements, which have been an important element in the success of the hairdressing salons, are progressively being introduced into The Body & Face Place outlets.

Sales and marketing

Alan Paul Hairdressing

A prime factor in the profitable expansion of the Alan Paul Hairdressing salons has been the image created by the Company. From the initial choice of location, through decoration and shopfitting, to the training of staff every effort is made to convey the image of a modern, fashionable salon providing the very latest techniques and styles in hairdressing. The strong emphasis on training and customer service ensures that each aspect of the business enhances the reputtion of the individual salons and of the Group as a whole.

Alan Paul actively participates in the local community and promotes its image through radio and press and by sponsorship of local events. A regular programme of in-salon promotions is used to maintain the Company's high profile.

There are estimated to be 28,000 hairdressing salons in the United Kingdom. Alan Paul operates a total of 60 of which 42 are already franchised. The Directors therefore foresee great potential for the development of its franchised salon network both at home and overseas.

The Body & Face Place

Since the acquisition of The Body & Face Place business with 11 outlets in 1987 the Company has established a further 41 located in central shopping areas. It is part of the Company's strategy to increase the number of The Body & Face Place outlets in the United Kingdom and then to expand overseas. Accordingly, the Company is creating a high retail profile for The Body & Face Place. The layout and decoration of the units using natural colours and materials produce a light and airy atmosphere which complements the products being sold.

The opening of each new outlet is supported by the distribution of leaflets, newspaper and magazine advertising and promotions. Regular new product launches, in-house promotions and changes in window dressing maintain and stimulate awarness of The Body & Face Place's image and product range. Packaged simply, in a selection of sizes, the natural base of the products is emphased, together with the fact that they are non-animal tested and are environmentally safe.

Retail outlets

Location and effective use of retail space is a key factor in the success of Alan Paul Hairdressing and The Body & Face Place.

The Group pursues an active policy of securing the right locations for its outlets at the centre of retailing activity in each particular area. The Group has a considerable advantage in running two retail businesses which complement each others it is able to consider larger sites in better locations which can be sub-divided into two units, one for Alan Paul Hairdresing and one for The Body & Face Place. In this way the Company is able to capitalise on its ability to utilise space by involving both businesses. At present there are 5 dual units and there are currently 2 further dual units under consideration.

The following table shows the growth in the number of retail outlets:

	Years ended 31st March				
	1985	1986	1987	1988	1989
Alan Paul Hairdresing	11	15	22	39	60
The Body & Face Place	–	–	–	18	52
Total	11	15	22	57	112

Note: The Body & Face Place had 11 outlets when acquired.

In common with many other retail businesses, some of the Group's retail outlets cannot use all the available space comprised in the units taken. In order to generate a return on this unused space, the Company has recently developed "Blueberry's" as a Twenties' style coffee shop which also provides a varied menu of light meals. These coffee shops are located above, or adjacent to the other businesses and provide an additional return on the available space and attract customers to the other outlets. It is the Company's intention to franchise the Blueberry's concept.

The Group also owns 13.33 per cent of the issued share capital of Salons Direct Limited, which carries out all shopfitting work on the Group's outlets as well as serving its own range of customer. This shareholding enables the Group to influence the service received and the quality of work undertaken.

The Group follows a regular programme of refurbishment of its units and it is a requirement of the franchise agreement of both Alan Paul Hairdressing and The Body & Face Place that each outlet is well maintained and is kept clean and tidy.

Details of the properties owned by the Company are set out in paragraph 5 of Statutory and General Information set out in Part III below.

Production and distribution

At St Cyrus the Company produces 70 per cent of the products retailed by The Body & Face Place. The recent introduction of new mixing equipment has improved the production process and will enable the Company to supply at least a further 150 retail outlets without any substantial investment in plant and equipment being required. The Body & Face Place is the major employer in this rural area and, historically, has had a low staff turnover enjoying considerable employee loyalty. There is an ample supply of labour for any expansion in production which the Company may wish to undertake.

The recent opening of a warehouse on the Wirral has improved the Company's distribution and has strengthened control and flexibility over the levels of stocking and production. The introduction of this warehouse has also released further space at St Cyrus for the expansion of production.

The Company contracts out the distribution of its products to independent hauliers who use vehicles painted in the Group's corporate style. It is Group policy to ensure that all orders are delivered within 48 hours of being placed.

Franchise arrangements

Both Alan Paul Hairdressing and The Body & Face Place are members of the British Franchise Association and their respective franchise agreements, packages and finance arrangements have been approved by this organisation. 11 franchisees have more than one Alan Paul Salon and 8 have both Alan Paul Hairdressing and The Body & Face Place franchises.

Alan Paul Hairdressing

Alan Paul has devised its own franchise package which is particularly suited to hairdressing salons. For an initial fee the franchisee is provided with a sublease and the business and goodwill of an established salon, assistance with funding arrangements, training and administration, all of which enable the franchisee to make the transition to ownership quickly and without interruption.

The principal source of income is the initial fee payable upon the grant of a franchise; further fees are charged on a percentage of turnover for which management and accounting services and Group advertising are provided. These continuing services are intended to assist the franchisee with many of the day to day difficulties associated with the ownership of a business. The franchisees must purchase of all the products needed by the salon through Alan Paul Hairdressing.

Alan Paul carefully vets all applicants for franchises, but given that the majority to date have been existing employees, the Company is usually fully aware of the applicant's calibre and potential. These arrangements enable the Directors to exercise continuing control over the franchisee's conduct and operation of the business and premises. As most franchisees do not have the necessary finances or market presence to secure the right retail locations, they benefit from the ability of Alan Paul Hairdressing to lease property at competitive rates.

The franchise period initially runs for five years, with an option for the franchisee to renew it for a further period of five years.

The Body & Face Place

The Body & Face Place concept is a more typical franchise operation and involves the retailing or products manufactured by the Company. Under this arrangement the lease and fixtures are sold to the franchise as part of the franchise package.

The Company charges an initial fee and makes a further charge based on turnover for ongoing services, enabling it to participate in increased sales. The main source of continuing revenue of The Body & Face Place comes from the sale of products to franchisees. Franchisees are required to purchase a minimum of 90 per cent of their stock through the Company. Unlike Alan Paul Hairdressing, The Body & Face Place does not provide any administrative services for its franchisees.

In addition to regular contact with The Body & Face Place franchisees through field co-ordinators, quarterly conferences of franchisees are held which provide an opportunity for an exchange of views and the co-ordination of Group policy.

Finance

Alan Paul has negotiated with The Royal Bank of Scotland plc arrangements whereby facilities are made available, with limited recourse to the Group, for Alan Paul Hairdressing salon franchisees. The facility involves the making of a loan with a flexible repayment holiday if required. The availability of this scheme, together with the accounting services provided, enables Alan Paul to maintain a tight control on all financial aspects of the franchise and allows the franchisee to concentrate on running the salon and providing the high quality of service required. Similar facilities are made available to franchisees of The Body & Face Place.

Management controls

The Group operates effective organizational and accounting controls over day to day activities. The Group management team, based at the Company's head office, supervises the running of both Company owned and franchised Alan Paul Hairdressing salons and The Body & Face Place retail outlets, with financial information being reported on a daily basis. The production and warehousing facilities are monitored closely to ensure that sufficient stock is produced and distributed to maximize retail sales.

The franchise agreements in respect of the salons and The Body & Face Place retail outlets give the Group a considerable degree of control over their operations. All Alan Paul Hairdressing salons have their accounts prepared by the Group, which makes all VAT and PAYE returns on their behalf, and during their regular visits the Group's managers check on The Body & Face Place outlet figures. All of The Body & Face Place outlets are equipped with electronic point of sale equipment which provider instant financial information enabling full sales details to be supplied to the Group head office.

The Group accounting team uses key ratios to monitor the performance of each salon and retail outlet and to give warning of any unit that is underperforming so that any necessary corrective action can be taken.

Appendix 17
THE WHITE PAPER

Opening Markets: New Policy on Restrictive Trade Practices (CM 727)

The White Paper contains good news for franchisors in the United Kingdom, and confirms that "the law should operate against only those agreements which have anti-competitive effects".

The object of the proposed new legislation, according to Lord Young, is to "prevent the development of blatant cartels and other restrictive agreements through which people in business co-operate to distort competition for their own benefit at the expense of their customers and others in the economy".

Basic Approach

It is intended that new legislation will replace the RTPA (the Restrictive Practices Court Act 1976) and probably the Resale Prices Act 1976 too. The new law will abandon the "form" approach of existing legislation and concentrate upon the object and effect of agreements and concerted practices. This approach is directly comparable to that of Article 85 of the Treaty of Rome and will aim at preventing the restriction or distortion of competition in the United Kingdom, thereby enabling the idea of a Single Market after 1992 to become more of a reality.

At one level, even a simple contract between two companies could be held to restrict competition because it prevents a particular sale to other competing suppliers. However, the new RTP law will aim to control only arrangements between independent firms which go beyond this and adversely affect competition in the relevant market taken as a whole. To achieve this, the prohibition in the legislation will be drawn widely. It will therefore be essential to identify, and give guidance to business on, those restrictions in agreements which, provided they are not operated in conjunction with other restrictions, are unlikely to have anti-competitive effects. It will also be necessary to identify agreements which, although restricting competition, have economic benefits which more than off-set their anti-competitive effects. These will be eligible for exemption from the prohibition.

Prohibited Practices

The new legislation will include a list of examples of practices falling within stated prohibition. These are described in Paragraph 2.10 of the White Paper and include:-

The Government have therefore concluded that the law should state that the prohibition will apply in particular to the following agreements and concerted practices:

(i)   those fixing prices and charges including any terms or conditions (eg resale prices, discounts, credit terms) which determine effective net prices;
(ii)   those which may be expected to lead to the fixing of prices, such as price information exchange agreements and recommendations on fees;
(iii)   collusive tendering;
(iv)   those sharing or allocating markets, customers, raw materials or other inputs, production or capacity;
(v)   collective refusals to supply or to deal with suppliers, collective discrimination in the terms on which different customers or classes of customer are supplied, and collective anti-competitive conditions of supply such as tie-ins, aggregated or loyalty rebates and "no competition" clauses.

To underline the Government's determination to stamp out price-fixing, except where it has been fully justified by a successful application for exemption, those who engage in price-fixing, including the imposition of resale price maintenance will not enjoy the benefit of any de minimis provision.

Investigations and Guidance

Responsibility for conducting preliminary investigations under the legislation will fall upon the Director General of Fair Trading. It will be his function to establish guidelines as to the kind of agreements that will be considered anti-competitive. The Director General will have a wide discretion and the practical effect of the legislation will to a considerable extent depend upon his decisions. These are likely to follow, to a large extent, the jurisprudence of the European Court of Justice considering Article 85. Indeed the new legislation will specifically provide for the Director General to be able to refer to such decisions for guidance. These are likely to include those which enforce objectively justified standards and certain licensing agreements for intellectual property rights which do no more than put limits on the authorised are of the licensed property (the so-called Ravenseft doctrine).

Enforcement and Penalties

The Government consider that the limited effectiveness of the RTPA has been in part due to the inadequate powers of investigation and the absence of sufficient penalties for most cases of abuse. These contrast with the powers held by the European Commission, already exercisable in the UK with the assistance of the OFT as one of the competent national authorities in this field. The Government are satisfied that if the legislation is to achieve its objectives, it must ensure that illegal agreements can be detected and the parties punished with a severity which is appropriate to the offence and sufficient to deter others.

Under the new law, the Director General of Fair Trading will be able to investigate on reasonable suspicion of a breach of the prohibition and will enjoy powers comparable to those available to the Monopolies and Mergers Commission in the Fair Trading Act 1973 and the Competition Act 1980. These powers will be exercised by giving the parties concerned due notice. However, if such notice is not complied with or there are grounds to suspect that evidence might be obtained, there will be the power to enter business premises, without warning and using reasonable force if necessary, to search for, examine and remove business records and take copies of them. It will be a criminal offence to obstruct the Director General of Fair

Trading or deliberately or recklessly to supply false or misleading information. Normal commercial confidentiality will, of course, apply, but the Director General will be able to use such information in the exercise of powers granted under other legislation such as the Fair Trading Act.

Whilst the usual rules of professional privilege apply, the Director General will have powers to obtain information from third parties.

The penalties to be imposed by the new legislation are somewhat draconian compared to the RTPA. Not only are the restrictions which cause an agreement to fall outside of the prohibition void and unenforceable, but the parties to the agreement INCLUDING THE DIRECTORS AND MANAGERS RESPONSIBLE FOR ITS NEGOTIATION OR IMPLEMENTATION will be liable to penalties. Businesses will also be liable to private action for recovery of damages.

Exemption or exceptions are therefore of great importance.

Exemptions and Exceptions

The Government believe it is right that the legislation should recognise that certain agreements, while involving restrictions on competition, also serve to provide benefits which would not otherwise be available. Such agreements should be capable of exemption from prohibition, if they are found to make a sufficient contribution of the production or distribution of goods or the provision of services, or to economic or technical progress, so as to countervail their restrictive effects and allow consumers to share adequately in the benefits.

The exemption test will thus be based closely on Article 85 (3) of the EEC Treaty, adapted as nececssary, in particular to make it clear that the legislation will apply equally to services. The improvement which an agreement brings about will be measured against the situation which would develop in the absence of the agreement and not necessarily that which held prior to the agreement. An exemption will not be available if an agreement eliminates competition so that there is no competition between the parties or from other suppliers.

In addition there will be certain exclusions such as where there is a conflict with existing law such as the Financial Services Act.

(1) *Individual Exemption*
The White Paper endorses the proposal contained in the Green Paper for a single general exemption and rejects the idea of an additional "public interest" exemption. Franchise Agreements such as those of Pronuptia, Service Master and Yves Rocher which have had to seek individual exemptions under Article 85 (3) will therefore be able to also obtain individual exemption under the new law

(2) *Block Exemptions*
The Government plans to maximise the benefits inherent in adopting a regime which is similar to EC legislation. Provision will therefore be made for agreements which are exempt under Article 85 (3), whether individually or by falling within a block exemption, to be exempt under the new legislation without the need for the parties to make separate application to the Director General. The law will also enable agreements which would fall within the terms of an EC block exemption, but for the fact that they do not affect trade between Member States, to be exempted in the UK. The White

Paper states that it would be unproductive for consideration of an agreement to focus solely on whether intra Community trade was affected or not and whether an agreement therefore fell within one jurisdiction (and was exempt) or the other (and was not).

Thus the proposed legislation will be welcomed by Franchisor in the UK. It will enable them to take advantage of a Block Exemption similar to the EC Block Exemption described in Chapter 4 above, and so further promote franchising in the UK.

(3) *de Minimis Exception*

The Government believes that the opportunities to distort competition through the operation of vertical agreements are somewhat less than through horizontal agreements and this will also be recognised in the legislation. Vertical agreements will qualify forde minimis exemption provided that no party has a turnover in excess of £30 million or such amount as may be fixed by secondary legislation. Many vertical agreements are also expected to fall within block exemptions. There will be no de minimis exception for an agreement involving retail price maintenance or any other form of price-fixing and the Director General's power to investigate de minimis agreements will apply whether the parties are competitors or customer and supplier.

Conclusion

Once the proposals contained in the White Paper are adopted, probably within the next two years, the legal environment in the UK will be far more positive towards franchising than it is at present.

BIBLIOGRAPHY

Franchising – Practice and Precedents in   Adams & Pritchard Jones
Business Format Franchising – (Butterworths)
1986

Les Procédures Européennes du Droit de la   Oliver Gast
Concurrence et de la Franchise – (Jupiter) 1989

Fraud Trials Committee Report (HMSO) 1986
ISBN 011380008 8

Commercial Agreements and Competition Law – Nicholas Green
Practice and Procedure in the UK and EEC
(Graham & Trotman) 1986

The European Challenge 1992 – The Benefits of   Paolo Cecchni
a Single Market (Wildwood House) 1989

The Journal of International Franchising and   Jean-Eric de Cockborne
Distribution Law (Frank Cass) Vol 3 No 3
March 1989

Nelson-Jones' Practical Tax Saving (Butterworths) Noble & Marks
4th Edition

Common Market Law of Competition (Sweet &   Bellamy & Child
Maxwell) 3rd Edition

Power Report on Franchising in the UK 1988   Michael Power
(Power Research Associates) 1988

Product Liability – The New Law Under the   Nelson-Jones and Stewart
Consumer Protection Act 1987 (Fourmat) 1988

Franchising for Profit (Institute of Chartered   Pollock & Golzen
Accountants) 1985

International Business Transactions (Kluwer) 1989 Nelson-Jones and Abell
Chapter 1 Business Format Franchising

Kerlys' Laws of Trade Marks and Trade Names   Blanco White and Jacob
(Sweet & Maxwell) 1986

Review of Restrictive Trade Practices Policy
(HMSO) March 1988

Opening Markets: New Policy on Restrictive Trade
Practices (HMSO) CM 727 July 1989

International Franchising;   Alexander S Konigsburg
Commonly Used Term.
Volume 1
(International Bar Association)

INDEX

liability, 90
obligations of, 51-53
protection, suggested
  procedure, 78-80
Free movement of capital, 106

General concept, 1-2
Goods
  franchisor, of, meaning, 37
Goodwill
  franchisee, obligations of, 53-54
Growth of franchising, 5-6

Identified meaning, 6
Import controls
  international franchising, 8
Individual exemptions, 26
Industries
  regulation of, 13-19
Infringement
  dangers of committing, 84
  See also Remedies against
    abuse
Injunction
  remedies against abuse, 83
Inspection
  franchisee, obligations of, 52
Intellectual property
  protection. *See* Protection
  single market, reforms
    relevant to, 104-105
Interim injunction
  remedies against abuse, 83
International franchising
  advantages of, 92-93
  commercial considerations, 91
  disadvantages of, 93
  exchange control, 98
  export controls, 98
  import controls, 98
  specific laws, 96
  structure of franchise, area
    developer, appointment of, 95

direct franchising, 94
generally, 93-96
joint venture, 95
overseas subsidiary, 94
taxation, 97-98
who participates in, 91-92
Investment business
  control of, 14-15
Investment franchise
  nature of, 7

Japan
  regulation in, 13
Joint venture
  franchising through, 95

Know-how
  meaning, 37, 76
  protection of, 76-77
  substantial, meaning, 38
Language
  single market, reforms
    relevant to, 108
Law Society
  regulation by, 14
Legal implications
  business expansion scheme, 88
  Consumer Credit Act 1974, 88-90
  EC law,
    Article 85, 22-23
    Article 86, 26
    block exemption. *See*
      Block exemption
    de minimis exemption, 24-25
    generally, 20-21
    individual exemptions, 26
    negative clearance, 26
    notification, 25
    Pronuptia case, 23-24
  English law,
    common law, 32
    Competition Act 1980, 32-33
    Fair Trading Act 1973, 33